THE WARRIOR MULLAH
The Horn Aflame 1892–1920

THE WARRIOR MULLAH

The Horn Aflame
1892–1920

Ray Beachey

BELLEW PUBLISHING
London

First published in Great Britain in 1990 by
Bellew Publishing Company Ltd,
7 Southampton Place,
London WC1A 2DR

Copyright © R. Beachey 1990

British Library Cataloguing in Publication Data
Beachey, Ray
The warrior mullah : the Horn aflame, 1892–1920.
1. Somalia, history
I. Title
967.73

ISBN 0 947792 43 0

Phototypeset by Input Typesetting Ltd, London

Printed and bound in Great Britain by
Billing & Sons Ltd

CONTENTS

ILLUSTRATIONS

Despite a lengthy search, no first-hand photograph of the Mullah appears to exist.

between pages 82–83

Maps

Acknowledgements

I am indebted to my son-in-law, Stephen M. Wallis, B.Sc., of Laurent
Giles Ltd., Naval Architects, Lymington, for providing the maps for
this book. For photographs and assistance in search for such, I am
indebted to J. A. Golding, C.V.O.; Lt. Colonel Eric Wilson, V.C.
(Hon. Secretary of the Anglo-Somali Society); D.R.C. West (Archivist,
Marlborough College); Professor B. W. Andrzejewski and John Fielder
Esq. I express my sincere thanks to the library staff of the Royal
Commonwealth Society and Foreign and Commonwealth Office for
their never-failing courtesy and help during my research for this book.
To my wife, Ursula, I owe my deepest gratitude for her support and
encouragement, and help in corrections and preparing the Index.

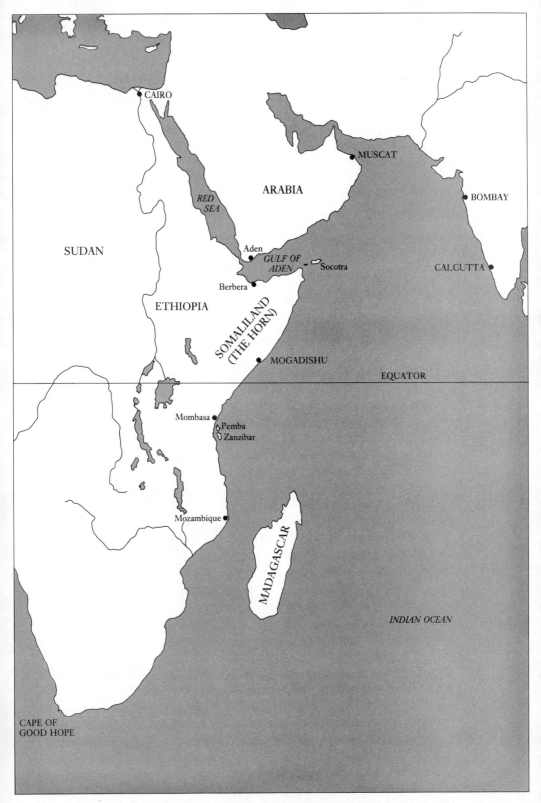

Somaliland and the Horn in relation to Africa and the Indian Ocean World

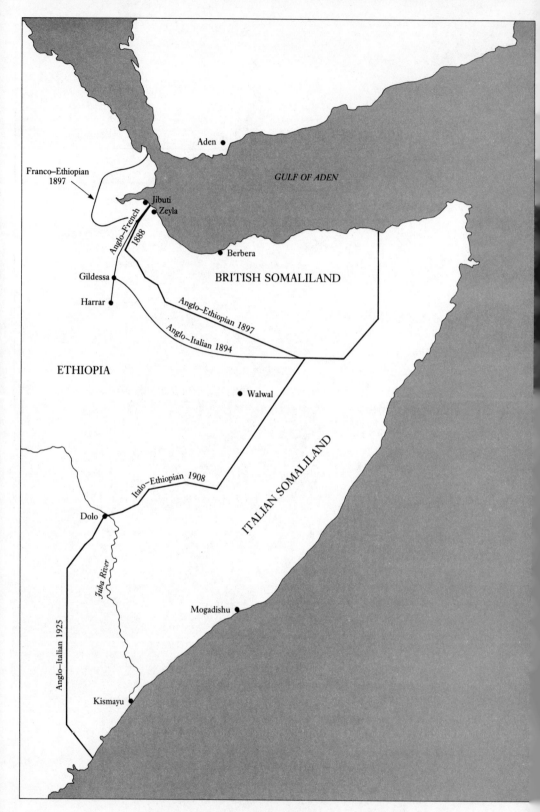

Demarcation of Somaliland boundaries, 1888–1925

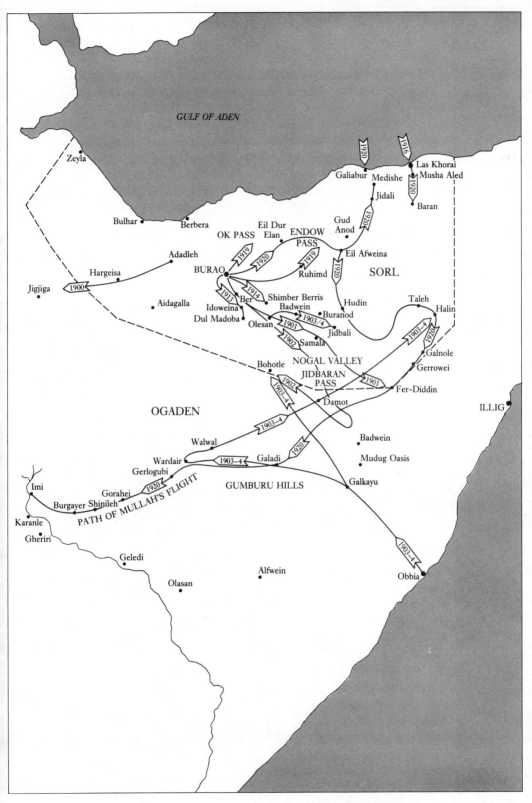

Area of operations and campaigns against the Mullah, 1900–20

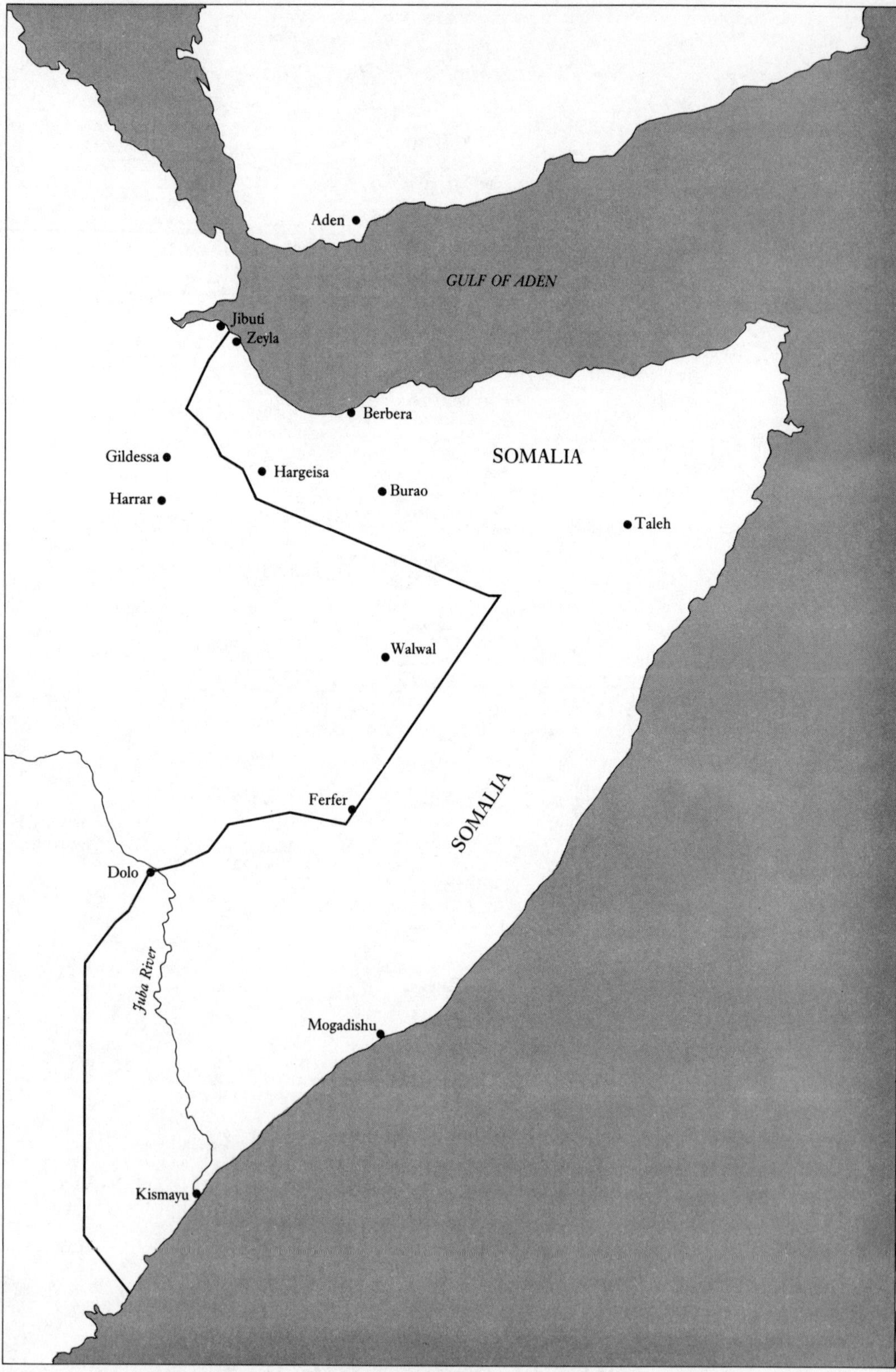
Aden
GULF OF ADEN
Jibuti
Zeyla
Berbera
SOMALIA
Gildessa
Hargeisa
Harrar
Burao
Taleh
Walwal
Ferfer
SOMALIA
Dolo
Juba River
Mogadishu
Kismayu

Present day (1990) Somalia

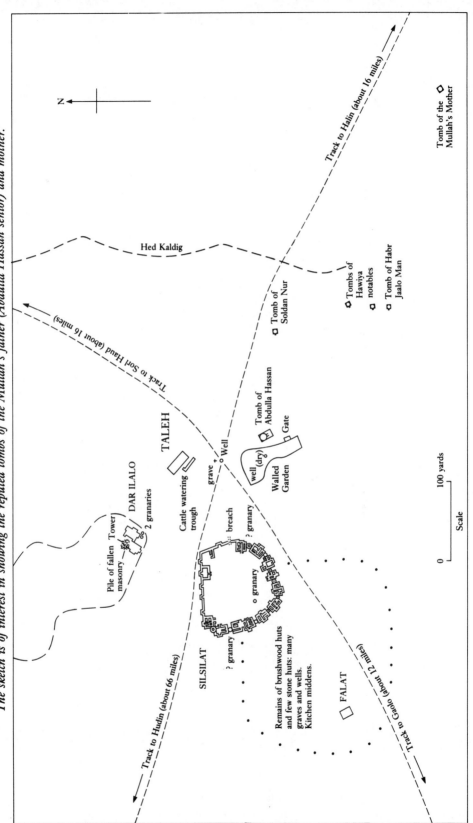

Sketch from *The Geographical Journal, Vol LXXVIII No 2, August 1931, p. 126, and accompanied a paper The Anglo-Italian Somaliland Boundary, read by Lt. Col. J. H. Stafford, R.E., (Senior British Commissioner on the Commission for the demarcation which took place in 1929–30). The sketch is of interest in showing the reputed tombs of the Mullah's father (Abdulla Hassan senior) and mother.*

N

Track to Halin (about 16 miles)

Tomb of the Mullah's Mother

Hed Kaldig

Tombs of Hawiya notables

Tomb of Soldan Nur

Tomb of Habr Jaalo Man

Track to Sorl Haud (about 16 miles)

TALEH

Well

grave

Tomb of Abdulla Hassan

Gate

Cattle watering trough

well (dry)

Walled Garden

DAR ILALO

2 granaries

Pile of fallen masonry Tower

breach

? granary

100 yards

Scale

0

granary

? granary

SILSILAT

Remains of brushwood huts and few stone huts: many graves and wells. Kitchen middens.

FALAT

Track to Hudin (about 66 miles)

Track to Gaolo (about 12 miles)

The Mullah's fortifications at Taleh

1

BACKGROUND TO SOMALILAND

THE Somali world lies cradled neatly in the Horn of Africa, between the Gulf of Aden and 'the Sualihi or Negroitic regions'. Its apex, like a great rhino horn, points north-eastwards into the Indian Ocean. This area, some 400,000 square miles in extent, had a population of about one million inhabitants at the end of the nineteenth century.

It is an old land historically, known to the ancients variously as Cush, Punt or Regio Araomatifera, and later, to Arab and Somali, as Bar-ajam or Bar-as-Somal – exotic names these, for this sun-baked and harsh land. The ancient seismic power which raised up the eastern half of Africa left the outer rim of the Horn with an immensely long and narrow coastal strip of bushless white sand. The real Somaliland lying behind this coastal strip is rarely seen by those who tread only its shores.

The traveller who crosses into the interior from the Gulf of Aden side first traverses a narrow strip of white sand shimmering in the heat, and then finds himself ascending an upward-tilted plateau broken by limestone crags, isolated peaks and deep ravines – a landscape of surpassing desolation. This is the Guban (to burn), so aptly named by the Somalis. Proceeding inland over the rising ground, at about 30 miles from the coast and at an elevation of about 3,500 feet, a different world is reached: the Ogo Highlands.

The Ogos, an eastwards extension of the Ethiopian highlands, form the main watershed between the interior plateaus and the coastal plain. They run from the Awash Valley on the west to Cape Guardafui on the east, and their spurs enclose the Darror and Nogal valleys on the south. The Ogos are at their most striking in that portion known as the Golis range, which lies immediately inland from the main port, Berbera. Rising to 6,000 feet or more in height, they are visible from out at sea. A lady traveller at the end of the last century thus described them:

1

Submerged in the shimmering ether we could discern, through the parting of the ways of the Maritime Range, the magnificent Golis, about thirty-five miles inland from Berbera, as the crow flies.

In this mountain world with air refreshingly cool, verdure luxuriant, and embowered amid aromatic flora, giant euphorbia and tall mountain cedar, the weary traveller finds a welcome retreat from the dust and heat of the coastal plains.

South of the Golis the land falls away to the great central grass plains of the Haud which, during the rains, provide the finest grazing land in the Horn. These are the so-called 'bans' of the Somalis. There are no permanent wells in the Haud, the nearest being in the Mudug oasis, far off to the south-east. The Haud and the area to the south of it, the Ogaden, shelve south-eastwards through a series of plateaus before descending abruptly to the alluvial plains of the Shibeli and Juba rivers. Both rivers rise in the Ethiopian highlands but only the Juba manages to empty its waters into the Indian Ocean; the Shibeli flounders and disappears in the sands a few miles from the sea.

Somaliland has probably one of the most inhospitable climates in Africa. In the Guban and maritime belt the heat is illimitable and the desert invincible, and at the coast this is compounded by the ceaseless kharif – a hot, labouring wind, heavy with sand. It is at its most appalling from May to September when, under a cerulean sky, temperatures rise to 110°F, and only a few thorn bushes cling to the burnt-out wastes. Nightfall brings no relief to this arid, silent coast. Annual rainfall barely reaches 3 inches a year, and this might fall in a single day, to be greedily sucked up by the parched sands.

During the dry season (*jiilaal*), January to April, there is wrought a delightful change at the coast. A cool breeze springs up. Temperatures are bearable. The long white sandy beaches invite the beachcomber, and the blue sea tempts the angler.

In the interior, on the upland plateaus, the climate throughout the year is hot in the daytime but cool, even cold, at night, especially from November to February. Rain may come twice yearly, from April to May and from September to October. The climate is dry and bracing and comparatively healthy, with enteric disease and malaria largely unknown. Temperatures are lower than at the coast, although during the dry season, and at the great heat of midday, sudden flurries of sand whip up sand devils, and the nomad, spreading his prayer mat, cannot but reflect on the wisdom of the Touareg veil. To the south, in the valleys of the Shibeli and Juba rivers, the weather is hot and humid, the rainfall generally higher than in the north and malaria is more prevalent.

In such a hot and arid country as Somalia the search for water is an eternal round, determining the rhythm of nomadic life. There is ceaseless migration from water hole to water hole, periodic trekking from grazing ground to grazing ground. Hence the wide familiarity with their own country which distinguishes the Somali. In September when the light rains are commencing to the north, the nomads from the Haud trek to the Guban, the eastern Ogaden and to the Mijjertein country where pasture and water are available. When heavy rains ensure pasture on the interior upland, the trek is reversed.

In such a harsh and forbidding land, life is hazardous in the extreme and fiercely competitive: there is much rivalry between lineage groups over ancient water rights and ancestral claims to grazing areas, and this frequently flares up into outright hostility and tribal warfare. Only the fiercely independent can survive. Just as the camel has been shaped by nature to reduce its dependence on water to a fine art, so has the Somali been shaped by the nature of his country into a finely wrought human being.

Whence came the ancestors of the Somalis? Traditional accounts refer to early Arab immigration from Arabia to the north Somali coast and intermarriage with the indigenous people, a process which continued after the rise of Islam. Vestiges of an older race are still to be seen in the short dark Midgan type of Somali, and in traces of old pagan customs, folklore and knowledge of agriculture. Continued influx from Arabia and acculturation with an increasingly Hamiticised African people, notably the Galla, would seem to have formed the Somali race. Richard (later Sir Richard) Burton's generalisation that the Somalis are a 'half-caste offshoot of the great Galla race, allied to the Caucasian type by a steady influx of pure Asiatic blood' seems near the mark. Somali pride in their purported Arab ancestry still exists, and is akin to that of people of Zanzibar who still flatteringly refer to their Persian descent. The name 'Somali' well might derive from 'so-mal' ('go and bring milk') or a founding ancestor, Samaale; equally plausible in this legendary land of milk, honey and incense is that it derives from the Arabic 'zu-mal' ('possessors of wealth').

The Somali peoples may be roughly divided into two groups. The larger of these, the Aji, are the self-styled 'true' Somalis, claiming Arabic descent. They comprise about 70 per cent of the total population and are made up of two confederations, the Darod and Irir, claiming descent from eponymous hero ancestors who arrived on the north

Somali coast from Arabia, in the early thirteenth century. As might be expected, the Darod and Irir tend to occupy the northern part of the territory, where their progenitors first settled. Nevertheless, elements of the powerful Darod group are found far afield; one branch, for example, in search of new grazing ground, moved south into the Ogaden region at an early stage in Darod migration. Another branch, the Herti, moved south across the Juba river as late as the mid-nineteenth century. Elements of the Darod are also found in north-eastern Kenya.

The Aji are largely nomadic pastoralists and Sunni Muslim in religion. Although seemingly a flux of tribes, clans and sub-clans, sections and lineage groups – a veritable paradise for the classificatory academic mind – they have a linguistic unity and a common republican society without the chiefs usually found elsewhere in African society. In this apparent welter of sub-tribes, clans, etc., there are strong permanent elements, such as family, kinship, patriarchism and the bond of the dia-paying group (a joint contract between senior adult men of related families to pay and exact compensation for crime or injury done by, or against, any member of their group).

The Sab, the other of the two main groups, and making up the balance of the Somalis, are looked upon as inferior and of mixed blood, the result of intermarriage with indigenous African stock. The Sab also consist of two large confederations, the Digil and Rahanwin. They are mainly cultivators occupying the fertile areas near the Shibeli and Juba rivers but are also widely dispersed among the Aji elsewhere in Somalia, and extend south into the Jubaland area towards the Tana river. An interesting community among the Sab at the end of the nineteenth century were the Wagosha occupying the district of Gosha some 100 miles up the Juba river. Some 25,000–50,000 in number, they were mainly runaway slaves, continually augmented by new arrivals from East Africa and the Galla country. They so effectively irrigated the banks of the Juba that their territory became known as the 'Dongola Province of the Juba': a veritable 'land of Goshen'.

The Sab have long had a tacit relationship with the Aji. Being protected by the tsetse-fly-infested forest fringe along the Shibeli and Juba, and by payment of annual tribute of ivory to the Aji, they have been able to negotiate their independence with the latter. Sab African origin is reflected in their stature and features, in their dialect 'Af-may', and in their predilection for native beer. They have adapted well to the more northern milieu. Among the Aji they perform the role of specialised minority groups known as Midgan, Yibir and Tomal, each with a distinctive cleverness of its own. The Midgan are skilful hunters and

4

trackers, using small poisoned arrows. The Tomal (supposedly the offspring of a Somali man and Midgan women) are renowned black-smiths, skilled in turning out bridle-bits, spears and knives. The Yibir, supposedly gifted with magical powers, sell amulets for occasions such as birth and marriage, and weave prayer mats. Their small, étui-like, leather cases, used for holding verses from the Koran and which are hung from the neck or arm by a leather thong, are especially highly esteemed. Superstitious Somalis aver that a Yibir at death simply disappears, and that no one has ever seen a Yibir corpse.

A vivid description of the physiognomy and anatomy of the Somali (Aji) type, is given by Richard Burton, who travelled in northern Somali-land in 1854–5. He described them as a tall slender people, of spare athletic frame, slim and wiry, and as agile as deer. Their proud bearing and superb carriage bespoke a consciousness of racial superiority, and also of physical toughness, the result of a hard life. In complexion they were slightly darker than the Arab, skin colour ranging from light to dark brown. In other respects they were very similar to the Arab, with their fine regular features, thin lips, often classic profile, fairly long, prominent and finely rounded forehead and high cheekbones. The nose was rather Grecian, the jaw prognathous and the lips full but not too thick nor everted. Teeth were large and white. The eyes were moderately large and deepset but brilliant and leaving the impression of a fierce and restless nature. Crowning these features was a mop of strong black (or bluey-black), wiry (or crinkly, ringlety) hair, which was frequently plastered straight up, as though whitewashed. Beards were sometimes seen, but these were only raised with difficulty, and usually in the form of minute curls. The hands and feet were usually small and delicately formed, shin-bones invariably curved and long in proportion to those of the thigh. Lark heels were not so common as among the negro.

The Somalis are a proud (some would say 'vain') people. Sir John Kirk, British consul at Zanzibar in the 1870s, marvelled at how little the Somalis were intimidated by British power. British East Africa officials, who came into contact with them in the Jubaland region at the turn of the century, were much impressed by them. Sir Arthur Hardinge, British consul at Zanzibar, fancifully likened their polity to that of nobles and chiefs of early English and Scottish history, and averred that they were:

a manly race . . . the older Sheikhs with their shapely bald heads and white beards, look like English farmers. Their clear eyes and quick intelligent gaze, were the outcome of a healthy life unaffected by the use of stimulants ... The race, in my opinion, has no equal in this part of Africa, either in intelligence or courage. They have come down from the north like a conquering host, driving the Gallas and Bajunes before them ... They are not afraid of Maxims, cannon or firearms ... A great recruiting field lies here virtually untapped.

A little later in time than Hardinge, Sir Charles Eliot, Commissioner in British East Africa, commented that the Somalis considered themselves equal to or superior to the British, 'and not infrequently prove it'.

The Somali character was a subject of endless discussion among European officers serving in Somaliland. There was decrial and encomium. The Somali character, they asserted, was a combination of opposites. There was levity and instability, a boisterous and warlike nature – so much so that Somalis on their arrival in Aden were usually disarmed by the British authorities there. There was improvidence and avarice, inordinate vanity and lordly dignity, irreverence and uncurbed insolence, such as spitting deliberately as the infidel passed by. There was much exaggerated pride, so much so as to leave him little open to suggestion: in his own opinion the Somali was not only equal to, but better than any man.

Yet, in contrast to this, there was independence and individualism, hospitality and frugality in his daily life; he was inured to danger and fatalistic to a degree, with bravery and toughness unparalleled. Completely at home in desert and thorn bush country, 'which was as the breath of life to him', his desert craft was superb. The Somalis were extremely formidable fighters, using deadly tactics. They carried small round shields of giraffe hide and fought in pairs with stabbing spears and knife, one man seizing his adversary while the other stabbed him. There was preference for ambushes and close fighting in thick bush.

This bravest, vainest and most merciless fighter was capable of greatness, ready to spill his blood on the barren rocks of his country. He would die contemptuously, 'taking the sabre straight and laughing'. He was little concerned about wounds, which were plastered over with camel dung and left to putrefy and heal. Speaking of his Somali guides, the explorer Captain J. H. Speke remarked that there was 'scarcely a man of them who does not show some scars of wounds ... some apparently so deep that it is marvellous how they ever recovered from them.'

European officers discovered that, under strict discipline and making allowance for their volatile temperament, Somalis made good police and military, although they were never willing to bend their backs as porters. Whether in the military, in British uniform, wearing sweater, shorts, puttees, khaki cummerbund and puggaree, or in native dress, striding along in dazzling white, flowing *tobe* or *khaili* of Scottish tartan pattern (more prized if carrying the blue stamp of a Manchester mill, or dipped in the muddy yellow waters of the pool at Milmil), the Somali cut a figure that caught the eye. And this was especially so when he was at his most austere, with a sheaf of the distinctive shaped spears of his tribe in one hand, and in the other a round target-shaped shield of giraffe-, rhino- or oryx-hide, and with a small leather case, containing a verse from the Koran, suspended from his neck by a thin leather strap, the ends of which fell down the back of his *tobe*, contrasting artistically with his burnished brown skin.

In religion the Somali was a good Muslim, a Sunni, albeit a feverish one, as when with another Dervish, or more especially in the presence of a Mullah holding a religious service before migration to a new pasture, or to ensure success when entering on a raid. As to the treatment of his women, the Somali stood out in the world of Islam: women were not kept in purdah and enjoyed a degree of freedom unheard of in the Arab world.

They were great travellers, these Somalis. Restless, travelling light and always on the move, they were known as 'the people without a pillow'. Their huts were of the slenderest kind, merely sticks placed in circular formation in the ground and drawn together at the top, and covered with thick, well-made mats of aloe fibre; they resembled the 'yurts' of the Turcoman tribes of Central Asia. A large band of Somalis on the move was an unforgettable sight: household belongings, dismantled hut – a strange contraption like a giant stork's nest – all hoisted high on the back of donkey or camel, and with men, women and children following on foot in a giant cloud of dust, and accompanied by thousands of head of stock.

The search for water and pasture absorbed the life of the Somali nomad. Watering places varied from the large and well-resorted-to, such as at Warabod, south of Zeyla, or the Afmadu wells (a veritable oasis) in the eastern Ogaden, to the many small wells dug in the bed of a dried-up watercourse, or those, short-lived, after the brief rains. The larger wells were usually funnel-shaped holes varying in breadth and depth according to the importance of the well. There was organisation and control at watering places. Some wells were under specific ownership and used for all requirements, human and stock. Others were organised in groups respectively assigned to camels, donkeys, etc. The method of raising water from the wells was by means of acorn-shaped buckets thrown from man to man from the bottom of the well to troughs at the top, a movement exceedingly graceful.

There were well-recognised tribal areas but there was also much overlapping and sidestepping into each other's territory, in a way often puzzling to the outsider. In years of drought a tribe might stray deep into its neighbour's territory, surprisingly without a blood battle. Amity would be arranged. An interesting feature of tribal life was that of marriage outside the recognised kinship circle. Although this might be pleasing to the eugenist, it had a more practical side: it gave the Somali male the right to visit his wife's family, and it secured for him additional grazing ground for his stock.

Among that stock one animal, the camel, stood out predominantly. It was the most cherished of all – so much so, that the highest benediction bestowed by camel herders was 'May God grant you camels and sons.' Camels are the most highly esteemed and valued animals in pastoral Somali society, and they figure prominently in Somali oral literature and are the subject of many proverbs: 'Give away camels never!', 'No camel means no milk, no milk means no life' and 'Miserable would always be the man who owns no camels.'

Nowhere in the world, except, perhaps, in Bikanir, India, or Arabia, does the camel (*Camelus dromedarius*) reign so supreme as in Somaliland, which today has the largest camel population of any country in the world, there being more camels here than people. The universality of the camel is strikingly apparent throughout the country; herds are numbered in thousands, even tens of thousands. The camel is the chief domestic animal, the ultimate provider and source of livelihood. It is unparalleled as a mount and beast of burden, its milk is excellent and highly nutritious, the meat of young gelded camels is as the finest veal, its thick hide is durable and with many uses, and so also the long hair when shorn. As an economic and social asset, the role of the camel in Somali life is comparable to that of cattle among Nilotic tribes in the interlacustrine region of East Africa.

The primacy of place enjoyed by the camel is evident at water points, where the largest and best group of wells is reserved for it, and the remainder for donkeys, sheep, goats and humans, respectively. Such is the value placed on a camel that the unsuspecting hirer or purchaser may not be aware that the original owner may claim the right to any subsequent offspring born to it.

Camels are excellent mounts, swift and hardy, unsurpassed for covering long arduous journeys. With the advent of the firearm they were not usually ridden in combat, for a rider hoisted high on a camel's back presented too easy a target. But as beasts of burden in desert conditions they remain unchallenged, and the caravan trade is still largely dependent on them. With marvellous capacity for conserving water in their bodies for long periods of time and under trying conditions, they are able to go without water for up to two weeks. They are easily fed, requiring no rations and able to live on tough thorny plants and dry hard shrubs which are masticated by the powerful front teeth. Carrying a load of 250 lb, and at an easy pace of two to three miles an hour, the camel can cover up to 20 miles a day. The ordinary Somali burden camel cost about 25 to 35 rupees (i.e. 30 shillings at the turn of the last century), and was easily obtainable in large numbers. The Arab trotting camel, generally obtained from Aden, was useful as a light baggage camel and as a mount for scouting and raiding, but it required water every two or three days and had to be fed on grain or good green grass. Maintaining a trotting pace of 5 to 6 miles an hour, and carrying a rider or light baggage, the Arab trotting camel could average from 45 to 50 miles a day. Their cost, however, was up to ten times as much as a Somali burden camel, and they were not easily obtainable, even in Arabia.

What a strange ruminant quadruped is the camel, so perfectly designed by nature for desert life, with its humped back, long neck, highly modified and cushioned feet with broad thick calloused soles and small hoofs at the end of each toe: surely a parody of the order *Ungulata*! Yet these features are a small price to pay for its physical attributes so precisely designed to suit its surroundings for long periods of time and under trying conditions. Much can be forgiven the camel's temper and sour attitude, and its attributes explain the half-mystical fellow-feeling that existed between Somalis and their beasts of burden.

This excellent beast, the Somali camel, gentler and more willing than that from Arabia or Bikanir, and unsurpassed in so many ways, nevertheless still retains a camel's character: 'Never tame, though not wide-awake enough to be exactly wild.' He would be easily tempted to stray from his path by any beckoning thorn or alluring green branch, was difficult and forbidding in the extreme when riled to anger, and most dangerous when rutting, with bubbling roar, lunging and fighting fiercely with his fellow camels.

However, all this could be forgotten when, on the long trek over baking desert plateaus and going for days without water or grazing, the desert 'devils' entrapped the traveller. Then the Somali camel, tough and durable like his master, uncomplaining and passive under its heavy load, would sink to its knees in the sandstorm and, stretching its neck along the sand, close its nostrils and remain motionless, providing a

9

bulwark and shelter for its master, until the sandstorm had cleared. Its stupidity and ingratitude could then be forgiven.

In this land, proverbial for its wealth in camels and the vast numbers of these, there were in addition large flocks of other stock. Sheep and goats abounded: the sheep, a variety of the Persian fat-tailed species, provided the so-called Somali skins, about one million of which were exported annually, and were much sought after by glove-makers abroad. There was also a long-standing trade in hides and meat on the hoof with Aden and as far away as Madagascar. There were also excellent asses used as pack animals. Somali mules were tough and useful, but troublesome to load on account of 'sore' backs. They could live on anything and go without water for two to three days. Their average rate of marching was about 3 miles an hour with a load of 100 lb. Their price was about 80 rupees. They were scarce, however, and difficult to obtain. The Somali donkey was similar to the mule, but could carry a load of only about 60 lb. It cost about 15 to 30 rupees. The Somali pony was a hardy type – those from the Dolbahanta country being especially prized. Their main defect was their vulnerability to African horse sickness, a fatal virus disease, characterised by fever, oedematous swellings and internal haemorrhage, and transmitted by certain biting flies, and which was endemic in large parts of the Horn. When this dread disease struck in force, it could halt British military operations or tribal warfare.

Cattle had a far less important role in the life of the Somalis than elsewhere in Africa, except in areas of more adequate rainfall, as in the western Ishaak and Gadabursi country, and in the trans-Juba region and Boran Somali country. British travellers in these regions in the late nineteenth century encountered, to their surprise, well-trained trek oxen. Goats foraged well on inhospitable grazing ground. Agile and sure-footed, they clambered on top of, and grazed on, low-growth trees and bush.

2

EARLY EUROPEAN CONTACT WITH SOMALILAND

OUTSIDE influences, Christian, Portuguese, Turkish and Ethiopian, barely touched Somaliland. Only Arabs and Islam placed their permanent seal on the Somali peoples at an early stage. The Horn remained almost inviolate from other outside incursions until the late nineteenth century, apart from a short-lived British contact at the end of the seventeenth century when Captain W. Kidd and fellow pirates, based on Madagascar, preyed on pilgrim ships bound for Mecca and made landfalls on the Somali coast for water and provisions. Captain W. F. Owen, during the course of his great hydrographical survey of the western Indian Ocean, 1823–35, also made landfalls there. The reception of these early British visitors on that coast was so hostile, however, as to leave an unfavourable impression of the Somali peoples. The first British treaty with a Somali tribe came about in 1827, following a Somali attack on a shipwrecked brig, the *Mary Ann*, near Berbera. By this treaty the Habr Awal agreed to pay compensation and to desist from further attacks on British ships.

The Napoleonic wars and invasion of Egypt, which led to a shift of British forces from the Cape to the Red Sea by way of the East African coast, brought increased familiarity with the Red Sea route, and so also the maritime surveys of the western Indian Ocean. But it was above all the capture of Aden in 1839, and its establishment as an important British port and garrison town, which directed attention to the north Somali coast lying directly opposite and only a day's sail away. The latter quickly became Aden's larder for meat and provisions.

There was, however, little attempt to penetrate the Somaliland interior. In the same year as the capture of Aden an Englishman, J. S. Leigh, claimed to have visited Harrar, some 200 miles south-west of Berbera. In 1843 Lt. R. Christopher reached the Webi Shibeli river which runs parallel to the east Somaliland coast, and named it 'Haines river', 'as a small tribute of respect' to Captain S.B. Haines, Political

11

Resident at Aden. In 1848, Lt. C. J. Cruttenden, working inland from Las Khorai on the north Somali coast, reached the Tug Darror, a great dry watercourse traversing northern Somaliland. Cruttenden's memoir on the Mijjertein is one of the first British accounts of a Somali tribe. An East India Company treaty in 1840 with the local sultan at Zeyla, whereby the latter agreed not to enter into treaty relations with any other power, anticipated the rivalry which was soon to develop between France and Britain in the area. The visit of Captain Guillain of the French Navy to the Somali coast in the early 1840s awakened French interest in acquiring a base in the Gulf of Tajurra.

Following a visit to Berbera, in 1842, of an East India Company official, and his recommendation that the Company acquire a greater knowledge of the 'unknown Somali country', two expeditions were mounted by the Company for that purpose. The first came to nothing, the proposed leaders dropping out at the last moment, fearful of the dangers awaiting them. For the second expedition, however, the Company found the ideal man to lead it in the person of an Indian Army officer, Richard Burton, fresh from a notable pilgrimage to Mecca in 1853. Burton, who was interested in seeking the sources of the Nile by working westwards from Somaliland, was not, in his own words, 'afraid of losing his cods'.

Burton, along with another Indian Army officer, Captain J. H. Speke (with whom he was to have a subsequent acrimonious relationship), drew up a joint plan whereby Speke would journey to the Nogal Valley in north-east Somaliland, to check on reputed gold deposits and the region's potential as a source of camels and pack animals. Burton, meanwhile, would visit the remote and forbidden town of Harrar, a replay of his romantic journey to Mecca. They departed on their respective missions in October 1854. Speke, proceeding inland from Bunder Goray, on the north Somali coast, journeyed through Warsangli country, crossed a mountain range to the south, and then dropped down into plateau country, 'a howling blank-looking desert, all hot and arid, and very wretched to look upon'. Here, still far from his goal and having overstayed his time, and being short of supplies and faced by mutinous Somali drivers and tricky guides, Speke was forced to turn back. His return journey was plagued by warring Dolbahanta, and it was not until 29 January 1855 that he arrived back at Bunder Goray. The tales of gold deposits had proved false, and so also the potential of the country as a source of baggage animals. Speke assessed his three months' expedition as 'a useless journey'.

Meanwhile Burton had reached Harrar on 3 January 1855, having discarded his Arab disguise on the way, and entering Harrar as an Englishman. His ten days' stay there left him with a greater respect for its climate than for the city itself: it was a mere 'pile of stones'. Burton's stay at Harrar was short, and he was back at Berbera by the end of January 1855.

After a short stay at Aden, Burton and Speke crossed over to Berbera again in April 1855, having planned another journey, into south-western Somaliland. They were thwarted, however, before they could start, by a Somali attack on their camp at Berbera in which a member of their party was killed and Speke severely wounded. The expedition was forced to retreat to Aden. British reprisals quickly followed. Berbera was blockaded by two East India Company cruisers, a hefty fine was levied on the Habr Awal tribe responsible for the attack, and a new treaty extracted from them whereby they promised to mend their ways, to assist in the suppression of the slave trade, and to acknowledge the right of the British to trade freely at Berbera and in Habr Awal territory.

Burton's account of his Somaliland venture, *First Footsteps in East Africa*, and its Appendix, 'Diary and Observations made by Lieutenant Speke, when attempting to Reach the Wady Nogal', provide our first British introduction to Somaliland, Burton claiming that he was probably the first European to enter Harrar. His account has many sage remarks, acute observations, much sardonic wit, and many memorable passages. He had met Somalis who had travelled much about the world and, after much 'knocking about', had acquired fluency in three or four languages and were excellent mimics of foreign manners and customs. He was surprised to find Somalis well apprised as to the latest developments in the Crimean War.

Burton's expedition was accused of showing 'want of that caution and vigilance' necessary when travelling among the Somalis, and it raised concern in Aden, lest its supplies from Somaliland be endangered by expeditions such as Burton's. It seems also to have stirred the French into rival action. In the same year as Burton's venture in Somaliland, the French obtained a concession to build the Suez Canal, and were soon directing their attention towards the Red Sea area. In 1857, in response to the British occupation of Perim Island in the Red Sea, the French probed the Gulf of Tajurra to obtain a rival base, and when a French official was murdered there in June 1859, they threatened reprisals unless the local sultan agreed to a treaty (March 1862) ceding Obokh. The latter port thus became a coaling and provisioning station rivalling Aden, until it was superseded by Jibuti, acquired by the French in 1896.

French action was paralleled by that of the Egyptians and Italians. Between 1866 and 1874, Egypt, then under the suzerainty of the Sublime Porte of Turkey, gained control over Massawa and various points on the African side of the Red Sea, and claimed jurisdiction over the north Somali coast as far east as Ras Hafun. In 1874 a formidable Egyptian force occupied Harrar Province. Britain, in view of her recent control of Suez Canal shares, and 'trusting in the friendly relations between England and Egypt', recognised these acquisitions as part of the Ottoman dominions under the hereditary rule of the Khedive of Egypt, on condition that Zeyla, Berbera, Tajurra and Bulhar remain free ports and that trade with Aden was not interrupted, and that Egypt enter into a formal engagement to prohibit the export of slaves in the territory she had occupied.

Egyptian administration brought considerable improvements at ports on the north Somali coast, the benefits of which ultimately fell to the British. Piped water supplies, piers, lighthouses, troop quarters, blockhouses and stockades were a civilised boon; less welcome was the institution of custom duties at these ports. The Egyptians soon overreached themselves. At Harrar their excesses resulted in the Khedive sending out General Gordon in 1879, to dismiss the culprits. At home the Egyptian government was faced with problems of its own: the rise of the Mahdi in the Sudan, the collapse of Ismail's regime, and the death of Gordon and loss of the Sudan. In 1884 the Egyptians had perforce to abandon their Somaliland colony and withdraw their garrisons, including that at Harrar. In this withdrawal they were assisted by British officers from Aden.

The departure of the Egyptians left the field open for the British, and Harrar Province, a fine, isolated upland region with rich coffee plantations and lush cultivation, was theirs for the taking. To the west of Harrar lay the great Awash depression and the Ethiopian kingdom of Shoa; to its south and east lay the illimitable desert reaches of Somaliland, still largely unexplored by Europeans. How different might have been the subsequent history of the Horn if Britain had moved in, in the wake of the departing Egyptians! Old Somali hands were still regretting the lost opportunity many years later.

Thus the rich, strategic and climatically attractive province of Harrar was returned to its ancient dynasty, helpless in the face of Ethiopian expansion at the end of the nineteenth century. Much was made at the time of British forbearance in refusing to occupy Harrar, but it was largely due to reluctance to spark off a scramble in the region by other European powers. The Indian government also did not conceal its aversion to taking on responsibility for this remote and seemingly incon-sequential territory. As a buffer state to keep the Ethiopians at bay, however, it would have been invaluable. Meanwhile the great influx of arms to Ethiopia was under way, fuelling the ebullient and expansionist mood that led to the defeat of Italy in 1896.

The north Somali coast was, however, a different matter from Harrar, strategically placed as it was on the sea route to India. Fearful lest another European power occupy it, Britain quickly moved in and took over Egyptian installations at Berbera, Bulhar, Zeyla and other points. Piped water supplies, wharves, piers, lighthouses and troop quarters all fell to the British. In 1884, L. P. Walsh, Assistant Resident at Aden, and J. Peyton, political officer, were directed to Berbera and Zeyla, to head the British administration of the north Somaliland coast. They were quick to acknowledge the debt owed to the departing Egyptians.*

The French also took advantage of the departure of the Egyptians. They occupied Obokh in 1883, and made treaties with Danakil chiefs to gain control of the Gulf of Tajurra.

In February 1885 Britain declared a protectorate over the north Somali coast from the south-west corner of the Gulf of Tajurra to Ras Galwein, at 48°E longitude. France responded by strengthening her position in the Gulf of Tajurra and converting Obokh into a major base with cable communication with the outside world. Owing, however, to the insalubrious climate of Obokh, its exposed harbour and surrounding hostile Danakil, the French soon had their eyes on the fine harbour of Jibuti, already mooted as the ocean terminus of a projected railway to Addis Ababa. Jibuti, however, lay within the coast protectorate declared by Britain in February 1885. Fortunately for the French, the British placed less value on Jibuti than on Zeyla, seeing the latter as an impor-tant base and terminus for a future railway to Harrar. An agreement was thus arrived at between the two powers on 8 February 1888, whereby Britain abandoned any claim to jurisdiction in the Gulf of Tajurra, including Jibuti and the islands of Musha and Bab. In return France recognised the British coast protectorate and her occupation of Zeyla. At the same time it was agreed that the boundary between the British and French spheres of influence (informal protectorates) was to run from Loyada at the coast (between Jibuti and Zeyla) in a south-westerly direction, and terminate at Gildessa, about 150 miles inland. There was also a stipulation that neither signatory would include Harrar in its sphere of influence.

*L. P. Walsh, *Under the Flag and Somali Coast Stories*, London, 1932

Before this agreement with the French, Britain had already been consolidating her position within her sphere of influence. Between May 1884 and March 1886, she had concluded treaties with five independent Somali clans from Zeyla eastwards (the Warsangli were included in January 1886) recognising their independence in return for a promise not to cede territory to any other power except Britain. Supplementary treaties in 1886 extended British protection over these clans (leaving only the Dolbahanta outside the arrangement). With these treaties in hand, Britain, on 20 July 1887, converted her sphere of influence into a British protectorate over the north Somali coast from Ras Jibuti on the west, to Bandar Ziada (at 49°E longitude) on the east, inland boundaries being left undefined. Thus were 68,000 square miles of territory, on the sea route to India, added to Britain's African empire. The responsibility for administering this new acquisition would devolve on the Government of India, through Aden.

To some extent it was German intrusion into Somaliland which forced the British to take the above action. The Germans, already established on the East African coast to the south, also aspired to control Berbera when it became apparent that the Egyptians would withdraw from there, and they negotiated to this end with both the Warsangli and the Egyptian Governor at Berbera. At this stage the British stepped in, and, as a result of British pressure, the Egyptian Governor and Germans were deported from Berbera on the eve of Egyptian withdrawal. The British also now renewed (for the third time) the treaty made with the Mijjertein sultan in 1862, and buttressed it with an annual payment to him of 360 Maria Theresa dollars. Soon, however, both German and British interests on the Mijjertein coast would be superseded by the arrival of the Italians there.

Following the intimation to France in February 1885 of the establishment of a British sphere of influence over the north Somali coast, an elementary British administration was set up there. Biladiers (country police) were appointed to protect caravan routes and prevent disruption of trade by feuding tribes. In administering justice in murder cases in the interior it became necessary to gain greater knowledge of the localities where these events occurred. This gave rise to a need for accurate surveys of the interior. In early survey work the names of the brothers Captain H. G. C. Swayne and Lieutenant E. J. E. Swayne, of the Indian Army, predominate. During the period 1885 to 1891 they surveyed much of British Somaliland. Their traverse surveys covered thousands of miles, caravan routes were mapped as far inland as Milmil, some 200 miles from the coast, and they gained an intimate acquaintance with Somali tribes. Captain (later Major) H. G. C. Swayne's *Seventeen Trips Through Somaliland* (London,1903) describes the Somali hinterland and its peoples in vivid and expressive prose. The Swayne brothers, unhappily, conferred on their maps such a plethora of place names, many derived from travellers' tales, as to make it almost impossible to identify them on current maps. As late as 1933–4 a Somaliland boundary commission report complained that these 'place names were a heavy task . . . We had 1,500 of them . . . and their varied spelling added to the task.'

The whole question of boundary surveys took on new importance with the formal declaration of a British protectorate and need for delimitation of boundaries with neighbouring territories, such as Italian Somaliland. Italian interest in the Horn of Africa quickly followed on the acquisition of the port of Assab at the southern end of the Red Sea by the Rubattini Steamship Company in 1870. In contrast to the Germans, Britain appeared well-disposed towards Italian adventurism in the southern Red Sea and the Horn. In February 1882, by an Anglo-Italian convention, Britain recognised Italy's claim to Assab, in return for Italy's support against the Mahdi in the Sudan. By further treaties with Danakil chiefs between 1883 and 1888, Italy acquired a protectorate over the Danakil coast, and in January 1890 these possessions, including Assab, were declared the Colony of Eritrea. In the previous year (1889) Italy concluded treaties with Mijjertein sultans whereby she acquired a protectorate over much of north-eastern Somaliland and annexed territory earmarked for Britain in the surveys recently carried out by the Swayne brothers.

Britain remained remarkably acquiescent in the face of Italian expansion in the Horn. Anglo-Italian protocols of 24 March and 15 April 1891 express mutual desire for demarcation of their respective spheres of influence. The need for such demarcation was accentuated when, in August 1892, Italy, on behalf of the Filonardi Company (succeeded in 1898 by the Benadir Company) extended her claims southward to the Juba and acquired a lease of the Benadir ports from the Sultan of Zanzibar. By an Anglo-Italian Protocol of 5 May 1894, Britain recognised an Italian protectorate over the Somali coast from 8° 15′N to Bandar Ziada, at 49°E longitude.* Inland their respective spheres were

*In January 1905 Italy acquired outright possession of the Benadir ports for a payment of £144,000 to the Sultan of Zanzibar. In 1905 Britain leased Italy land near Kismayu, to facilitate communication with the Benadir country. In 1908, by royal decree, the country between the Juba and the southern Mijjertein was placed under an Italian civil governor.

delimited by a line running from Gildessa south-east to the intersection of the 8°N parallel and the meridian 44°E longitude, and thence along the parallel of 8°N latitude to its intersection with the 48°E meridian, thence it ran north-east to the intersection of 9°N latitude with 49°E longitude, (which was assumed to correspond with the Mijjertein/Dolbahanta border), and then north along this meridian to the Gulf of Aden. By the boundary line as outlined, Gildessa, Jigjiga and Milmil, places included in the British sphere by the Swaynes' surveys, were now in the Italian sphere.

There was more to the Anglo-Italian protocol of 5 May 1894 than the boundary arrangements might indicate. There was tacit recognition in it that Italy was the protecting power over Ethiopia, and by a secret codicil to the protocol Britain recognised that Harrar and Milmil were in the Italian sphere, but Britain had the right to enter Harrar and Milmil if necessary to safeguard the British protectorate's interests, as for example, trade or border peace. Within the month the secret section was leaked to the French by the Italian Foreign Minister. It brought vigorous French protest that it was a violation of the Anglo-French agreement of February 1888, whereby neither signatory was to include Harrar in its sphere of action. Britain hastened to assure the French that there was no such violation, and that Britain would limit her action to Milmil.

The most advanced point of Italian occupation in the southern Somaliland hinterland was at Lugh, a station founded by Captain Bottego in 1895. By the treaty of Adua, 1896, Italy recognised the independence of Ethiopia, and an Italian-Ethiopian agreement of August 1897 defined the Italian-Ethiopian frontier as a geographical line drawn from the point of intersection of the 47 meridian with the 8 parallel, and running south-west (parallel to and at a distance of 180 miles from the Indian Ocean) to Lugh, on the upper Juba river. In return for an indemnity of £120,000 to the Emperor Menelik in 1907 and ratified by a convention of May 1908, Italy entered into an agreement with Menelik that:

> from the Webi Shibeli the frontier takes a north-easterly direction according to the line of 1897. All territory belonging to tribes towards the coast is to remain under the dependence of Italy; and all territory of tribes towards the Ogaden is to remain under the dependence of Abyssinia.

Under this agreement the Italian hinterland boundary was extended to Dolo, on the Juba, north of Lugh. Thus did Italy attain, despite the grievous setback of Adua, an acceptable hinterland for her Benadir coastal strip.

Profoundly important for subsequent events in the Horn was the

18

death of King John of Tigre in battle against the Dervishes at Gallabat in 1889. Before his death Europeans (including the British) tended to associate Ethiopia with the great plateaus and mountainous area north-west of the Awash valley, encompassing the provinces of Tigre and Amhara and, possibly, Gondar and Wollo Galla. This was the area traversed by Napier in 1867–8 and over which King Theodore and King John in succession held sway. Shoa, to the immediate south-east of the Awash valley, was less well-known. While European eyes were on events in the northern provinces in the later nineteenth century, Menelik, ruler of Shoa, was actively consolidating his southern king-dom, and when the death of John seated him firmly on the throne of a greater Ethiopia, the centre of power was shifted from north to south. Thus could Count Gleichen (*With the Mission to Menelik, 1897*, p. 113) note that the country south-east of the Awash, previously separate from Abyssinia, was now, 'to all intents and purposes', part of it.

It was under Menelik that there took place that expansion eastwards which brought the Ethiopians into traditional Somali country. Harrar and the neighbouring highlands were occupied and Menelik's nephew, Ras Makonnen, appointed governor. Makonnen's 'Fitauraris' (com-manders) established permanent Ethiopian military posts at Jigjiga, Gildessa and Biyo-Kaboba – traditionally Somali country, and soon to be assigned to Italy by the Anglo-Italian agreement of 1894. Ethiopian soldiery, quartered on the surrounding people, wrought cruel execution on Somali tribes in the upper Shibeli and western Ogaden region. The Swayne brothers, surveying on the upper Fafan river not far from Harrar in 1892–3, were well placed to observe Ethiopian expansion in this region. They found it difficult to reconcile this attractive upland world, with its fresh air, the scent of sweet jasmine and flowering shrubs, with the ravages of the Ethiopian predators. Lord Wolverton, travelling in the area some 200 miles south of Berbera in 1893, com-mented on Ethiopian aggression and their looting of Somali stock. Ethiopia had availed herself of the preferential treatment accorded her under the Brussels General Act of 1890 and had built up her armed strength to an extraordinary degree. In the face of well-armed Ethiopian aggression the Somalis were in a parlous state. They had no treaties of protection with the British, and at the same time they were denied arms owing to British adherence to the Brussels treaty, which forbade the import of arms through ports under British control. The Somalis thus suffered grievously, and the Swayne brothers noted that Mullahs were preaching jihad (holy war) against the Ethiopians. H. G. C. Swayne claimed that the Somalis looked to the British for protection against the Ethiopians, and had interpreted the arrival of the cruiser, HMS *Kingfisher*, at Berbera in February 1891, as British intention to intervene on their behalf against the Ethiopians. The Swayne brothers were accorded the royal salute, 'reserved only for a sultan or the British'; and Somali men, women and children clutched at their saddles, crying out that they should lead them against the Ethiopians. When these pleas went unrequited the Somalis turned to their Mullahs. When a Mullah, greater than all, appeared among them he would be greeted as the Messiah. As for the British, not only did they fail to protect the Somalis against the Ethiopians, but they appeared to align themselves on the side of the Ethiopians. The struggle in Islamic eyes thus became doubly holy: Ethiopian and European Christian against Muslim. How different might the future of the Horn have been if Britain had come down on the side of the Somali instead of acquiescing in Ethiopian expansion into traditional Somali territory.

According to H. G. C. Swayne, visiting Harrar in the spring of 1893, the dolorous plight of the Somalis in the face of Ethiopian aggression arose from the superior armament of the latter. The Ethiopians were obtaining arms, including the latest Remingtons, by way of Jibuti. The Italians also, seemingly unaware that they were shaping a rod for their own backs, were supplying the Ethiopians with arms, ultimately to be used against themselves. When Swayne remonstrated against the presence of Makonnen's heavily armed soldiery in Somali territory, Makonnen informed him that the price of calling them off would be the cession of the port of Zeyla to Ethiopia. Lord Delamere, who had a shooting lodge near Hargeisa, also commented, when big-game hunting in Somaliland in 1895, on the large numbers of heavily armed Ethiopians in the vicinity.

The ambivalent attitude of the Italians towards Ethiopian expansion in the region of Harrar in the years immediately before the treaty of Adua (1896) is the key to events there during those years. Despite the Anglo-Italian agreement of 1894 which assigned this region, including Milmil, Biyo-Kaboba, Jigjiga and Gildessa, to the Italian sphere, the Ethiopians moved in and occupied these places. Italy, mesmerised by her view that an Ethiopian occupation was preferable to that of the Somalis, looked on with benevolent eye and acquiesced in it.

The Italian attitude derives from earlier Italian experience with the Somalis in this region. The massacre of Count Porri's government-backed expedition near Gildessa, by Somalis in 1885, and that of another party of Italians near Zeyla in 1886, caused Italy to view the Somalis as less of a stabilising force in the interior than the Ethiopians.

20

Menelik, fearing the Italians would annex Harrar in revenge, entered into a treaty with Italy on 2 May 1889, whereby in return for arms he would discipline the Somalis responsible for these attacks. Following her defeat at Adua in March 1896, Italy had neither the will nor the means to occupy the area assigned to her under the Anglo-Italian agreement of 1894. Thus one of the main consequences of Adua was the abandonment by Italy of the Somali Ogaden to Ethiopia.

The Ethiopians also expanded into the British sphere. In September 1896 the Ethiopian flag was hoisted at Alola in Gadabursi territory and an Ethiopian fort was built at Biyo-Kaboba in British territory, as fixed by boundary agreement with the French on 2 February 1888. Writing on 24 November 1896, Dr Donaldson Smith, the American explorer, who travelled from the Gulf of Aden to Lake Rudolf at the time, stated that:

> a line run from Imi, on the Shibeli River, to a point immediately below Bongo, in Kaffa, will mark the southern limits of any country to which Menelik can at present lay claims, either by virtue of peaceful occupation by treaties with native chiefs, or by conquest. To the west Abyssinia is bound by a line running north and south along the western border of Kaffa.

Between 1897 and 1900 the Ethiopians pushed south and east of the upper Fafan and Shibeli rivers and as far south as the upper Juba where they made an unsuccessful bid to occupy Lugh.

Adua was a turning point in the history of the Horn. It left Ethiopia as a power to be reckoned with. Menelik, full of overweening pride, claimed dominion over a vast area, insisting that he was only reconstituting the ancient limits of Ethiopia. This claim impinged on the spheres of European powers and resulted in their sending missions to Menelik to come to an understanding in the matter. The French were the most successful in achieving this. A concession for the construction of a railway from Jibuti to the interior had already been granted by Menelik to a French company in 1894. Further accord was reached in March 1897 by a French-Ethiopian convention fixing the limits inland of the French protectorate over the Gulf of Tajurra. The French colony of Obokh-Jibuti controlled the main channel of access to Ethiopia, and the governor of the colony, M. Lagarde, was in friendly diplomatic relations with Menelik. The latter had permitted a French expedition to move from the west by way of Ethiopia to link up with a French expedition moving eastwards from Upper Ubanghi towards the upper Nile.

The Russians similarly enjoyed a favourable position with the Ethiopians, tending to exploit their purported religious affinity with the Ethiopians. Russian interest in this part of the world derived from the establishment of a Russian evangelistic mission at Sagallo on the north shore of the Gulf of Tajurra by Captain Achinov in January 1889 (seemingly unaware that this was in the French protectorate). Although disavowed by the Russian government and viewed as a bizarre attempt on the part of religious zealots to force the hand of their own government into protecting them, its effect was similar to that of the socialist experiment by the Freelanders, farther south on the East African coast, at about the same time. The episode caused much excitement in Paris and Moscow, coinciding as it did with the conducting of a party of Ethiopians to Moscow by M. Leontieff, and revealing Russian aspirations in Ethiopia. It is tempting to read too much into the episode. Little could come of it, for Russia at the end of the nineteenth century was faced with major difficulties at home, and soon, overshadowing all, there was the Russo-Japanese war.

The British position *vis-à-vis* Menelik was less favourable than that of the French. The British Somaliland protectorate lay in the orbit of Menelik's dreams, but at the same time, Britain needed his co-operation against the Dervishes in the Sudan. She also had to retain his goodwill in the face of European rivalry in the Horn, especially that of the French. Although Ethiopians were now ensconced in areas assigned to Italy and Britain under the Anglo-Italian agreement of 1894, and this seriously affected the traditional pasture rights of British protected tribes, there was no overt British reaction to it. However, when in early 1897 the French and Ethiopians began negotiations which resulted in a French-Ethiopian convention in March of that year, whereby the limits inland of the French colony of Obokh-Jibuti were fixed, it was evident that there were vital questions between Ethiopia and Britain to be cleared up. Hence the decision to send a British mission to Menelik, in March 1897.

The mission was led by James Rennel Rodd, diplomatist and scholar, previously at Zanzibar, and lately Cairo. It was in the tradition of former British missions to Ethiopia in the latter nineteenth century, such as that of Sir William Hewett, in 1884, to obtain King John's assistance in evacuating garrisons from the eastern Sudan, and that of Sir Gerald Portal, in 1887, to arrange peace between King John and the Italians. Rodd's task was to secure a friendly neutral Ethiopia in the face of a British advance on the Upper Nile to oust the Dervishes, and he was to come to an agreement with Menelik as to frontier delimitation between Ethiopia and the British Somaliland protectorate. He was instructed to make whatever concessions were necessary to achieve these two goals, so long as Aden's food supply was secured and British prestige upheld. There must be no impression of a sell-out.

It was an impressive mission which gathered at Zeyla in mid-March 1897, in preparation for the trek to Addis Ababa. The mission's 200 camels and 30 mules were laden with munificent gifts, meant to surpass the supposedly 'very magnificent' ones of a Russian mission rumoured to be on its way to Addis Ababa at the time. There was bullion and silver plate, there were carpets, jewelled crosses, silks, and *objets d'art*, exhibiting the finest examples of London craftmanship. There was a grand escort of Sikhs and Rajputs, symbolic of the power of the British Raj in India. Most striking, however, was the coterie of British giants, five in all, who made up the British party. Ranging in height from 'Speedy', at 6'6", to H. G. C. Swayne, the smallest, a mere 6'3", their thumping size would surely impress the Ethiopians.

Leaving the reed- and coral-built village of Zeyla on 20 March 1897, the mission wended its way through desert growth, mimosa and Red Sea apple shrub to the Warabod wells, 8 miles from Zeyla. Here, they were met by spear-bearing Essa tribesmen whose initial hostility soon turned to obsequious friendliness in the face of the obvious strength and formidable panoply of the mission. A further 10 miles' march brought the mission to the Gildessa springs, whose opulent vegetation betokened a different world from the harsh Somali desert, now left behind. From Gildessa onwards there began the gradual ascent to Harrar, through groves of wild olive, jasmine and hairy-leaved heliotrope with its striking purplish flowers. Another two weeks' march brought the mission to Harrar. They found it much changed from Burton's description of it nearly 40 years before. Since then it had become much more open to the outside world. Its bazaar was mostly inhabited by Indians – British subjects – as the chief bankers and merchants. Ethiopians seemed to be everywhere, and in armed strength.

At Harrar there commenced that off-loading of gifts which was supposed to smooth the path of the mission. Those for Makonnen, Governor of Harrar, included two great braziers, a sword of honour, an eight-bore rifle and 300 rounds of ammunition, a gold-plated Martini rifle and a Colt repeater. For Makonnen's wife there were fine silks and embroideries. The giving of these gifts completed, provisioning and recruitment of additional mules done, the mission resumed its journey to Addis.

After it dropped down into the Awash Valley, a few days' march brought the mission to the steep acclivity of the mountain massif of

Ethiopia. From there on to Addis Ababa they were in a different world, an upland world of bearded Ethiopians. Addis was reached in early April 1897. Here every man seemed to be armed, and nearly every type of firearm was represented. There was no doubt now as to the rumours of Ethiopia being one large arsenal!

The mission's appearance at Addis Ababa did not cause the surprise that might have been expected. Addis Ababa had become used to the bizarre and unusual. Following their meeting with M. Ilg, Menelik's Swiss adviser, there again took place the ritual 'giving of presents'. Those for Menelik were truly marvellous. There were 'wonderfully warm' buffalo robes and a magnificent polar bear skin from North America. There was silver galore – two large silver salvers engraved with the Lion of Judah, four silver branch-candlesticks, an ornate silver-gilt ewer and basin, four silver-gilt rice bowls, a magnificent large silver-mounted looking-glass – and, especially for Menelik's wife, diamonds, an emerald necklace, silk embroideries and a beautiful silk Persian carpet. There were two superb gold inlaid double-barrelled rifles and a .450 Holland Express, a pair of the best field-glasses obtainable. To round off this munificent list there was a splendidly bound volume of *A Life of Alexander the Great*, 'especially printed in Ethiopic'. In contrast to this British munificence, that of the Russians seemed paltry indeed: a gramophone, a few Russian Cossacks on loan, and some 40 instruments for the formation of a brass band.

The official reception for the British mission at Addis was on the grand scale amid scenes of barbaric splendour and pomp. There was much pride and panopoly and archaic rude ceremony. The Ethiopians, flushed by their recent victory over the Italians, were intent on impressing Europeans at their court. Scenes of Ruritanian sumptuousness were laid on for their benefit, a splendid repast for the hot and wearied travellers from the coast.

Menelik's court was cosmopolitan. There were 15 high-ranking Europeans, the doyen of whom was the Swiss M. Ilg, Counsellor to Menelik, being seated at his right hand. The French contingent predominated. Prince Henri d'Orléans and le Vicomte Edmond de Poncins bore high titles, Menelik having sprinkled his encomiums most liberally. A number of Europeans had undergone a remarkable metamorphosis since their arrival at his court: M. Lagarde and M. Leontieff were now Duke of Entotto and Count Leontieff respectively. There were, in addition to these bemedalled Europeans at this exotic court, Russian Cossacks, the Ethiopian royal household with its Rases (Governors), and high-ranking military: Dejazmachs (Generals), Kanyazmachs and Gerazmachs (Commanders).

Even before he got down to business Rodd learnt the extent of

Ethiopian ambitions. On the eve of Rodd's arrival, 4 May 1897, Menelik had issued a circular letter to European powers, outlining his territorial claims. He meant to restore the ancient frontiers of Ethiopia. To the north-west and south they extended to Khartoum and Lake Nyanza, and on the east they included much of the northern Horn. Rodd came to the conclusion that the 'Ethiopian Empire', at least in the mind of Menelik, extended much beyond that portion usually marked on maps as 'Abyssinia', especially to the south-east, where her feelers were in measurable distance of the coast south of Cape Guardafui. To the north-west, in the Sudan and Dervish* country, the stark desert plains were a deterrent to Ethiopian advance in that direction. The attractive fertile province of Harrar and the foothills to its immediate east were much more to the liking of these men of the hills.

Rodd started negotiations with Menelik on 13 May 1897, mindful of his instructions as to making necessary concessions, including adjustments to the frontiers as defined in the protocol with Italy of 5 May 1894 (Britain appears to have written off Italy at this stage), and the transfer to Ethiopia of tribes under British protection, with the proviso: 'You will be careful to obtain pledges that they will be treated with justice and consideration.' The opening conversation with Menelik did not augur well. The latter claimed that the Somalis from time immemorial had a lesser role in the Horn. They were traditional cattle-keepers for the Ethiopians who, because of their 'delicate constitutions', could not themselves live in the low countries. The problem for the mission in supporting Somali claims was that they were based on a tribal or clan basis and there was no central government or authority to invoke to back them up in the way Menelik or Makonnen could do for the Ethiopians. If only the Somalis had a king/emperor to speak for them!

Swayne, present during the discussion on Somali frontiers, argued against Britain's entering into a bilateral treaty with Ethiopia, as irreconcilable with Britain's treaties of protection with Somali tribes and the fact that these tribes had grown accustomed to British rule. In the discussion on the need for accurate boundaries and precise maps, Menelik feigned ignorance of such matters, insisting that Rodd await the arrival from Harrar of Ras Makonnen, who was much more versed in the subject. Rodd, however, could not wait, as he was anxious to complete his business before the start of the rains. Finally it was agreed that he would finalise negotiations with Makonnen at Harrar, on his way back to the coast.

*'Dervish' (from Turkish dervis or Persian darvésh) refers to those valiant and ardent fighters for Islam vowed to a life of poverty and austerity.

The main aspects of the treaty to which Menelik gave his seal at Addis, on 14 May 1897, were secured with little difficulty, apart from those pertaining to boundary matters. There was to be permanent British representation at the Emperor's court, and most-favoured-nation treatment for Britain in matters of commerce. The caravan route between Zeyla and Harrar by way of Gildessa was to be open to the commerce of both nations and Ethiopian goods were to go through Zeyla free of duty. Menelik, on his part, agreed to prevent munitions of war going to the Dervishes by way of Ethiopia. On the whole, Rodd had achieved his aims.

The mission's send-off from Addis was in the grand manner: there was a military pageant of 20,000 soldiers, accompanied by more giving of gifts, this time by Menelik. Rodd was presented with 'ten horses with silver-studded saddles and bridles'. Rodd and party, apart from Swayne, were much impressed by all this. They described Menelik as 'verily a great man ... clear-headed and acute, but simple-minded withal', and dreadfully fearful of being taken in by enigmatic phrases and conditions within conditions, so dear to the diplomatic mind. The lesson derived from the wording of the Uccialli Treaty was still much in Menelik's mind. To set his mind at rest in this regard, the wording of his treaty with the British was also made out in French, the classic diplomatic language.

The members of the British mission thought that the Ethiopians, on the whole, had been much maligned by the outside world. Stories of atrocities committed by Ethiopians against Italian prisoners were much exaggerated. There were some authentic cases of mutilation, no doubt, but these were traceable to the half-savage allies or subjects of Ethiopia. The mission left Addis with the memory of a virile and intelligent people, and they were Christians!

Arriving at Harrar on 31 May 1897, on the return journey to the coast, Rodd negotiated with Makonnen the boundary arrangements to be incorporated in the main treaty made with Menelik on 14 May. Rodd describes Makonnen as a 'perfect Abyssinian gentleman', who freely admitted that the Ethiopians had considerably encroached into the British protectorate, to the east of Gildessa, but said that Somalis had burnt Ethiopian huts in the disputed area. Rodd argued strenuously for the right of tribes to resort to their traditional grazing grounds even though these were now occupied by the Ethiopians. Makonnen's opening bid was to claim 33,000 square miles of territory lying within the British protectorate, including Hargeisa. Rodd, in a counter bid, offered 13,500 square miles in the south-west of the British protectorate, taking in the wells and grazing area of the Essa and Habr Awal tribes and giving control of the Gildessa-Zeyla trade route, a most tempting offer! Makonnen, feigning injured feelings at what he termed a measly offer, complained that the English were 'hard bargainers', who took all the good land for themselves and left him only desert country. In the upshot, however, he accepted Rodd's offer, which was generous in the extreme.

Rodd later justified his concession as being in the spirit of his instructions to conciliate Ethiopia, and this was especially needful now that the British campaign against the Dervishes in the Sudan was in its last phase. The concession, so he argued, would also end further Ethiopian incursion into British territory, and it would be nigh impossible to dislodge them from the posts they presently occupied without recourse to armed warfare.

His business with Makonnen finished, Rodd continued his journey coastward by way of Gildessa, meeting the notorious adventurer, Carl Inger, on the way down. On 14 June 1897 he arrived at Zeyla where he was met by Colonel Hayes-Sadler, the political agent there, and thence was conveyed to Aden by the steamship, *Mento*.

Rodd arrived back in a London of cosmopolitan splendour and gaiety, for it was the year of the Diamond Jubilee, and almost overwhelming in its impression of contrast to what he had left behind: the scenes of wild pageantry and barbarism of Ethiopia, and the wild wastes of the Somali deserts. He had little time, however, for such reflections. There was a long interview with Lord Salisbury (Prime Minister and Foreign Secretary), already apprised by a confidential letter from Rodd at Addis Ababa, dated 13 May 1897, as to the annexionist appetite of the Ethiopians and their encroachment on British protected territory, and the difficulty in negotiating a joint frontier with them.

There is a note of rueful regret and some self-reproach in Rodd's account of his interview with Salisbury. He found the latter much more preoccupied with events in the Sudan and the French advance on the upper Nile than with Ethiopian encroachment into Somaliland. Salisbury appeared more interested in that portion of Rodd's treaty with Menelik whereby the latter bound himself to prevent arms reaching the Dervishes than in the securing of grazing rights for comparatively unknown Somali tribesmen. In all, however, Rodd's mission to Ethiopia was considered a substantial success. It earned him the Companionship of the Order of the Bath, and a reputation as an 'African expert'. In 1902 Rodd was transferred from Cairo to Rome, where he assisted in negotiating Anglo-Italian treaties for the delimitation of their territories in Africa.

The frontiers of the British Somaliland protectorate as negotiated by Rodd with Makonnen at Harrar on 4 June 1897, and set out in annexture to the main treaty with Menelik (ratified by Queen Victoria on 28 July 1897), were based on tribal divisions, points occupied by the Ethiopians, and, to some extent, on natural features (the Ethiopians claimed ignorance as to such things as meridians and parallels of latitude). The boundary line of the British protectorate with Ethiopia retraced the line of the Anglo-French Agreement of 9 February 1888, as far as the hill of Somadu (half-way between Gildessa and the coast, and designated as Beio Ano on modern maps), then south-east in irregular fashion, along the line of the Sau mountains and Egu hills to a point, Moga Madei, whence it ran in a direct line to a point, Aran Areh (at intersection of latitude 8°N with longitude 44°E), and thence in a straight line to the intersection of latitude 8°N with longitude 47°E. From here on it followed the line of demarcation of the British protectorate as agreed by the Anglo-Italian protocol of 5 May 1894.

This boundary line gave Ethiopia not only 13,500 square miles of British protected territory but also territory (including Gildessa, Jigjiga and Milmil) assigned to Italy by the Anglo-Italian protocol of 5 May 1894. As a saving grace, there was a provision in the agreement that tribes on either side of the line had right of access to grazing and wells on the other side, but they would then be under the jurisdiction of the territorial authority concerned. There was neither Italian nor Somali participation in this treaty-making, although their vital interests were concerned. It might be argued that the Somalis had no central government or authority to act on their behalf, no overall spokesman. However, there was no attempt to consult Somali tribal elders in the matter. Even the doughty Swayne, despite his grave doubts as to the morality of it all, did not speak up on behalf of the Somalis. As for the Italians, they were still licking their wounds from Adua, and seemed not to have the will to demur.

One indirect result of Rodd's mission to Addis Ababa was the revival of the project for a railway to Harrar, from either Zeyla or Berbera. M. Ilg had made no secret to Rodd as to French plans for a railway from Jibuti, by way of Harrar, to Addis, and possibly to the Upper Nile. The French had already, in 1894, obtained a concession for such a railway. The British mission had also learnt of Somali opposition to any joint French-Ethiopian railway running through their territory, although they would not demur if it were under British auspices. Rodd, while in

London, urged the early construction of a light railway from Zeyla to Harrar. It would pre-empt the French project, and would confer untold benefits on what was at present an unprofitable possession under a slight coastal administration and with an indeterminate hinterland. A railway would develop the interior and secure a monopoly of its trade, and raise Zeyla to the status of a major port. In his advocacy of such a railway, Rodd had the full support of Hayes-Sadler, now Consul, except that Hayes-Sadler, with more local knowledge than Rodd, would make Berbera, rather than Zeyla, the seaport terminus of the railway.

It was not an auspicious time for Rodd to raise the subject of a railway in northern Somaliland. With the Anglo-Ethiopian agreement signed, there was a feeling that the future of British Somaliland (albeit with some loss of territory) was secured. There was already a lessening of Aden's dependence on Somaliland as a source of meat. The advent of refrigeration on ocean-going vessels meant that frozen meat from Australia and New Zealand was now readily available at Aden, although fresh meat on the hoof was still preferred there. The factor most heavily weighing against the construction of the railway, however, was the opposition of the British Treasury. It could see no rational argument in its favour. The cost would be prohibitive, even in the modified form of a light railway to the Haud and a branch to Gildessa, as suggested by Rodd. Thus the railway proposal was quashed. Years later, Rodd was still rueing the fact that the railway had not been built. Otherwise, the 'fanatical Mad Mullah' would never have become so formidable . . . we might have been spared the many valuable lives lost, the millions spent in thankless expeditions against that elusive enemy who gave us so much trouble over a period of 20 years.' Rodd was prescient, for the need for such a railway was to crop up again.

There was renewed assessment of British interests in the Horn following Rodd's mission and the Anglo-Ethiopian Agreement of 1897. The importance of Ethiopia as a political force to be reckoned with, and so also her ambitions in the Horn, rivalling those of Italy and France, were now recognised by Britain. The diplomatic task of dealing with these contending rivalries could not be left to the Indian Government, ill-equipped as it was by temperament and interest for such a clever game, despite its being disappointed at not being consulted in the conceding of Somaliland territory in the recent negotiations with Ethiopia. India itself was faced with warfare on her frontiers and by numerous demands on her military forces for service in Jubaland, Uganda and other parts of the Empire.

It thus came as no surprise when, on 1 October 1898, the administration of the Somaliland Coast Protectorate was transferred from the Indian Government to the Foreign Office. Colonel Hayes-Sadler, an old East Africa hand, was raised from Consul to Consul-General for the Protectorate. By Order-in-Council (1899) the new territory became the British Somaliland Coast Protectorate. There was much optimism as to its future. It was the only British territory in eastern Africa which was self-supporting. There were high hopes for the development of its mineral, agricultural and commercial resources, and there was its traditional trade in frankincense and gums, skins and meat. The British Treasury, always chary with its plaudits, expressed much satisfaction at the surplus, albeit small, for the first two financial years, 1898–9 and 1899–1900, under Foreign Office control.

This auspicious beginning was fleeting, for soon a holy man, a Wadad, Mohammed Abdille Hassan, the 'Mad Mullah', so termed by the British, would challenge the very foundation of British rule in the protectorate. In March 1899 Hayes-Sadler wrote accusing him of abetting the theft of a government rifle. The Mullah's reply, couched in what was to become his familiar epistolaric style, was lofty, proud and defiant:

> There is no god but Allah, and Mohammed is his messenger. Nought have I stolen from you or any other. Seek what you want from him who robbed you. Serve whom you have chosen to serve.

There had been no shortage of holy men in the Muslim world. The British had recently strained with might and sinew in fighting the Dervishes and meeting the challenge of the Mahdi and Khalifa in the Sudan. Earlier in the century they had contended with Dan Fodio in West Africa. Now they faced a similar challenge in the Horn. Whence came this holy man of the Somalis?

3

GENESIS OF A MULLAH

THE scene is a small valley in the Nogal Dolbahanta country in northern Somaliland. In front of a cleft in high rock walls overlooking a dry river bed, the evening camp fire cast strange shadows over the small group of Somali tribesmen clustered around it. The imagination can easily conjure up the apparition of a genie rising in the spiral of smoke. The wizened old Yibir, famed for his bone-setting and the centre of attention, faced an awesome task. He wrinkled his nose as he puffed the cinders into life in the small forge, heating the murky water in the small copper bowl resting on two stones and straddling a small fire. Neatly laid out and close by were the crude tools of his trade: instruments for 'letting out devils'. There was a small lancet-shaped knife, a tiny saw of the European key-hole type, a perforator (on the principle of a centre bit), a chisel-like tool, hardened thorns up to 2 inches in length, the screws or fasteners, finally the main drill, crudely made and one-eighth of an inch in diameter. These 'surgeon's' implements were placed in a bowl of steaming water, sterilised and ready for use.

Meanwhile the patient, a lad of not more than ten years of age, lay drugged in a heavy sleep induced by inhaling the smoke from burning leaves of the quat and *Datura stramonium* plants along with infusions from the wildpoppy. The old Yibir carefully donned his leather cape and placed it over the holy amulet strung on a thong around his neck. Muttering incantations, he prepared his patient. The boy's head was shaved, the skin then rendered aseptic by daubings of juice from the arentac tree. The Yibir then began the operation. With his sharp lancet knife he turned back a horseshoe-shaped flap of skin, about 2 inches by 3 inches in size, laying bare the skull underneath. With the aid of the larger drill and then the smaller centre-bit, he outlined a disc of bone (the trepan) about the size of an English crown coin or a napkin-ring. With his minute crown saw he quickly removed the small disc from the skull wall, thus opening up the dura mater. Continuing his mutterings, the Yibir worked quickly and deftly. Then a sudden grunt affirmed his discovery, the cause of the compression: a small tumour, about one-quarter of an inch in diameter. This was quickly removed by a neat undercut.

The trepanning was quickly and dexterously done. The disc of bone, kept in a warm bowl of camel's milk throughout the operation, was now cut into small pieces which, as in a miniature jigsaw puzzle, were then packed back into the opening and the skull flap was brought back into position. Over the whole there was then applied a poultice of crushed leaves of the evergreen haroun bush, and on top of this was placed a plaster of topaz-yellow resin from the famous Dolbahanta yehar incense tree.

Throughout the operation the young lad had breathed easily, scarcely stirring. Drugged, and in deep sleep, he did not waken until two hours later. He then sat up and, with serene and almost adult gaze, looked round at the silent figures gathered in mute reverence at the scene they had just witnessed. Although in modern psychological parlance he had had what would be termed a 'personality disorder', it was for these tribesmen truly a metamorphosis, the genesis of a Muslim saint. Had not Haji Sahadi Hassin, most holy of name, undergone a similar operation by trepanning in his youth?

The father and uncles of the young lad had watched with bated breath throughout the operation. They now hastened to give prayers of thanks to Allah and the Prophet. Had not they themselves noticed, and had they not often affirmed that the young boy, Mohammed, had shown signs of holiness from his earliest years. Mohammed's parents were from wide-ranging backgrounds. His father, Abdullah Hassan, a poor camel owner of no special repute, belonged to the Habr Suleiman or Bagheri section of the southern Ogaden, and the child had visited the main watering place, Galadi, of his father's people, deep in south-east Ogaden. His mother, Malali, was of the Ali Gheri, a sub-tribe of the powerful Dolbahanta, and came from near Kirrit, some 200 miles north of Galadi, and it was here that the child looked to as his main home. He himself was born (1864?) and nurtured at Kob Faradod, near Kirrit, in the Dolbahanta country, some 180 miles south-east of Berbera.

From his earliest years he was introduced into the world of the nomad. Scarcely more than a babe, wrapped in a small *tobe* and strapped to his mother's back while she marched at the rear of the camel caravan with the other Somali women, querulously shouting abuse or running forward to beat into line a refractory camel, little Mohammed was joggled about like a rag doll. Docile after the fashion of Somali children, he emitted scarcely a cry during these arduous journeys under the burning sun. By the age of six, Mohammed was herding the stock of his mother's tribe, ranging on his own for distances of up to 10 miles from his birthplace. Soon these lesser perambulations would be interspersed with longer journeys to the outside world, including Berbera, a place which loomed large in the trade of these hinterland tribes. A mere slip of a lad, he made the ten-day, 180-mile trek on foot, up-hill and down, over sun-scorched rocks and sand, along dried-out watercourses, his bare feet blistered and blackened, hardened into endurance by the sand blast of the hot winds.

During these long trips, between Berbera and Kirrit, and from Kirrit to the land of his father's people in the southern Ogaden, young Mohammed displayed the conceit and spirit of independence of his mother's tribe, and the zeal for prayer and religious instruction that characterised his father's family. He showed a remarkably intense and precocious interest in the words of the Mullahs on their frequent visits to his tribe or when accompanying them on their perennial migrations. Sitting under the shade of a friendly tree, spellbound at the feet of some Mullah of purported erudition and beauty of holiness, expounding the oral revelations of the Prophet and passages from the Holy Koran, Mohammed listened with rapt gaze. It was during one of these catechical tuitions, that the old Mullah, Haji Abdullah Faradi, a Seyyid, reputed descendant of the Prophet and, as such, wearing the blue turban, and with the green waistband of a Haji, recited a passage from the Koran with unfailing memory, and then narrated a superb prose passage describing the martyrdom of their patron saint. His voice was like a bell, and there was such sweetness of intonation and piety that his listeners were moved to tears. It was a great oratorical performance, accompanied by wonderful and expressive gestures. It was during one of these reverent and spellbinding devotions that Haji Abdullah, noticing the small cupola-shaped protuberance on the child's head, exclaimed: 'Verily, Allah has chosen thee!'

Mohammed was 11 years old when he accompanied an uncle to Berbera, and from there travelled by dhow to Zeyla and Aden. During the journey he was assigned to bundling up hides and preparing produce for sale at Aden, tending the live sheep on board, and serving ghee and rice to the ragamuffin crew. His arrival at Aden presented for him a new world: the great liners and naval vessels at anchorage in the busy harbour, the bustling docks, and the British soldiers, *en route* to and from India, upright and proud, marching in step to a rousing military band through the twisting streets of the old town. It was young Mohammed's first glimpse of Britain's imperial might, then at its high noon. Berbera, previously for him a wondrous port, now paled into insignificance in the face of what he saw at Aden.

Before returning to Berbera, the dhow on which he travelled sailed up the Arabian coast to Mukalla, where goods from Aden were exchanged for dates brought down from Basra. At Mukalla, as at Aden, Mohammed visited mosques and conversed with the Mullahs, showing himself, despite his tender age, to be well versed in the Koran and the Sharia (Islamic law). He endeavoured to speak Arabic, the language beloved of the Prophet. How widespread, so it seemed to him with his limited background and untutored ideas of geography, was the religion of Islam. Truly, God was great.

Four more journeys were undertaken to Aden in the next few years, each bringing new experiences to young Mohammed. In the Somali quarter of Aden he heard tales of the wider world where the infidel reigned supreme, and of Islamic countries administered by the British Raj, where good Muslims were held in subordination and their Mullahs were looked upon as religious oddities. It was on one of these journeys, at the age of 17, that he made the momentous decision to see the wider world of the Red Sea. He enrolled as assistant fireman on a steamer of the Italian Lloyd Trestino Line, which called at the port of Jedda, the gateway to Mecca.

Jedda, lying towards the northern side of a western-facing bay, on a low sandy plain, and backed by a range of hills some 10 miles distant, is enclosed by a wall, with towers at intervals. Its three gates are well named: the Medina gate on the north, the Mecca gate on the east, and the Yemen gate on the south. Inside the Medina gate, and close to the town, were the Turkish barracks, and beyond these the tomb of 'mother Eve', the most holy place in Jedda. The town of Jedda itself, with its houses of corraline rock, had little in the way of architectural merit to commend it. The magic of Jedda lies in its being the portal to Mecca, some 60 miles away. Mohammed, finding himself so close to that holy of holiest places, was in an exalted state, almost a religious trance.

Yet for all his salaams, earnestness and pleading, the captain of the Lloyd Trestino steamer refused him the few days' leave he requested, to visit the shrine of the Prophet. Mohammed, bitterly disappointed, sulkily acquiesced, but did not forget the Italians. He departed the gateway to the Holy City, without setting eyes on the sublimest of all places this side of Paradise, but with a deep inner resolve to return.

Within the year he was once more at Jedda, making the sacred pilgrimage, a pilgrimage which metamorphosed his spiritual and emotional being. It was an unforgettable experience and transported him to such heights of religious fervour that he seemed to surmount all worldly aspirations and worries. The burden of this life on earth was irrelevant in relation to the vision of Paradise.

He was only 18 years of age, a tall, slim, lithe and sinewy youth, with dark Afro/Semitic features, and already sprouting the small goatee beard which was to characterise his later appearance, and now he was performing the pilgrimage, one of the five pillars of Islam. He had worked his way up from Berbera to Zeyla by dhow, and thence to Jedda. Leaving his fellow crew members at the docks, he entered the Yemen gate and, once into the town, lost no time before passing through the Mecca gate. He was on his way to the shrine of the Prophet, to the holy shrine.

He made what was usually a two-day ride to Mecca in half that time, by a quick change of riding mules. Entering the sacred *haram* of the Holy City from the west, he was greeted by a sight which has made the hearts of millions of pilgrims vibrate. Months of weary journey and deprivation were now forgotten in the face of the wondrous sight lying before the eyes of the aspirant Haji. The great mosque of Mecca and the Holy Kaaba within it were the supreme affirmation of that promise of heart's ease which had sustained the sorefoot pilgrim on the long and exhausting road to the seat of the Prophet. Verily, it was second only to seeing the face of the Prophet himself. There was a spiritual ecstacy in the air of Mecca which lifted up Mohammed quite beyond himself.

With his hired *mutauwif* (guide) he was manoeuvred into the intricacies of the Haj ritual. Mohammed donned the *ihram*, meanwhile exclaiming, 'Here am I, O God, here am I!' Since this was the Dhu'l Hijja, the final month of the Muslim year (Arabic calendar), and since he had come on the ninth day of that month, his was no ordinary 'Umra', but the real pilgrimage enjoined by the Prophet: the Haj, the once-in-a-lifetime holy pilgrimage to the shrine of the Prophet, to his birthplace, not to his tomb, for that was in Medina where he died.

Around the Kaaba, seven times, in clockwise direction, did Mohammed perform the *tawaf* or circumambulation. Next came the kissing of the holies of holies, the small black stone, surely the most precious in the world, fixed in the south-east corner of the Kaaba. Its smooth surface could only be touched through the elaborate silver filigree which enclosed the broken pieces ever since it had been riven by fire during the siege of AD 683. (The silver network had miraculously saved it during the sack of AD 930 by the Carmathians, and had preserved it during a 22-year exile, until it was ransomed and restored to its abiding home.)

How fortunate for the young devotee that he had arrived at the Kaaba on one of the rare days when its small door, some 7 feet above floor level, was opened! Again, how favoured was he to be among the half-dozen pilgrims permitted to mount the short flight of steps and to peer in, to experience the inner transfiguration from the beatific vision within, so wonderful as not be described in the words of ordinary mortals.

Here now, in 1884, already Sheikh, and still only in his teens, Mohammed swore at the Prophet's shrine to rid Somaliland of the infidel who had violated his land. The rare vision of the Kaaba's interior seems to have given Mohammed superhuman powers, for he not only made the quick runs, to and fro, seven times over, along the Al Mas'a, 'the place of running', but, with hair now cut in pilgrim fashion, he encompassed the most arduous part of the pilgrimage, the 30-mile trek from Mecca to Mount Arafa ('Mount of Mercy') in record time and without slaking his thirst or partaking of food. Such worldly appetites had no place during these hallowed hours.

Returning to Mecca, Mohammed drank of the holy waters of the well, Zemzem, in the court of the great mosque. Finally, he circum-ambulated the Kaaba for the last time. The pilgrimage was completed. Before leaving the Holy City the young Haj, for he was now one of the elect, met the Grand Sheriff of Mecca himself. Truly Allah is great!

The intoxicating and exalting effect of the Haj is well known. Its effect on young Mohammed was remarkable and pregnant in the extreme. To cap it all there was his meeting with Mohammed ibn Salih al Rashidi, founder of the Salihiya brotherhood, who imparted to him the fanatical tenets of his harsh and uncompromising interpretation of the Prophet's teachings. The Salihiya stressed the strict observance of Islamic laws: austerity and the avoidance of alcohol, smoking and chewing of *kat*, and foreign imports and influences. Thus at the age of 19, how blessed was he, young Mohammed, to have made the pilgrimage. He had lived for a few days in the very empyrean of Islamic sainthood. Never did a more ardent disciple emerge from the great Madrassi of the Holy City.

Mohammed traversed the return road from Mecca to Jedda as one in a dream, as though inspired. On the dhow journey homeward, he remained deeply immersed in the Koran, oblivious to those around him. Word spread among the crew members that there was a saint on board, and he was treated with great respect. At Suakin, on the western side of the Red Sea, the young Haj heard of the Mahdi and his successor, the Khalifa, who had converted the Muslims in the vast Sudan to a more holy and rigorous way of life. Was there not a message for him from Allah in all this? Might not he too be a Mahdi ('guide'), divinely appointed to regenerate Somaliland?

The next ten years were deeply formative in Mohammed's life. He made six more visits to Mecca, and by the time he had made the last of these, in 1895 at the age of 30, his spiritual training was rounded out: he was now more than a mere Wadad; he was a Sheikh and Khalifa, the chief priest of the sect of Mohammed ibn Salih in Somaliland.

The intervals between his pilgrimages to Mecca had been mostly spent as a travelling Wadad among his mother's people, the Ali Gheri of the Dolbahanta, and his father's people, the Habr Suleiman or Bagheri in the southern Ogaden. On his return from his last pilgrimage in 1895, Mohammed attempted to introduce at Berbera the strict teachings of his master, Salih. He came, however, into conflict with older and well-established Islamic brotherhoods: the Qaadiriya, Dandaara-wiya and Ahmadiya. It was abominable, in his view, that they should tolerate, before their eyes, the planting of Christianity at Berbera, where a Catholic mission had been operating for some years with some success, especially among the flotsam population of that port, and was taking under its protection homeless children who became its converts. The sight of the latter wearing crucifixes around their necks was especially repugnant to Mohammed, for were not such images anathema to Islam? He found that his own stern Salihiya doctrines and puritan reforms were uncongenial to the people of Berbera, and now convinced that only a jihad would succeed against unbelievers, he made for the hinterland.

Making his base at Mudug in the southern Haud, well out of range of the British at Berbera, he acquired much influence among the southern Dolbahanta, into the Ali Gheri branch of which he married. He also won over many followers from among the Adan Madoba, including Haji Sudi, formerly interpreter on a British ship, widely travelled, and who was to become Mohammed's trusted lieutenant. Within a year of establishing himself at Mudug, Mohammed extended his bases to Bohotle and points in the Nogal Valley from where he traversed widely afield and into the Protectorate. Within the British Protectorate he won over Ahmed Farah and Rer Yusuf, of the Habr Toljaala near the northern coast to the east of Berbera, and the Musa Ismail of the eastern Habr Yunis, and Sultan Nur of the Habr Gerhajis south of Berbera. He continued to be active among his father's tribe in the southern Ogaden.

Here Mohammed's jihad, for such it appeared, was directed more clearly against the Ethiopians than the British at this stage. Mohammed had travelled as a Wadad in the area of Ethiopian encroachment in the southern and western Ogaden in the early 1890s, and was preaching there at the same time that the Swayne brothers were on the upper Shibeli in 1893, reporting on the jihad-preaching activity of Wadads in the region, although they made no special reference to Mohammed at the time. Mohammed now brought under his teaching the Rer Ibrahim (Mukabil) and the Ba Hawadle (Miyirwalal) of the southern Ogaden. It was among these people that he became fully apprised as to the wrongs inflicted on them by the Ethiopians: the experience left him with a burning hatred for these Christian Africans.

The Ethiopians, even before their victory over the Italians at Adua, were much puffed up and imperialistically minded, sending invading expeditions deep into the Ogaden, as Swayne had observed during his visits there in 1893. Following Adua the Ethiopians were vainglorious beyond restraint. Compared to the Somalis they were well armed with modern rifles, and Swayne, at Harrar in 1897, saw these modern arms being brought in by the mule-load. Also paraded before his eyes were Somali prisoners-of-war from the Ogaden.

The British at Berbera at first saw Mohammed only as a devout Wadad, and had no reason to believe that he was other than such, nor that he intended to drive out the British. He seemed an earnest seeker after the truth, and there was room, in British eyes, for the introduction among the wild Somalis of the interior of a strict and austere asceticism, as preached by the Salihiya sect. Mohammed's influence at first appeared beneficent: his teachings enjoined strict observance of the tenets of Islam, and an interdiction of *kat*, the stimulant drug. He settled disputes among remote tribes, warned against inter-tribal warfare, and seemed to be on the side of law and order. Occasionally he corresponded with the Vice-Consul at Berbera on tribal matters, and even sent down prisoners for trial at the Vice-Consular Court there, such was his apparent faith in British justice.

This halcyon period did not last. Mohammed acquired considerable influence over hinterland tribes, and they in turn increasingly preferred his brand of rough-and-ready justice based on Islamic law to making the long journey to Berbera. Even so, the British continued to look upon his activities with much tolerance – even indulgence. His adjudication of legal cases sensibly concurred with those dealt with by the British authorities. He continued to exhort strict adherence to Allah's commandments. Tribes previously cantankerous were now more peaceful. As Mohammed's influence grew, however, there became discernible, a notable change in his utterances and so also a gradual reshaping of his views. They were increasingly tinged with anti-Britishness. In a few months reports were filtering into Berbera that Mohammed was urging the expulsion of all Europeans from the Horn, and challenging the right of the British to levy customs dues at the coast.

In these early years, Mohammed was quietly disciplining his followers, damping down inter-tribal hostility, asserting his own ascendancy, and substituting his authority for that of the tribal elders.

4

THE EXPEDITION PERIOD, 1900–5

BY early 1899, the Mullah had based himself at Sheikh in the Golis range some 40 miles south of Berbera. His name, however, soon became increasingly associated with raids on tribes friendly to the British, and there were reports of his collecting arms and men, and preaching fanaticism akin to a jihad. The culmination came in March 1899, when this self-proclaimed holy man of Islam sent a taunting letter, a veritable challenge of war, to the British Consul-General at Berbera. The latter acted quickly. The Mullah was declared an outlaw, and a young political officer, Haji Musa Farah (henceforth a veritable *bête noire* to the Mullah) was sent to arrest him. The latter, forewarned, slipped away over the Golis range and southwards into the vast Haud region. Thus began a drama which would last for 21 years and involve the deployment of British imperial forces over much of the northern part of the Horn. In its nature it was to be akin to that long-drawn-out struggle between the Dervishes and the British in the Sudan, only recently concluded, and to the jihad led by Usman dan Fodio in northern Nigeria, earlier in the nineteenth century.

Throughout the summer of 1899 the Mullah forayed and raided, preached much, and whipped up fanaticism. Tribesmen who did not join him were denounced as infidels, and he boasted that he would drive the British back into the sea whence they had come. News of these doings, and of the Mullah's threats, soon reached Berbera and there was much panic among the Indian merchants there. They hurriedly stowed away their families and goods on board ship, ready for a quick departure. The timely arrival of two Royal Marine ships, however, allayed the alarm, and soon Indian merchants, families and goods were once more back on shore.

Not all tribes joined the Mullah, many standing firm by their treaties with the British, and others – alienated by the Mullah's cruelty or disappointed with promised booty – defected from his cause. The

Mullah, however, had so infected the Dolbahanta with his fanaticism that neighbouring tribes appealed for British protection, and when at the end of 1899 it seemed the British would move against him, the Mullah moved farther south into the remote region of the western Ogaden, into territory claimed by Ethiopia. Here his success in raising adherents among tribesmen much disaffected by Ethiopian rule so alarmed the Ethiopians that they sent a large force against him. Failing to locate the elusive enemy, the Ethiopians retired to Harrar and Jigjiga. It was now that the Mullah displayed his mastery of those wily tactics which made him such a formidable foe.

The Dervishes, as the Mullah's fanatical followers were now referred to, remained well out of reach of the Ethiopians but continued to be much apprised as to the latter's movements. At Jigjiga, at the end of March 1900, the Dervishes, keyed up and in the full flush of a jihad, and mindless of their losses (over 1,000 were killed), hurled themselves on the unsuspecting and hated enemy. The Dervish attack, although finally repulsed, so shook the Ethiopians that they well might have exclaimed: 'One more such victory and we are lost!'

Inflamed by this engagement with the Ethiopians, and with arms from Jibuti reaching them even in the remote Ogaden, the Mullah and Dervishes raided British-protected tribes resorting to their traditional grazing grounds, and menaced in the direction of Hargeisa in British territory. The danger was such that it forced the British to call in Central African troops, already much overstretched by demands made on them for the Ashanti campaign in West Africa. Major A. W. V. Plunkett, in command, making his headquarters at Adadleh about 50 miles south of Berbera, set up detachments at Hargeisa, Sheikh, Burao and Odweina. In mid-September 1900 when the Mullah appeared about to pounce on Hargeisa, Plunkett, to prevent him crossing into British territory, marched to the frontier.

The Mullah, unaware of his approach, was placidly resting in camp immediately across the frontier on the Ethiopian side, with his camel herds and cattle out grazing. Lt-Colonel J. S. Graham, of the Central African Rifles, describes the incident:

> I well remember our dismay and Plunkett's ire when, the day we were to make our night dash to seize the Mullah, the runner arrived from the Consul-General at Berbera . . . with the order forbidding us on any account to cross the frontier. Our information was that the Mullah had no idea that we had even left Hargeisa. We could see his camp fires and from a spy knew exactly which hut he was in. He was, however, just over the frontier and Plunkett did not dare disobey the order. We were all convinced, and I

shall always remain so, that we should have got him with some certainty that night and also have caused very heavy casualties among his followers. As it was we had to make an ignominious retreat to Hargeisa, causing much trouble and expense in the following years.

Regimental records confirm Graham's story, although the Consul-General's despatches from Berbera make no mention of it, merely referring to the Central African Rifles demonstrating in the direction of the frontier. But for that frontier, laid down by the Anglo-Ethiopian agreement of 1897, Plunkett would likely have snatched his prize.

Efforts were now directed to prevent the Mullah crossing back into British territory, and during the closing months of 1900 there was much toilsome marching, amid a constant drain on forces to meet imperial commitments in South Africa. The Boer War was now overshadowing all else: the war against the Mullah was minor compared to it. By late December 1900 the last companies of the Central African Rifles departed Berbera, much to the relief of the local townspeople, who had found the Yao contingent from the Nyasa region especially troublesome.

Somaliland must now rely on its own forces, and it was also expected that Ethiopia would now play a much greater part in the struggle against the Mullah. To this end two British officers, Major Hanbury-Tracy and Captain Cobbold, were assigned as advisers to the Ethiopian army. Plans were drawn up at the end of the year for an Ethiopian advance into the western Ogaden, while a Somali force under Captain E. J. E. Swayne would hold the Dolbahanta in the east.

The Ethiopian campaign, which began early in the new year, proved to be, like that of the previous year, a sorry tale: defective supply arrangements, lack of water (rain washings mixed with animal excreta were not to the liking of the Ethiopian troops), the intense heat of the lowlands, disease and defection of guides – all wrought a heavy toll. Despite additional recruitment of forces – to the number of 14,000 by May 1901, many attracted by promises of plunder – the Ethiopians failed to get farther east than the Gerlogubi wells. By July 1901 they were back at Harrar, looting on their retreat and leaving much bitterness in their wake. The weight of the campaign now fell on the newly formed Somali Levy which Captain E. J. E. Swayne had raised in the early months of 1901.

It comprised a Somali force of 1,500 men, made up of 1,000 infantry and 500 mounted men, all whipped into shape by 20 British officers and 50 Punjabi drill instructors. In four months a mass of raw Somali spearmen was turned into a disciplined force expert in handling the

Martini-Enfield rifle, sword and bayonet and Maxim gun. It was expected that this Somali Levy, combining as it did the natural-born fighting instinct of the Somali with the sterling discipline of the British army, would far outweigh the difference in numbers posed by the Mullah's force of 5,000 hard-core Dervishes (rifle and spearmen) and up to 20,000 tribal spearmen.

The Somali Levy had been raised none too soon. Scarcely was it ready to take the field than news came that the Mullah had crossed back into British territory. He had returned to his beloved Dolbahanta country, and was awaiting the British at Yahel, fully confident that, with the withdrawal of British forces overseas, and in view of the recent poor showing of the Ethiopians, his own star was in the ascendant. The newly formed Somali Levy was early called upon to prove its worth.

The Levy made an impressive show of strength as it marched out from base camp at Burao in late May 1901 and headed in a south-easterly direction. In early June, at Samala, 100 miles south-east of Burao, and deep in Dolbahanta country, the Levy split into two columns. The smaller, under Captain M. McNeill, remained at Samala to guard stores and captured stock. The main column of 1,000 men, under Swayne, headed south-east in flying formation to attack the Mullah's forces. The Levy, however, made a grave miscalculation in thinking their movements secret. Dervish scouts had been watching them carefully, and no sooner had the main column under Swayne left Samala than 5,000 Dervishes led by the Mullah in person, threw themselves on McNeill's camp. It was an early baptism of fire for the Levy. Its training now stood it in good stead. The Maxim was handled with great dexterity, and a concerted and disciplined fire held the Dervishes down at a distance of 150 yards, although a few fanatical spearmen managed to penetrate the outer line of the camp before being killed. Time and again throughout the long day and into early evening the Dervishes rushed the camp, but the Levy stood firm. At last, faced with unsustainable losses (over 600 dead), the Mullah ordered a general retreat, he himself leading the way at a furious pace. A shock awaited him, for he and his bodyguard blundered into Swayne's flying column which had camped across their line of flight. The surprise was complete and the disarray total. It ended in the headlong pursuit by the flying column of the Mullah and Dervishes until the latter disappeared into Italian territory. Swayne had no authority to follow them there. The Mullah had quickly become aware of the safety conferred by international boundaries! It was with much chagrin that Swayne called off the pursuit. Little remained for him to do except punish the hardened

Dolbahanta who had supported the Mullah. This took the form of appropriating much of their stock.

Swayne had scarcely returned to camp at Bohotle in early July 1901 when news came that the Mullah was back in British territory, just inside the frontier line near Fer-Diddin. Without resting, the Somali Levy again took the field. In mid-July, when within a few miles of Fer-Diddin, Swayne received orders of recall. He had to make a quick and hard decision. Either retreat through hostile and highly excited tribesmen, or advance on the Mullah. He chose the latter. A hard night's march brought contact with the Mullah's large force. Many of the tribesmen who were with Swayne now fled, such was their terror in the near presence of the Mullah. A sudden and heavy burst of gun fire unleashed on the column announced contact with the enemy. Aware that a large Dervish force faced them in bush cover, Swayne fell back on tried tactics. Victory must be obtained in the open field, and this meant converting the marching column and firing line into the traditional British square, and hoisting the tattered remnant of the regimental flag as a rallying point in case of ensuing mêlée.

Regrouping and forming a new front while guarding against flank attacks from the concealed Dervishes was no easy task. Maxims had to be disentangled from dead camels, stock had to be prevented from stampeding, and supplies guarded. Meanwhile the Levy continued to direct a hot fire against the Dervishes to flush them out of the bush cover. Despite it all, the Levy managed to form square. A formidable fire power, including that of the Maxims, was now unleashed on the Dervishes. In the face of it the Mullah retired in haste into the thick bush, leaving behind many dead, among them two of his brothers. Swayne now took up immediate pursuit, giving the Mullah no respite until the latter reached the Italian frontier line and literally flung himself across it. Swayne, debarred from crossing that line, called off the pursuit. His wounded were in sore need of care, water was scarce and there was a shortage of remounts.

The Mullah, now in Italian territory, fled without stopping for several days. His line of retreat was well marked by abandoned water-vessels, camel mats, many dead, and chained prisoners – some of whom later escaped into the desert only to die of thirst. Although Swayne obeyed instructions not to cross into Italian territory, not so his Somali scouts. They continued the pursuit and, at one stage, emptied their bandoliers at a small group of horsemen jogging ahead on weary ponies. Little did they realise that the group of horsemen included the Mullah, his son, and the ever-faithful Haji Sudi. At this stage in their flight the Mullah and his bodyguard were reduced to drinking the water found in the bellies of dead camels. It was a tale later to be told around Dervish camp fires!

The first phase ('First Expedition' as it was known) of operations against the Mullah, although prematurely closed by instructions from London in July 1901, was nevertheless deemed by Swayne to have been a success. With the field force withdrawn to Burao by the end of 1901 and with a vast booty of stock in British hands, he assessed the results before taking his well-earned home leave. In the final ten weeks' campaign the Levy had thrice inflicted defeat on the Mullah in stand-up fights, and had twice chased him out of British territory. It had inflicted heavy casualties on the Dervishes: over 1,000 killed and wounded and 800 prisoners taken. British losses were 40 killed and wounded, among the dead being the brave Captain Friederichs, recently arrived from South Africa, and one of the first officers to return to Somaliland from that arena of war. He had been killed while helping a wounded man.

The surmise of British officials and the Dolbahanta tribes that the Mullah would soon be back in the Protectorate was not belied. His retreat into Italian territory had brought him a new source of strength. He found a fervent supporter for his fanaticism in Osman Mahmoud, the Mijjertein sultan, who fed the Mullah with arms and allowed the Dervishes to occupy Illig, an important port of entry in his territory for arms and supplies. Revitalised by this, the Mullah slipped back into British territory at the beginning of the year. Again there was the familiar pattern of looting and raiding of British-protected tribes. In January 1902 Swayne was hurried back from leave, to face the Mullah anew.

Now, however, Swayne held the full-blown rank of Commissioner, with wide civil and military powers. He had the support of his home government, for it had been rudely shaken by the Mullah's resurgence. Most important, however, was that permission had now been obtained from the Italians to enter their territory. This concession was to be invaluable, for scarcely had Swayne set foot in Somaliland again before the Mullah, as though in response to the return of his old adversary, flitted back into Italian territory, this time to the Mudug oasis, south of the British Protectorate.

Swayne's plans were prolonged and carefully laid. His strategy was based on making a daring bid to winkle out the Mullah from the Mudug oasis. The oasis lay inland about 130 miles from the Indian Ocean, and about 100 miles south of the British frontier line. It was a place of much importance for the nomads. It was no ordinary oasis, being an

45

area of some 40 miles across, from north to south, and about 80 miles long, from west to east. Its repute as an 'oasis' largely derived from the series of wells cut into the white rocky soil and which provided a copious supply of deceptively clear tempting waters. But the imbibers of these waters, in Swayne's words, experienced uncomfortable results, and were much 'astir'. Nevertheless the wells were much resorted to by man and beast during the dry season. Captain M. S. Wellby, who made a long circuitous journey through the Horn in 1895, visited the Mudug oasis during the wet season, and gave a glowing picture of its grassy plains, verdant patches of bush, and 'immense numbers of sheep and goats, camels and cows, dotted all over the country'. Mudug was also a trade centre for caravans journeying between the coast and the interior. Cloths, dates, sheep, gum and ghi, and a surprising variety of trade goods were obtainable here, and in the wet season, caravans would tarry while fattening up their stock before continuing their trek into the Haud. Mudug had much to offer the Mullah.

Swayne laid his plans during the spring of 1902. The ending of the Boer War in May 1902 placed additional forces at his disposal, and these, along with two companies of the King's African Rifles recently returned from West Africa, a detachment of Sikhs from Aden and the 1,500-man Somali Levy, gave him a force of 2,400 rifles to pose against the Mullah's 12,000 mounted men and 1,500 riflemen. Swayne had the use of the heliograph for communication, and he constructed stone forts at Burao and Bohotle. He was disappointed that his request to land a force at the port of Obbia was not granted, for he had intended that this force, linking up with the pro-British sultan, Yusuf Ali, would have contained the Mullah on the east.

News that Brigadier-General Manning was proceeding to Somaliland to study the military situation there on behalf of the War Office stirred Swayne on with his plans. If he could achieve a quick success before Manning's arrival, it would redound to his, Swayne's, credit. There was much interest in Britain at the time in eastern Africa and the Cape-to-Cairo scheme. To those whose ideas of African geography were vague, the Horn might well seem part of that scheme. With the Boer War over, there was renewed interest in Somaliland. Swayne lost no time in acting. His first step was to seal off the Mullah's arms supply from Mijjertein country, by pushing down the Nogal Valley.

On the morning of 29 September 1902, there emerged from the Jidbaran Pass on the south-eastern side of the Nogal Valley an extraordinary mobile force, the pick of the Levy. Arabian riding camels, fleet and light of foot, made up the sprightly advance, then came the more stolid Somali camels and following behind was the mass of riflemen. Taking up the rear came 2,000 transport camels carrying water tanks, and then followed another 2,000 catering camels for rations. This impressive force faced a 100-mile advance across the waterless Haud to the Mudug oasis.

On 4 October Swayne's scouts reported the enemy only a day's march ahead. The column encamped the night of the 5th at Erigo and by early dawn the next day was moving through the dense bush towards the enemy. From tree perches, scouts on both sides watched each other's movements. A captured prisoner led Swayne into believing that the bush was less dense ahead than it really was and, but for a timely warning from one of his scouts, he would have been ambushed. A halt was called, and three sides of a square were formed with the transport in the middle, and three companies taking up the rear. The dressing of this formation in dense bush, with the restless camels in the centre, was no small achievement.

Swayne's forces were now in the worst and blindest bush that the Haud could produce, and with visibility less than 5 yards in front. Suddenly, with a rush, the enemy attacked from three sides, firing madly and reaching to within a few yards of the line. The recently raised Somali troops on the left, under Colonel Phillips, now fell back and panicked. Their fear proved contagious. The rest of the flank also now broke, except for the Yao of the Central African Rifles who stood firm. During the ensuing mêlée the precious Maxim machine gun was lost. (Not recaptured until 1920, its loss caused a Court of Inquiry.) The half-company on the front, under Swayne, held their ground until he gave the order, when they charged forward and drove off the enemy. The rear and the companies on the right also stood firm. It was a desperately contested affair, with the enemy darting in and out of the bush, crying out 'Allah!', 'Allah!' while pouring deadly fire. Their fanaticism, fed by ample ammunition, was unbelievable. As though welcoming death, they charged so close that their clothing was set on fire by the discharge of grapeshot. The Somalis on the British side, under Christian officers, were under much stress, for they were of the same blood and religion as the enemy. Many had brothers and cousins among the Dervishes and they were taunted by the latter for their infidelity to Islam.

The crucial point came when hundreds of enemy spearmen circled the left flank and rushed the square. They attacked as fanatics, regardless of death, lying down behind cover a few yards away, and continually firing into the square. This stampeded the camels, scattering the water tanks and ammunition boxes and causing a scene of great terror and confusion. Under Swayne's direction the companies reformed, and in the face of their concentrated rifle fire and that of the two 7-pounders, the enemy fell back and the ground was cleared. There followed fierce hand-to-hand fighting. Great casualties were inflicted on the Dervishes, who lost 1,400 spearmen and riflemen. Within a belt of 20 yards of the front face of the square, there were 62 bodies, among them Hadjis, Mullahs and Emirs, lying amid a heap of spent cartridge shells. Among the enemy dead were those from tribes as far away as the upper Juba and even the Sudan, showing how far away the Mullah had won adherents to his cause. The British took a large number of prisoners, and a vast herd of stock: thousands of camels, sheep, cattle and horses.

Losses on the British side were two officers killed (Colonel Phillips, while trying to rally his men following the loss of the Maxim, and Captain Angus, while in charge of a 7-pounder). There were other individual acts of bravery: Lieutenant Everett severely wounded while attending to Colonel Phillips, and Colonel Cobbe who continued to serve his guns with only one Somali sergeant, and for which he later received the Victoria Cross. In the final tally British losses, compared to those of the Dervishes, were light: 56 levies and 43 spearmen killed.

With the enemy apparently worsted, the British force formed *zariba* (camp), while driving off some of the enemy when they showed up, and also recovering most of the stampeded camels (although not two cases of whisky which had been lost)*. That same evening they buried their dead in the presence of the officers. The next morning, the 7th, the force moved 6 miles away to an open plain where there was water. Swayne, believing that the enemy was encamped 10 miles to the south, moved out with a lightly equipped column which included three companies of the Yaos to stiffen the Somali levies. There was much apprehension as to how the latter would perform, for they were in superstitious awe of the Mullah, some even likening his career to that of the Prophet, who always recovered from reverses. Perhaps the Mullah was immortal!

In view of the whereabouts and strength of the enemy being uncertain, the damaged morale of his own troops and the difficulty of travelling through dense bush and unmapped country by compass bearing only, Swayne called off the pursuit. Mudug lay 40 miles ahead through dense bush, and with the large transport train and thousands of head of captured stock, the many prisoners, and his own sick and wounded,

*Subsequently returned by the Mullah with a note that they were no use to him, and that the British should give him a seaport instead.

it would have been hazardous for him to advance further. He had already achieved much, for apart from the loss of the Maxim, victory had gone to the British.

Retirement to Bohotle was carried out in orderly fashion with no sign of haste, lest a precipitate retreat invite a full-scale onslaught from the enemy: a column on the march in Somali country was extremely vulnerable. Bohotle was reached on 17 October 1902, and Swayne, after seeing his force into safety, was himself struck down by fever. He now resumed his home leave, so abruptly interrupted at the beginning of the year. The last news of the Mullah was that he had retired to the Galadi wells, west of Mudug but still in Italian territory. Thus ended the Second Expedition.

Hard lessons had been learned from it. The Somali irregulars had come up against the unbelievable fanaticism of the Dervishes at first-hand and had been shaken and unnerved. Had they stood firm, Swayne's losses would have been much smaller. It was an unforgettable experience. General Manning was later to claim that it was Swayne's over-attachment to and reliance on his Somali irregulars that had incurred a near defeat. Swayne, for his part, would never concede that the Yaos had saved the day. It was undeniable, however, that henceforth the loyalty of the Somali levies would be suspect. A lesson had also been learned as to the danger of a quickly disorganised transport caught in thick bush: a stampeded transport was a nightmare thought!

At home, too, in Britain, there was much concern over the near defeat at Erigo, disillusionment with the Somali Levy, and worry over Dervish resurgence. At a Foreign Office conference in mid-October 1902, retirement from and even abandonment of the protectorate was debated, but ruled out as it would seriously affect Aden's source of supplies and British control over the north Somali ports; it would also leave loyal Somali tribes at the mercy of the Mullah. As to alternatives to retirement or abandonment, a frontier defence force was considered, but was deemed unrealistic: it would mean guarding a boundary of over 500 miles and would require a veritable army and entail an expense quite unacceptable to the Imperial Treasury. In the discussion as to the most appropriate policy for the Somali Protectorate, the experience of recent events in the Sudan was much in mind. The policy of letting the Sudan 'stew in its own juice', which had been followed for a time prior to the defeat of the Khalifa, had eventually to be forsaken in the face of the increasing Dervish threat and their widening influence. Similarly, in Somaliland, the Mullah, unless scotched quickly, would pose an ever-increasing threat. Full-scale action against him was the answer, and as soon as possible. The Conference lost no time in deciding on this, and there quickly followed consultation with the War Office as to the forces required for the operation.

There would be less reliance on the Somali Levy. Regular troops were now returning from South Africa, the King's African Rifles were available from East Africa, the 2nd Bombay Grenadiers, the 23rd Bombay Rifles and 2nd Sikhs from India. In a generous gesture of loyalty to the British Raj, the Maharajahs of Bikinir and Jodhpur and the Nawab of Bahawalpur offered camel corps. A field hospital was available from Aden. In December 1902, Italian co-operation was obtained in the form of permission to land British forces at the port of Obbia. The Ethiopians agreed to send a force of 5,000 rifles down the Webi Shibeli, to bar the Mullah's retreat westward. Previous experience, however, showed that not too much should be expected from the Ethiopians: they were allies to be shunned.

Against his enemy the Mullah could muster up to 40,000–50,000 men, of whom possibly 2,000 were riflemen. His forces were on the move, ranging south of the Nogal Valley as far as the Mudug oasis, and to the west as far as Galadi. There was much conjecture on the British side as to whether the Mullah would make a stand at Mudug or withdraw farther east into Italian territory, or go west into the Ethiopian Ogaden. He could not be left undefeated at Mudug, for his power would then increase and his influence spread – it was already felt as far away as the Jubaland Province of British East Africa, and there was a rumour that the Mullah planned, in an emergency, to take refuge at Lugh, on the upper Juba.

There was a sense of urgency in launching the Third Expedition which was to oust the Mullah from Mudug. It was under War Office direction and the command of Brigadier-General Manning, recently arrived in Somaliland. That Swayne was still on leave was just as well, in view of his immense objection to the use of regular troops. He had argued that they required too much transport and were ponderously slow, as compared to the mobile and lightly laden Somali forces.

Manning planned to advance on Mudug from the port of Obbia on the east, while a column from Bohotle would advance on Mudug from the west. The two would join up at Mudug. The Obbia column, under Manning, numbered 2,000 fighting ranks including mounted infantry and Bikanir Camel Corps. The Bohotle column consisted of 850 men, including mounted infantry and camelry, a Pioneer Regiment for handling communication and transport, and a telegraph section from the Royal Engineers. The task of getting the two columns to Mudug through the waterless Haud was a formidable challenge. It meant passing a large force through desolate country and against an inscrutable enemy with no bases and extremely agile in its movements. Transport and water were crucial. It meant ensuring that some 1,500 transport camels and hundreds of catering camels would be available at Obbia, in preparation for the trek to Mudug. The main base for the overall expedition was at Berbera, and that port soon hummed with activity. Amid the salvoes of troopships entering the harbour, the landing of forces took place and also a vast array of impedimenta: guns, stores, ordinance, saddlery and food supplies. Around the outskirts of Berbera there arose a city of canvas. Press correspondents from the main English newspapers flocked to Berbera, much as had happened at the Cape during the Boer War, so recently concluded. It was a cosmopolitan scene, with forces from all parts of the Empire represented. Most of the troops were from India, but with few Muslims among them, for there was fear they might sympathise with the Mullah. The Indian troops found Berbera a depressing place with its dearth of good curry, and no polo games organised for them! The sight of unveiled Somali women was little consolation, for before their arrival at Berbera they had been warned against consorting with local females.

News of all this activity at Berbera soon reached the Mullah. He put his own construction on it. It indicated, he said, how much the British feared him, if they had to rally such a vast array against him.

By 3 January 1903 the Obbia column under Manning had landed. Owing to lack of transport (Sultan Yusuf Ali of Obbia had not fulfilled his promise to provide this),* it was not until 22 February that the column left Obbia. By 24 March it had joined up with a portion of the Bohotle column at Galkayu, in preparation for a joint advance on Galadi. A quick reconnaissance by the Bikanir Camel Corps had reported that the Mullah was camped there. By 31 March, the remainder of the Bohotle column having come up, the combined force was at Galadi. It was now discovered that the Mullah had retreated west, into the Ogaden. Following reprovisioning with stores and water at Galadi, a column of 500 men armed with 9-pounders and Maxims, under Lieutenant-Colonel Cobbe, set out for Wardair where the Mullah was reported to have taken up position. Cobbe, after some tough skirmishes with the enemy on the way, in one of which Captain Chichester was killed, and being short of water and scarcely knowing his way in the

---

*It resulted in the Italians deporting him to Aden and then to Massawa, and replacing him by his son, Ali Yusuf. Yusuf Ali was brought back to Obbia in 1904, much broken in mind and body, and nearly blind.

impenetrable bush, sent forward a reconnaissance force of 250 men under Colonel Plunkett and seven British officers.

Unaware of the Dervish spy system and their use of bonfire signals to warn of British troop movements, Plunkett's force rashly pursued, and was lured into the dense bush of the Gumburu hills. The Mullah, choosing a well-sheltered spot, laid his trap, and was ready for them. The British force was vastly outnumbered by the Mullah's horsemen and spearmen, and in the two-and-a-half hours of fierce fighting that ensued, it was virtually cut to pieces. The Dervishes, charging from the dense bush, repeatedly hurled themselves on the hastily formed British square, regardless of death, and impelled on by the shrill cries of their women in the rear. Only when British ammunition was exhausted, and the Maxims had been broken up lest they fall into the hands of the enemy, did a fierce onrush break the square. A desperate bayonet charge to get clear brought near annihilation. Nearly the whole British force, to the number of 200, including Colonel Plunkett and the other British officers and a detachment of Sikhs, were killed. Only a few Yaos survived and managed to reach Cobbe, to tell the tale.

Dervish casualties were over 2,000. Their dead lay 'piled in heaps', in front of the now defunct Maxims. Gumburu may have been a disaster for the British, but for the Dervishes it was equally so: they almost despaired that Allah could allow this small infidel force to wreak such havoc on them.

In the face of the Gumburu disaster, Cobbe retired to Galadi. On the way there he met General Manning, and the combined force proceeded to Galadi, and thence to Galkayu. The main Bohotle column, oblivious of events at Gumburu, had proceeded to Danot, 45 miles south-west of Bohotle, from where, in late April, a flying column under Major Gough pushed on to Walwal in the Ogaden. En route it was attacked by a large force of Dervishes flushed with their success at Gumburu, and some of them incongruously sporting the uniforms and topees of British officers who had fallen on the field at Gumburu: hence the rumour that renegade white men were in the Mullah's ranks! Gough's column was severely mauled in the clash with the Dervishes, and had to withdraw to Danot, where they buried Captains Bruce and Godfrey who had been killed in the fighting, and laid a funeral pyre for the dead Sikhs. This sad task completed, the entire Bohotle force withdrew to Bohotle where, at the end of June 1903, they were joined by the Obbia forces. Angus Hamilton, Reuter's correspondent who accompanied the Third Expeditionary Force, left a graphic description of the march back to Bohotle, in which he distinguished himself in a charge against the enemy. He well describes the subdued air of the withdrawal: the Gumburu disaster had hurt deeply. Hamilton could report, however, that the Somali soldiers had displayed great steadiness and personal bravery during the retreat, thus reversing the poor opinion they had earned for themselves at Erigo.

There was little of a cheery nature to report from the Ethiopian side. Their role in this campaign was as inglorious as in the previous one. According to Colonel Rochfort, the British officer accompanying the Ethiopian force, there was much bizarre staging in Ethiopian military tactics. Their commander (fitaurari), would dress himself in a lion skin and, surrounded by his staff, would sit at the door of an elegant tent, whence he issued orders in a grand manner to his men in the field. Rochfort claimed that the Ethiopians were over-confident. Their series of unbroken successes against the Italians and the Egyptians had gone to their heads. However, it was a different matter when they were up against the Somalis. The Ethiopians were hesitant and out of their depth in the semi-desert country of the western Ogaden, where lack of water and grain supplies made them peculiarly vulnerable. They claimed to have occupied Bari on the upper Shibeli and to have inflicted crushing defeats on the Mullah's spearmen, and to have blocked the Dervish advance westward. Although they did fall in with and kill some Dervishes, there were nothing like the numbers they so lavishly claimed. Their markmanship was poor, they were over-exuberant: any small victory was the occasion for much wild ceremony and savage *feux de joie*. News of the Gumburu disaster reached the Ethiopians after they had withdrawn to Harrar, although they tried to use it as justification for their withdrawal there, and also for their failure to link up with the British forces. Lack of communication and good organisation was not confined to the Ethiopian side: it had also prevented simultaneous action between the Obbia and Bohotle columns. The Mullah, wily and crafty leader that he was, made the most of the situation, and his excellent spy system and sources of information kept him fully apprised as to enemy movements.

With pressure on him relieved by the withdrawal of the British and Ethiopians from the field, it might have been thought that the Mullah would have remained in the Ogaden. However, in early June he made a daring and successful movement north-eastwards to the Nogal Valley, crossing the British frontier between Bohotle and Damot, virtually through the British lines, and cutting communication between those places by removing several miles of telegraph wire. It was a rapid and unexpected movement, so well executed and so well covered by the

Mullah's horsemen that General Manning learned of it only on 12 June, when it was too late to act. Nor was Manning's temper improved by the letter he received from the Mullah which was penned while the latter was en route to the Nogal Valley. It was addressed 'to the English People', and was aggressive and threatening in tone. The Mullah still spoke of taking Berbera and driving the British into the sea. He adjured them to heed his words: he liked war, Allah was on his side, and so also was the geography of the country – for it consisted only of ant-heaps and desert under a burning sun. His wealth consisted of stock, easily moved about; and there was no other wealth which the British could lay hands on, no property, gold or silver. His men were with him: those who had fallen in battle had received their supreme reward, the delights of Paradise. The only way of peace for the British was to leave the country. As a final taunt, he reminded them of the machine-gun captured at Erigo in October 1902. He offered to return it in exchange for ammunition.

The British had little time for the Mullah's sallies. They were pondering much on the failure of the Third Expedition. Should they have waited until the *jilal* (dry season) was over and there was a good flush of pasture and water? It would have much eased the operations of the mounted South African troops and Bikanir Camel Corps. The tenuous lines of communication, from advance points, Bohotle and Galadi, to Berbera and Obbia, were vastly over-extended and difficult to guard, and highlighted the lack of transport, supplies and water. The lack of mounted scouts, the scanty and unreliable information as to enemy movements, and too little knowledge of the terrain of the country, had all hindered troop movements. There was a special need for up-to-date maps for this still largely unexplored and unknown country. There were none, apart from sketch maps made by the Swayne brothers – surprisingly accurate though these were. These maps were usually based on compass sketches executed at night around the camp fire, and covering the day's travel. Distances were usually judged by time and the rate of travelling. The Somali, when in bush or desert country, was guided by the sun and stars and, although having a marvellous sense of direction and distance, was not always accurate in passing on this information. The situation as regards maps was somewhat remedied by the War Office map of 1907 which drew largely on the sketches of the Swayne brothers and other miscellaneous information, but it was over-detailed. Hundreds of place-names marked on it are unlocatable on modern maps.

The autopsy on the failure of the Third Expedition had scarcely been completed before plans were under way for another, greater expedition against the Mullah. The latter, after his long march from the Ogaden, was now strongly entrenched in the eastern Nogal Valley, in British territory, and with his Kharias spread out in the triangle marked by Halin–Gerrowei–Kallis. His morale was high, and his recent successes had attracted thousands more supporters to his side, from as far away as the Gallas and Adones on the upper Shibeli. He could put 2,000 armed mounted men and up to 20,000 spearmen into the field, and his herds were numbered in tens of thousands.

Lord Roberts, Commander-in-Chief at the War Office, saw grave danger in the Mullah's daring move back into British territory. He must be destroyed or expelled. To lead the new drive against the Mullah, a new commander, General Sir C. Egerton, was appointed (in place of Brigadier-General Manning) the Inspector-General of the King's African Rifles. Unlike Manning, Egerton was a tried soldier, a proto-Field Marshal, much experienced in fighting Muslim zealots on the North-west Frontier of India and in the Sudan.

Egerton, finding what he termed 'an exhausted force' on his arrival in Somaliland from Bombay in early June 1903, set about building it up. There was to be an 8,000-man field force, the core of which – about one-third of the whole – would come from India: two brigades of infantry, a mounted corps and divisional troops. The remainder would be made up of locally recruited corps, such as the Gadabursi and Tribal Horse, and irregular mounted scouts (*illalos*). Egerton placed great emphasis on transport: an immense number of camels, at least 10,000, would be needed. Even before his arrival at Berbera, he had arranged for 5,000 camels to be shipped from that great repository, India. The Indian camel could carry a 400 lb load, but could not go for long periods without water, as could the Somali camel. Egerton bought up or hired over 4,000 of the latter. The Somali camel, although carrying only a 160 lb load, was priceless for its power of endurance. There were also – the cream of the camel force – 700 fleet-pacing Arabian camels from Aden, ideal for scout work. The Fourth Expedition's appetite for camels proved to be almost insatiable. The wonder is that the breeding proclivities of the animal could sustain the demands made upon it.

A strange array of wheeled vehicles was collected: buckwagons from South Africa, camel carts and *ekkas* (light two-wheeled, one-horse, one-passenger carriages) from India – a great novelty in Somaliland. There was much talk of railway construction at the time: the recently completed Uganda Railway had enabled troops to get to Uganda quickly to put down a mutiny there. By November 1903 surveys for a light railway from Berbera to Bohotle and Harrar, with a branch line to Adadleh, had been completed by Major S. L. Craster, R. E. In the upshot the railway was never built, and it would have been too late anyway, to have been of use to Egerton. Road construction was, however, undertaken by a coolie corps and Sikhs from India, and two companies of sappers and miners. In the organisation of staff, supplies and transport for the Fourth Expedition, all the practical needs for war in harsh desert conditions seem to have been envisaged. There was a special 'Water-boring Establishment' to preside over the installation of water supply plants at various points along the lines of communication.

The Mullah, the object of all this preparation, was strategically well placed, with his headquarters at Halin, advance posts at Jidbali and Buranod, and he was in occupation of Illig, through which came his arms. The central core of his force were the 8,000 Dervishes based at Jidbali, and it was here that the British estimated the Mullah would make his stand. It was 150 miles from the nearest British post, and from Jidbali, if necessary, the Mullah could retreat north, south or east, as circumstances dictated. It would be difficult to pin him down.

Egerton's original grand design was to occupy the line of wells across the southern Haud, from Gerlogubi to the sea, and confine the Mullah to the north of this line. He would also bring in the powerful Dolbahanta tribe (with whom the British had no treaties, and who had proved so troublesome in the past and had usually supported the Mullah) on to the British side. The Home Government, however, was averse to enter-ing into treaties with the Dolbahanta at this stage: it would be a risky business, entailing their protection and assuming further liabilities on their behalf. As for Egerton's cordon from Gerlogubi to the sea, it would mean operating on over-extended lines and stretching resources to the limit. A much more limited approach was needed, and above all there must be a quick blow at the Mullah. So Egerton's modified plan was as follows: Manning's and Fasken's brigades would move eastward from Olesan (half-way between Burao and Bohotle) in a two-pronged action. The more northern column under Fasken would establish posts in the northern Nogal Valley and advance on Halin, while the southern column under Manning would move into the southern Nogal towards Gerrowei, occupying Damot and with some gesturing towards Mudug to give the Mullah the impression that the British controlled the latter. The Ethiopian force, with seven British officers attached to it, and generously supplied with British money, equipment, water tanks, etc., would occupy the Galadi and Galkayu wells and deny the Mullah access to the Ogaden. The Ethiopians, despite their vaunted military prowess, were slow in mobilising, and there was much squabbling between the Emperor and Ras Makonnen, Governor of Harrar. Egerton had reservations as to their usefulness, and in view of the Ethiopians getting no farther east than Wardair, provision was made for Manning to occupy Galadi. The primary object of these so-called stops was to drive the Mullah north and bring him to battle. In the south-east a naval demonstration at Obbia (200 miles down the coast south of Illig) was meant to lead the Mullah into thinking a force was landing there to deny him access to the southern Mijjertein. In the north-east, Osman Mahmoud, Sultan of northern Mijjertein, undertook on certain conditions to keep the Mullah out of his territory.

Preparations went ahead slowly. Supplies, transport and water-supply plant were pushed forward along the anticipated line of advance. Concentration of troops proceeded so well that by November they were nearly all at Bohotle and Eil Dab, despite Manning having to march to Galadi to make good the Ethiopian failure to occupy that place. A naval demonstration at Obbia in May 1903 resulted in the installation of Ali Yusuf (son of banned Sultan Yusuf Ali). In mid-November 1903 four naval vessels under Commander E. R. Pears, RN, made a naval demonstration at Obbia, and this, along with a supply of arms to him, persuaded the wavering local sultan, Ali Yusuf, to support the British by occupying the Galkayu wells. Commander Pears then proceeded north to Illig where there was another naval demonstration, and it was also ascertained that it was impracticable to land at Illig during the height of the north-east monsoon.

Meanwhile, before the concentration of troops at Olesan had been completed, scouts had ascertained that the Dervishes were strongly entrenched at Jidbali. Finding the Dervishes in overwhelming strength, the column and infantry support withdrew to Badwein on 20 December 1903. There then followed a hurried concentration of all the forces at a point 20 miles east of Jidbali: they included Fasken's brigade, the mounted troops, and Manning's command, including the Galadi garrison (which was to withdraw to Eil Dab by 15 January 1904). On 10 January 1904, the combined force moved off in double echelon formation. It contained the best and most seasoned troops at the Empire's disposal, a train of transport, mountain batteries, baggage, water-tins and other impedimenta.

When they were within half a mile of Jidbali, the force formed a square. The transport camels were hobbled and tied down by the forelegs in the centre of the square, the mountain batteries were unlimbered and brought to the fore, while the infantry at the front knelt or lay down. Scarcely had the officers checked that all was ready, in these few brief moments of high tension, than the Dervish onslaught began. A mass of thousands of Dervish spearmen bore down on the square, while hundreds of Dervish horsemen appeared out of this mass, to gallop to and fro along the British lines. Suddenly, amid cries of 'Allah and the Prophet', gesturings and execrations against the infidel, there arose a wild and terrible shout. It was the signal for a mad rush on the square, which was still holding its fire. Its response was quick: the Maxim from its corner, and deadly rifle fire from the front and right flanks, and a barrage from the batteries to the fore, delivered an overwhelming fire power. In the face of it the Dervishes were forced to break and pull back. But only momentarily. They came on again, in short rushes, from cover to cover, and lying down behind the barest concealment. The British officers could not but notice that Dervish tactics were remarkably similar to those of the Boers, against whom they had fought so recently. The square, however, held firm, and the concentrated fire from its ranks, relentlessly applied, forced the Dervishes finally to break and flee. The Bikanir camelry and ponymen quickly took up the pursuit. Egerton rued the fact that he had no cavalrymen: they with their lance and sword would have plied their trade with good effect.

The chase was deadly, with scarcely time to count the prizes, and there were many: over 1,000 Dervishes killed (contemporary Somali scholarship puts the figure much higher, but sees it as a glorious entry into Paradise for the fallen), hundreds of prisoners taken, and such a collection of ancient rifles as would delight the heart of the connoisseur. Egerton would have pushed the pursuit to the limit, but for the delay in the return of the Galadi garrison, the late arrival of supplies, and, above all, lack of water – the wells at Jidbali were choked with debris and dead bodies until the engineering staff cleared them out. Two days after the Jidbali engagement Egerton called the pursuit off. No matter, for the British already counted it as an overwhelming victory, the greatest so far against the Mullah, and at a small cost – 27 killed, including three British officers. Telegrams of congratulation soon came from King Edward VII, Lord Roberts and Lord Kitchener, Commanders-in-Chief in the UK and India, respectively.

The Mullah had not been present at Jidbali; he was in the Buranod Hills a few miles to the west. On learning of the defeat of his forces and faced with numerous desertions from his ranks, he retired northward with his main force.

It would seem that the Mullah had risked Jidbali because he apparently believed the naval demonstration at Obbia had cut him off from the south, that the British were in occupation of Damot and Galadi, and that the Ogaden was debarred to him. In the northern Mijjertein his alienation from Osman Mahmoud made that area unattractive to him. Thus he made his stand at Jidbali, and when it went against him, there was only one line of retreat: through the Anane Pass, across the Sorl Haud and north towards Jidali, in the north-east corner of the British Protectorate. From here there were no escape routes except by sea or into Italian territory – provided he was granted asylum in the latter.

Egerton now set about sealing off the southern Haud and cornering the Mullah in the region of Jidali (the similarity of this name with Jidbali caused much confusion). Manning's brigade was assigned the task of holding the eastern Nogal, including Halin, and Fasken was to draw on garrisons at Sheikh and Las Dureh for an advance to Jidali and the Warsangli country. By mid-March 1904, these operations had been accomplished, with Fasken based at Eil Afweina in the north, and Manning occupying Halin. Meanwhile Egerton had sent surrender terms to the Mullah: in return for the two Maxims captured at Erigo and Gumburu and the surrender of 1,400 rifles, his life and the lives of his family would be spared. His future residence would be decided by His Majesty's Government. This offer brought no reply. There is no indication that the Mullah ever received Egerton's letter.

There now began a cat-and-mouse game. The Mullah, learning of Fasken's advance to Eil Afweina, retreated to Baran, and when Fasken, after occupying Jidali on 21 March, pushed on to Baran and then Higli Gab on the Italian frontier, which he reached on 29 March, the Mullah kept one jump ahead, his line of flight clearly marked by debris and dead until it vanished over the Italian border, across which British operations were prohibited. Having ascertained that the Mullah was receiving supplies through the port of Las Khorai on the north coast, and failing the promised support of the Warsangli, Fasken directed some of his forces to Las Khorai, whence, after leaving a token force there, they were to embark for Berbera, the mounted troops returning to Las Dureh. Meanwhile some Somali levies held Baran.

On 7 April 1904 came news of the consent of Italy to operations across her border (which, if received ten days earlier, would have been invaluable). New instructions were issued immediately. The force at Las Khorai was to remain there. Mounted troops were halted on their return to Las Dureh, and there was to be a concentration of forces between the Eil Afweina and Rat areas, preparatory to ascertaining the exact whereabouts of the Mullah in Italian territory. There were many false leads, the last news being that the Mullah had headed south to Halin, but learning that it was occupied by Manning's brigade, he had turned east towards Illig where he had a garrison of 200 riflemen and 500 spearmen.

Egerton had already surmised that the Mullah, if cornered in the north-east, would make for Illig. Illig was, however, a fortified place and very difficult to attack from the landward side. It was separated from Halin, the nearest British post in the Protectorate, by some 200 miles, much of it dense waterless bush. The answer was an attack by sea. On 31 March 1904, Italian consent was obtained for a British force to land at Illig, in the presence of an Italian warship. Three British naval vessels, *Hyacinth*, *Fox* and *Mohawk*, arrived there in the early hours of 21 April. After first feigning a landing near Illig village, a party of seamen and marines with Maxim and battery guns were towed ashore in steam launches farther up the coast and seized the plateau heights a few miles north of Illig (much in the same way that Wolfe had seized the Heights of Abraham in the capture of Quebec). The force then turned southward and encircled Illig on its landward side. Meanwhile signal communication was maintained with the naval vessels who fired on the Dervishes as they were cleared out of their stone defences and caves, in which they had sought shelter, and fled south along the coast.

With the Dervishes ousted from Illig, there was little more for Egerton to do but roll up his telegraph lines and evacuate his posts in the Nogal Valley, leaving only a signalling post at Hudin. The forces in the northern part of the Protectorate either withdrew to the coast at Las Khorai or marched overland to Sheikh, in the Golis range. The last news of the Mullah's whereabouts came at the end of April 1904. He had taken up residence in Italian territory and had established himself near Gerrowei, on the Italian side of the frontier, a perch from which he could drop down into either territory as best suited his purpose. Final notice of recall of the British forces came on 2 May 1904, and with it, for all purposes, the Fourth Expedition may be assumed to have ended. Jidbali in a sense marked the end of the 'Expeditionary Period'. As with the earlier expeditions against the Mullah, much hindsight was at play in pointing out weaknesses in the Fourth Expedition, such as the failure of the northern Mijjertein and their sultan, Osman Mahmoud, to co-operate as promised. Osman Mahmoud had played false and had patched up his quarrel with the Mullah, and had abetted and aided his escape into Italian territory. The rains had broken at a critical moment and this had allowed the Mullah to move freely about without regard to wells. There was the shortage of transport and the crippling problem of lack of water during the dry season. The heterogeneous nature of the large field force, its elements being drawn from far corners of the Empire, and their dietary requirements being of a most varied kind, made catering an exasperating task. As in previous expeditions there was need for accurate intelligence and good maps.

British failure to follow up Jidbali was unfortunate, for the Mullah might well have been finished off at this stage. Sir Reginald Wingate, with long experience in fighting Dervishes in the Sudan, certainly thought a great opportunity had been lost. With the Mullah out of the way a measure of local government might have been introduced, as in the Sudan after the fall of the Khalifa. The Third and Fourth campaigns, although costing the British Exchequer over five million pounds and the lives of many valuable British officers, had failed to encompass the Mullah's downfall. He was still very much alive, in Italian territory. Old Somali hands warned that he would soon be back.

Egerton's large force was now withdrawn, and there remained only local troops and a temporary garrison of the 33rd Punjabi Infantry on a one-year lease, after which the Protectorate would have to look to its own defence. The relaxed view and apparent calm of British authorities in the summer of 1904, as regards events in Somaliland, after the strenuous efforts of the Fourth Expedition, is largely explained by plans afoot to bring in the Italians in any further confrontation with the Mullah.

The Dervishes obtained an important source of arms when they occupied the port of Illig in the summer of 1901. They also gained a formidable foothold in Italian territory, and injected a new element into the rivalry between the Sultans of Obbia and the northern Mijjertein which was a cause of concern to the Italians. Hitherto the Italians had been little affected by the Dervishes and the Mullah. Now, however, with the Mullah ensconced in Italian territory, the British gain was an Italian loss. The Italians saw the solution to this new problem in an agreement with the Mullah. To this end, Cavalier G. Pestalozza, Italian Consul at Aden, was directed by the Italian Government to open negotiations with the Mullah. In mid-September 1904, he sent a letter penned in flowery Arabic (in which language he was fluent) to the Mullah proposing a meeting in the following month. To this the Mullah agreed.

When Pestalozza arrived at Illig on 15 October, the Mullah was awaiting him. It was the first encounter between the Italians and what they termed 'the terrible armed Dervishes and blood-thirsty Mullah'. The Italians had come with some trepidation, for Pestalozza was unarmed, trusting in the Mullah's promise of immunity from harm. To the relief of the Italians they were received with civility, albeit with much suspicion and dislike of the infidel.

Illig was a formidable port at which to land at any time and, during the monsoon, almost impossible. Pestalozza planned his arrival to miss the monsoon, but found the harbour blocked by a sand bar. Eventually landing, he faced a climb up a steep slope to a crest from which there spread out a rocky expanse littered with half-completed buildings and piles of stones. Some 400 yards from the crest stood a high-walled enclosure through which a gate faced seawards. Before he could advance towards this enclosure, Pestalozza and party (including the Mullah's emissary, Abdullah Shahari) were surrounded on all sides by armed men. They were then ushered towards the enclosure in front of which some 150 mounted armed men were drawn up. Detached from them, and seated on a handsome Somali horse of light bay colour, was the Mullah. His clean robes and turban stood out with startling whiteness against the plumes of bright red wool decorating the head and front pieces of the Somali harness.

Following an inspection to ensure that they were not armed, the Mullah and a small group of notables led Pestalozza and party into the enclosure, which proved to be a large compound with an inner fortress. There was a halt and a prayer, and after some delay the Mullah wheeled his pony around, stopping ten paces in front of Pestalozza, while the other horsemen circled the party. The Mullah, master of the long silence, now maintained one for five minutes, after which, turning to Pestalozza, he started the dialogue of introduction.

The Italians, he said, were the first Europeans to come into the midst of 'our Dervishes'. They must affirm the object of their coming – was it peace? Pestalozza, in reply, affirmed that it was, and that he sought peace for both Somalis and Italians. He deftly side-stepped the Mullah's further question whether this meant peace for the British too. He was sure that the Mullah, being a man of law and observer of the Holy Book, would hear him out. He, Pestalozza, although not having full plenipotentiary powers, did have the full trust and backing of his own government in negotiations with the Mullah, and the wishes of the latter would be transmitted back to them in full.

These preliminaries completed, Pestalozza was led into the building, still surrounded by armed men. The meeting now began – the first face-to-face confrontation between the Mullah and a European: Pestalozza, quick, perceptive and with lounging Latin grace, versus the Mullah, tall, impressive, fit-looking – not yet taking on the corpulence which marked his later years – his dark, fuliginous complexion, Semitic features and small chin beard leaving little doubt as to his Afro-Somali origin. His luminous eyes scarcely veiled the zealotry which was his driving force. Most striking was the horny ridge on his forehead, the result of that operation performed on him as a small boy. Pestalozza would long retain a vivid memory of this meeting. He counted himself favoured in having met the Mullah in person. An interpreter was scarcely needed, since Pestalozza was fluent in Arabic, and when the Mullah heard that beloved tongue from the Italian's lips, the latter had practically won his case.

In the negotiations which followed, the Mullah quickly indicated his wishes: a fixed residence in Italian territory, rule over his own tribes, freedom of religion (presumably his own brand of Salihism) and freedom of trade. In return, he guaranteed cessation of hostilities and, most important for the Italians, would acknowledge the semi-independent Sultanates of Obbia and the Mijjertein, in the Italian sphere. He would bond these concessions and promises with money and hostages, if the other party would do likewise.

This first meeting between Pestalozza and the Mullah augured well. Further details had to be worked out, and to obtain British accord (obtained in November 1904) for an agreement with the Mullah there were meetings between Pestalozza and the British Commissioner, Swayne, as to differences between the Dervishes and British-protected tribes over pasture rights: Swayne was much concerned over Ethiopian reaction to the Italian proposal to grant the Dervishes pasture rights in territory claimed by the Ethiopians.

On 5 March 1905, Pestalozza and the Mullah met again at Illig and signed the Protocol (in Arabic) of the final agreement. Under it the Mullah received a most generous concession: his own state within the Italian sphere of influence. It took in much of the lower Nogal and Haud. On the seaward side it included the port of Illig and territory from Ras Bowen down to Ras Aswad, a distance of nearly 200 miles. This territory encroached much on that claimed by the Sultans of Obbia and the northern Mijjertein, and they, with much chagrin, now saw the Mullah raised to greater status than themselves within the Italian sphere. Likewise, the expansive gesture of the Italians in assigning to the Mullah pasture areas to the west almost as far as Kurmis (7° 50′, 46°), in territory claimed by the Ethiopians, was bitterly resented and contested by the latter.

The Mullah, in return for all this, gave general affirmation of lasting peace and accord between the Dervishes and all other peoples. There was to be free trade and security for caravans passing through his territory, and the Dervishes would refrain from trade in arms and slaves. Differences between the Dervishes and their neighbours were to be settled in the traditional peaceful manner of *ergo* (negotiation by a mission), under Italian aegis. In return for the political and religious freedom he would enjoy in his territory, the Mullah promised to govern his subjects with equity and justice.

The Illig Agreement was welcomed by both the Italian and British governments, and received favourable notice in the press of both countries. For the Italians the settlement was meant to provide a way out of the acrimonious dispute between the Sultans of Obbia and the Mijjertein, by introducing a new element into the situation. The assigning of pasture rights to the Mullah, in territory claimed by the Ethiopians, was meant to provide a buffer against the latter. The Illig Agreement also smoothed the way for the Italians who, in taking over a troublesome Mullah, obtained British support for the cession to Italy by the Sultan of Zanzibar of his sovereign rights in the Benadir ports, in return for a payment of £144,000, and for the cession to Italy in 1905, by Britain, of a piece of land near Kismayu to facilitate communication with the Benadir country. In the upshot, the Italians acquired a very awkward subject who would give them more trouble than they had bargained for, and give them a taste of what the British had endured.

For the British, Illig cost nothing and promised much – an end to the long and costly war with the Mullah. He was now Italy's problem. And with the transfer of the Protectorate from Foreign Office to Colonial Office control on 1 April 1905, the way seemed open to its development – as was the case with Uganda and Kenya in East Africa, where a similar transfer had recently taken place. In contrast to the Foreign Office policy of retrenchment and withdrawal to the coast, the Colonial Office supported Swayne's view that such withdrawal would mean domination of one tribal group by another, and disaffected tribes might well again turn to the Mullah. British treaty obligations to interior tribes must also be honoured: any retraction of these would have serious repercussions elsewhere, as in East Africa and the Sudan. Complete evacuation was out of the question in view of northern Somaliland's importance for the route to India and British control of Aden. It would also go against the whole trend of the time, expansion of Empire rather than contraction. The only suitable course was vigorous administration, and this could best be done by a tribal militia under British political officers. Illig had brought these questions to the fore.

The Colonial Office would fain have the Protectorate transferred to the India Office. The latter, however, wished no part of it. Until the transfer was completed and until arrangements were made for a militia scheme, and as a temporary compromise, armed camps were established, the most important being those at Eil Dab and Bohotle with a few hundred rifles each; a much larger force, however, was established among the Warsangli to keep watch against arms coming from the coast. The militia scheme was finally completed by the end of August 1905, and in September the 33rd Punjabi Infantry were withdrawn. The militia scheme was a compromise between the views of Swayne, Manning and Cordeaux. The two latter wanted a standing militia, Swayne wanted a flexible tribal militia (*karia*). These different views (although in a sense all favouring a form of indirect rule, much in vogue in Africa at the time) derived from their differing interpretations of the extent of the Mullah's defeat at Jidbali. Manning and Cordeaux held that the Dervishes, especially the Dolbahanta, the Mullah's mainstay, had received such a drubbing at Jidbali as to be in great disarray. Swayne, however, held that neither Jidbali nor the Illig Agreement had ended the Mullah's menace.

Reaction to the proposed militia scheme came in early August when Cordeaux addressed an assembly of elders at Sheikh, informing them that regular troops would be withdrawn from the interior. Faced with this dire prospect they pleaded for arms and promised a common front against the Dervishes.

The militia scheme involved full military strength of 1,500 men, of whom half were Standing Militia, with headquarters in Sheikh. The remainder, the Tribal Militia, was made up of some 20 tribal sections whose main task was to protect their grazing grounds. They would receive periodical training at Sheikh, where they would be replenished with arms and in turn would report on security in their areas. The militia system was under the command of Captain Smitheman (later replaced by Major McNeill) who was aided by seven political officers, one of whom, W. H. Byatt, was a civilian with Somali experience.

The political officers had a double role, administrative and military – no easy task. The Standing Militia was a levy of irregulars, a conglomeration of tribes, and soon revealed strains at being tethered to Sheikh. Their military training much preoccupied the political officers. At the same time the Tribal Militia, slackly supervised and with no specific role, and with more arms in their hands than the political officers were aware of, chafed under checks imposed on them. Both Standing and Tribal Militia, having abundant arms and minimal attention from political officers, took to game-shooting, hitherto the pastime of a few English sportsmen visiting Somaliland. The Tribal Militia were reputed to have double the number of rifles officially recorded by the political officers.

Recruitment to the Tribal Militia was difficult. The Somali, a nomad at heart, had no love for regimented life, even if only part-time, or for the regular periods of square-bashing at Sheikh, under the hard eye of a British sergeant-major. Tribal elders were only too pleased to send off their ne'er-do-wells and misfits for this periodical training, and to appropriate the arms they brought back at the end of it. Swayne was well aware of these defects. He would have had a real *Karia*, a fleet desert force of Somalis, led by a Lawrence of Arabia figure. Good use should be made of those very qualities which Manning and others derided, and who claimed that 'The Somali does not make a good soldier for garrison life, his ways are nomadic and he hates the routine of garrison work . . . the Somali are too much influenced by local and tribal sympathies to be relied on.' Attempts to remove defects were not always successful. When, in October 1905, Indian troops replaced Somali troops at Berbera, Bulhar and Zeyla for coast defence and the replaced Somalis were formed into two infantry companies, the latter saw this as a down-grading, and were much disgruntled and troublesome. More satisfactory was the appointment of additional military officers to supervise the Standing Militia at Sheikh, thus leaving the political officers to supervise the Tribal Militia more closely. Fortunately, while these corrections were being made, there were no calls on the militia system. The Illig Agreement seemed to be holding.

It is doubtful, however, whether any of the interested parties had faith in the Illig arrangement. Some officials thought that the Mullah had entered into it merely to gain time and recover from his Jidbali defeat. In April 1905, when the Mullah's deputation was in Berbera, and the British signature was added to the Illig Agreement, he was already muttering of 'eternal fighting' between himself and the British, and in a letter of 11 April 1905, he warned the British Commissioner of further fighting because of a telegraph line between Berbera and Burao, left behind by the Fourth Expedition, and which in Dervish eyes was a 'devilish device'. He complained that he and his followers had been relegated to a land of bush, stones and ravines, and wished to return to their own country, in British territory, and from which the British should get out at once. As expected, the Mullah would not settle down among diverse tribes, far removed from his original haunts and beloved Dolbahanta, from which derived much of his authority.

In late April 1905 the Dervishes were on the war-path again, raiding deep into the Ogaden as far as Walwal, where they confronted the Ethiopians. In July 1905 they raided into the British Protectorate as far as Jidbali, some parties even reaching Bohotle and Eil Dab. In the autumn of 1905 they looted over 1,000 camels, including prized 'meat camels' (young gelded males) from the Mudug oasis, and occupied the wells between Illig and the Bagheri country. Italian citizenship rested easily on the Mullah. He evicted the Italian consular agent, Heri Ismail, at Bunder Kassim in late 1905, and the latter had to be rescued by a British vessel. The Dervishes raided the southern Mijjertein, and by mid-summer 1906 forayed as far as Wal, Adadero and Mudug, driving the Esa Mahmud section of the Mijjertein and the Rer Mahal into British territory where they encroached on already over-grazed pastures. The British, aware of the merciless reception awaiting these tribes if they were returned, were loth to send them back.

The contentious issue of pasture claims persisted. The Illig Agreement had insufficiently defined these, and also which tribes were to enjoy these rights. Thus a supplementary British-Italian agreement of 19 March 1907 authorised the Mullah's 'followers', not 'tribes' as designated at Illig, to enter British territory, and resort to their traditional pasture area as outlined by the wells at Halin, Hudin, Tifafleh and Damot. In return, the Mullah recognised the British boundary and promised to desist from raiding tribes under British and Ethiopian protection. He also acknowledged that the Mudug oasis and Galkayu wells were under the control of Yusuf Ali and his sons. Another aspect of Illig was that it appears to have created a host of hangers-on and talebearers, seeking to sell their services either to the British for cash, or to the Mullah as reassurance for the future. In conjunction with this the arms trade flourished. Cessation of outright hostilities seems to have accelerated its prosperity.

Despite the supplementary agreement of March 1907, there was discernible a mutual distrust between Britain and Italy as regards their approach to the Mullah. There were counter-accusations of ineffective administration in their respective spheres, and an Italian charge that the British would not join them in a naval blockade of the northern coast to prevent entry of arms for the Mullah. British Treasury opposition to increased expenditure meant that reliance was made on two old dhows manned by raffish crews, euphemistically described as 'two small armed revenue cutters'. The Italians, unwilling to act without British support, acquiesced in non-activity, blaming this on the British, and were of an increasing cynical view that by accepting the Mullah into their sphere they had played into British hands. The latter were suspicious that the Italians wished to draw them into joint action against the Mullah.

The paralysis that had descended on the Italians following their defeat at the hands of the Ethiopians at Adua seems to have persisted in their policy in the Horn. Already in August 1905 Pestalozza voiced his doubts to Swayne as to Italian inability to restrain the Mullah. The Italians had other problems to contend with: the Bimal tribe, in the immediate interior of Merka, were insurgent between 1905 and 1906, for a time cutting communication between Merka and Mogadishu and diverting trade to Zanzibar. The Mijjerteins in the northern Italian sphere had repudiated the 1889 treaty with the Filondari Company whereby they acknowledged Italian authority, and were seeking control over the Benadir coast. The Italian response was one of 'divide and rule', inciting southern Mijjertein to press northwards against the northern Mijjertein, and to bombard the coast of the latter to force the capitulation.

By early 1906 the Italians were openly admitting their precarious position in the Horn. The British saw the Italians as a 'broken reed', and because of this the Mullah might find it safer to raid within their sphere. However, the Ogaden and unpoliced Italian border to the west provided escape routes for the Dervishes, and their incursions added to the tribal counter-raiding and Ethiopian incursions that were taking place there. In the British sphere Dervish incursion into traditional pasture areas led to counter-claims of an intricate and exasperating kind. In one instance British forces were engaged in a two-month punitive action in settling a stock-transfer agreement made in Jigjiga.

The Illig Agreement was not working. Swayne expected the Mullah to return to British territory, and was still holding forth as to the merits of a tribal militia to contain him if he did return. Manning, less immersed in the Somali scene and anxious to get away, was becoming increasingly detached. As for the Mullah and his staunch supporters, they still retained their vision of an all-Islamic Horn, with no place in it for the infidel. And brooding over it all was this harsh and uncompromising land. Into this picture came a new and inspiriting presence, seeing all with a fresh and encompassing eye. In October 1907 young Winston Churchill, the 33-year-old Under Secretary of State for the Colonies, visited Somaliland in the course of a grand tour of inspection which took him to Malta, Aden, the Horn, Kenya and Uganda, and back to England by way of the Sudan and Egypt. Vigorous and able, with a quick and perceptive eye, Churchill's summing up of the position in British Somaliland was lucid and sharp.

5

CHURCHILL'S VISIT AND WINGATE'S MISSION

CHURCHILL'S stop-over at Berbera was brief, a few days only (his critics said 'a few hours'), although during his visit he managed a short incursion a few miles inland to the foot of the Golis range, the double journey embracing a whole day. His visit to Somaliland does appear fleeting, but Churchill had at hand full information on the state of affairs there and was plied with much advice by officials at Berbera.

Churchill described Somaliland as a land of dust and poverty, an opinion he saw no reason to change, and which was in fact reinforced after seeing the lush tropical greenness of Uganda, a territory which he compared to Somaliland, much to the disadvantage of the latter. Churchill's 'Minute on the Somaliland Protectorate', written after leaving Berbera, and dated 28 October 1907, is much more than a Minute. It is a substantial report, fresh and acute in its assessment of the situation. An eminent Treasury official referred to it as a 'weighty and statesmanlike pronouncement'. It carries an air of cogency and authority. Somaliland was, Churchill said, a wilderness of stone and scrub, a land marked by utter poverty. It was peopled by rifle-armed zealots with more than their share of 'wadads'. Yet this sterile and useless acquisition had cost Britain much: on one campaign against the Mullah she had spent nearly as much as the whole annual grant-in-aid to Uganda, a wonderful and fruitful land inhabited by a docile people. The sole reason for the retention of the Somaliland Protectorate was the need of Aden for supplies from there. It certainly had no other claim to be included in the cluster of valuable colonial possessions elsewhere in Africa and which were ripe for development. For itself, the Somaliland Protectorate should be left to live on frankincense and myrrh!

Churchill's report made no great impact at the Colonial Office, where it was discussed on 20 and 25 November 1907. The Colonial Office still did not take seriously the situation in Somaliland, and with Churchill still in Africa, the report did not receive the attention it deserved. Within a year, however, it came to the fore. By November 1908 the military situation in Somaliland was such as to warrant serious Cabinet consideration. On 24 November 1908, Churchill, now at the Board of Trade, circulated to his Cabinet colleagues the report which had lain dormant for almost a year. It made an immediate and important impact on them.

The report opens with the blunt statement that the general position in Somaliland was most unsatisfactory – from either a financial or military point of view. The modest revenue raised by duties at the coast was barely sufficient to support a skeletal civil and military authority at the coast, let alone administer the interior and give security to its people who lived under the shadow of the Mullah's advance. It was a dismal financial sheet that Churchill presented.

A dreary prospect faced the Somaliland Protectorate, if the recent past was any guide. With revenue for the past four years averaging £37,000 a year, and with yearly average expenditure running at £105,000 (and this did not take into account the special war expenditure of £2,300,000 for the 1903 and 1904 Expeditions), a grant-in-aid of well over £60,000 might be anticipated for the years to come. There was no indication that the territory would yield any extra revenue in ensuing years.

Churchill tersely summed up the military situation, exposing in dramatic fashion the weakness and vulnerable position of the paltry forces, more adapted to checking raiding parties than pinning down the Mullah's formidable Dervish host. The British forces comprised the 6th Battalion, King's African Rifles (400 Indian soldiers) and the Somali Standing Militia (350 mounted and 100 unmounted Somalis), both under British officers. There were also 180 armed police, and 100 camel-mounted Somali escorts for the political officers. In all, a pitifully small military presence, considering the magnitude of the task facing them.

The regular forces were distributed as follows. The political officers and escorts were posted along a triangular 'line of observation and intelligence', from Hargeisa to Las Dureh by way of Ber. On the coastal side of this line 650 mounted men were fairly evenly distributed at the bases at Burao, Sheikh and Suksodeh. In addition to these forces, there was a 'highly irregular militia' of friendly tribes armed by the British whose gadfly tactics – raids on unarmed neighbours and depredations – made them more of an incubus than a benefit.

In case of an advance by the Mullah, the following strategy would unfold. There would be a quick muster of mounted troops at Ber, to hold the position until the arrival of large reinforcements from Aden and India, and, if forced to retire before this, it would be to Berbera. And this, exclaimed Churchill, was 'the pearl' of the situation, for in the event of such a retirement it would leave only 'two garrisons of 50 infantry men each', in the forts of Burao and Sheikh, with the ineluctable prospect of their being destroyed while awaiting relief from an overseas expeditionary force which itself would cost three to four million pounds. No provision appears to have been made for the position of friendly tribes and tribal militia in such circumstances. 'And,' Churchill asked, 'could one imagine a more uncomfortable position?'

Despite military expenditure 'utterly disproportionate to the resources or value of Somaliland', there was still no effective security. Britain's hold on her territory was precarious, the greater part of the Protectorate remained undefended, and British obligations to friendly tribes were in default. The choice was stark: either defend the territory at immense cost or abandon it in the face of an attack from the Mullah. Churchill harked back to the two 'pitifully weak' garrisons tethered to Burao and Sheikh, pending arrival of powerful overseas forces, and who would await rescue or destruction. Churchill had seen on the north-west frontier of India and in the Sudan the folly of establishing undefendable small forts in the heart of enemy country. At any time, in the Muslim world, there could be an upsurge of rifle-armed fanaticism, with the advantage lying with the enemy, despite careful planning and well-laid lines of advance by the Imperial power. The choice in such cases was ineluctable: success at any cost or stark destruction.

As a war correspondent on the north-west frontier of India, Churchill had argued for a 'Forward Policy', but this was because 'our Empire in India is worth holding.' Not so with British Somaliland, a stark and arid land. Bases at Burao and Sheikh had nothing to offer; they only gratuitously courted danger. Looking at the overall position, the options were clear, if unattractive.

There were two choices: occupy the country and hold its wells, and join with the Italians in crushing the Mullah, regardless of cost and size of forces necessary; or withdraw to the coast, leaving only a tenuous line of observation from Hargeisa to Las Dureh supervised by political officers and escorts, and patrolled by two small companies of mounted Somalis. Behind the line of the Golis there should be left only forts at Sheikh and Burao as a token of British strength. Withdraw all Maxims from the interior; leave only a fortnight's stores and ammunition at these posts. The main line of resistance and source of revenue (duties) would be the coast, and it could be held by garrisons of 300 men at Berbera and 115 men each at Bulhar and Zeyla. These small garrisons could still resort to hot-weather retreats, such as Sheikh in the Golis, if the political officers considered it safe to do so. To compensate for the more trying climate conditions at the coast, leave conditions for service there should be improved. To complement these garrisons at the coast the two small revenue cutters at present in service should be increased in number to four.

Churchill saw much that was anomalous in the defence of the territory: lack of telegraph communication between Berbera and the outside world, although there had been telegraphic communication with Aden, India, Zanzibar and South Africa since the late 1870s. At present, Berbera's contact with the outside world was by some days' camel journey to Jibuti, and from there by French telegraph (with all the secrecy that this involved) to Aden. To rectify this anomaly all that was needed was a short line of direct cable from Berbera to Aden. Installation was not costly and annual expense of wireless stations would run to no more than a few hundred pounds. The advantages, however, were enormous. Reinforcements when needed could be obtained by wireless telegraph from Aden within the day. And the knowledge that 'the English were talking to Aden and India, where British soldiers were based, by a post without wires' would not be lost upon the Mullah.

After Churchill had pointed out the reduction in forces his plan involved, and although regretting the 'use of the paring knife upon these smart companies of Somalis mounted on their wiry active little ponies or perched on their camels', the military establishment resulting (including wireless telegraphy and two more revenue cutters), small and flexible in character, would be effective, and its cost only £25,100 annually, compared to the current charge of £54,600.

Apart from these savings, his proposals, Churchill maintained, would ensure peaceful penetration in the interior; the line of observation could quickly be drawn in, if necessary; there would be no hostages in the interior. The forts would remain to scare the enemy, 'though not to trap ourselves'. The coast would be effectively held, with forces always available at Aden.

His proposal, Churchill claimed, was essentially self-contained and final; it would limit precisely the liabilities of the British Government and close altogether 'the vistas of expenditure and expeditions which now lie painfully and even deliberately exposed'.

Of course the whole picture might be quickly changed by what happened to the Mullah. He might even die! In which case there could be a return to the more lighthearted ways of a self-supporting Protectorate as existed before the Mullah emerged as the dominant concern of the British administration and the major threat to the Protectorate. But, precluding the Mullah's death, welcome as it would be, there were ineluctable facts to be faced: Britain could not really resist the Mullah's assertion of influence among the interior tribes if he seriously pressed it: 'These wild peoples have always lived in anarchy and strife among themselves or with their neighbours.' Hitherto millions of British taxpayers' money had been 'squandered' vainly in interfering with this state of affairs.

The ultimate and not unacceptable solution for Churchill was to leave the Mullah *in situ* in the interior, and, providing he treated the friendly tribes properly, the British would allow him to trade with the posts they controlled at the sea, holding always the threat of blockade in the event of his misbehaviour. It was not an heroic policy but there was much to justify it; there were many examples of such policy on the north-west Indian frontier. Finally, in view of the utter poverty of this wilderness of stone and scrub, and the military strength of its fanatical inhabitants, it was the only worthwhile policy for the British Government to pursue.

Churchill saw only a small portion and not the best of the Protectorate during his short stop-over at Berbera, and he saw it at the worst time of year. He appears to have had no idea of the hinterland, and his views were certainly not applicable to the whole of the Protectorate; he knew nothing of the fertile river valleys of the upper Juba and Webi Shibeli, the pasture lands of the Haud and Ogaden, or the superior climate of the Golis range and upland area behind it, to which British officers resorted as an escape from the exhausting heat at the coast.

Churchill's report was considered at the Colonial Office on 25 November 1907, while Churchill himself was still in East Africa, prior to returning home by way of the Nile and seeing much better lands than Somaliland, especially Uganda, *en route*. He did not arrive back in England until the end of the year. Meanwhile Colonial Office views were expressed regarding his report. C. P. Lucas, eminent Colonial Office official and historian of the Empire, and soon to head the newly formed Dominion Department at the Colonial Office, considered the report dangerous in advocating an abrupt change of policy from that previously followed, viz., the carefully thought out and judicious compromise of a standing militia and tribal force – one which gave the Somalis time to organise their own defence while holding the interior until this was attained. Lucas was all for gradualism in the development of a colony. Churchill, however, would have the British shut themselves up at one or two ports leaving the interior to take care of itself. It would never work! It was impossible to hold the coast without control of the interior.

Other officials at the meeting on 25 November 1907 affirmed Lucas's view. Commissioner Cordeaux, on leave from Somaliland, argued that the coast could not be held without control of the interior, and pointed out that British treaty and moral obligations to friendly tribes should be not forsaken. There was also the treaty obligation to Ethiopia in the matter of ending the illicit trade in slaves, arms and contraband goods. Ethiopia had previously honoured her commitment not to support the Dervishes in the Sudan, and Britain should honour her commitment in return. Withdrawal to the coast would be a blow to British prestige. There were current rumours of instability and possible collapse of the régime in Ethiopia, and if this came about it might be the signal for a general scramble in the Horn, a scramble in which Britain would be at a grave disadvantage if she lost control of the interior of her Protectorate.

Sir Edward Grey, at the Foreign Office – an Office only a few years previously relieved of the irksome Somaliland territory – opposed Churchill's recommendations. So also did H. J. (later Sir Hubert) Read, senior official at the Colonial Office, who was profoundly knowledgeable about Africa, having served as head of the Office's East and West African Departments. Grey and he argued that such withdrawal would be seen by the Mullah as a sign of British weakness, and as giving him a free hand in the interior, while the British remained locked up in their enclaves at Berbera, Bulhar and Zeyla.

Replying to his critics on 19 January 1908, shortly after his return from Africa, Churchill challenged them to refute his facts. They could not deny that friendly tribes, armed by the British, did indeed raid their neighbours with these weapons; that an advance by the Mullah would leave the Ishaak tribes at his mercy and so also the isolated posts at Sheikh and Burao pending the arrival of large reinforcements. Churchill remained convinced that the policy of coastal concentration was the right one. Neither the Italians nor the French were 'such fools as to waste their money in attempting to control the interior of this spheres of influence'.

Resolute in his convictions, Churchill did, however, contemplate an alternative to the present form of administration of the territory: amalgamation with Aden. In a letter of 14 December 1907 to Sir Francis Hopwood, Permanent Secretary at the Colonial Office, Churchill eloquently argued for such an amalgamation: were not the destinies of Aden and British Somaliland 'inextricably intertwined'? British Somaliland had originally been acquired because of British interests at Aden, the one place where all the threads of the Somaliland question combined; if Aden were closed to Somaliland trade, every tribe right up to the Ethiopian or Italian frontier could be 'pinched'. The military and administrative advantages of amalgamation were obvious. Much duplication would be avoided and there would be much economy: one overall administrative officer; joint armed forces; flexible interchange of subordinate political officers; mutual drawing on of military forces in case of need, such as disturbance or siege. Churchill argued his case for amalgamation with cogency and compelling force.

It drew more support than his recommendations for coastal concentration, especially one aspect which Churchill had not dwelt on. Amalgamation with Aden would throw the responsibility for administering British Somaliland back into the lap of the India Office, and the Colonial Office would be pleased to see it returned there. One official, R. L. Antrobus, stressed the ease of management of Somaliland through Aden rather than London, and pointed out that when the Colonial Office originally took over the Protectorate from the Foreign Office, it had urged that it be administered by the India Office, but the latter had managed to persuade the Cabinet against this. The India Office in 1908, however, was no more inclined to take on the irksome responsibility for the Protectorate than it had been in 1898, and so Somaliland remained with the Colonial Office. By now Churchill had removed himself from the whole question, and was directing his energies and ability to another great office of State: in April 1908 he became President of the Board of Trade.

While Churchill visited and departed from Somali shores the Mullah remained entrenched in the eastern part of the Protectorate, where he controlled Las Khorai, the port of entry for his arms. He had brought into his fold some of the Warsangli (British subjects), Bagheri and southern Mijjertein and, thanks be to Allah, he had trusted agents, 'eminent Dervishes of authority . . . wise and faithful', such as Osman Dervish and Ibrahim Hassan. 'God is Merciful,' the nine divisions of his forces were under loyal commanders, mostly relatives, including three wives, one of whom, Hasna Doreh, being as warlike as Boadicea.

The Mullah, while renewing his fighting strength, kept up his usual running correspondence with the British, in which he complained of their blockade and its 'spoiling' of prices, and of the Dolbahanta who raided his people and refused to pay blood money for their crimes. He demanded the return of his 17 wives held by the British (in truth they held only eight of them). He complained that he was surrounded by a world of intriguers and of these the British and Ethiopians were by far the worst. As for the Italians, they were pestiferous gadflies who had poisoned one of his sons. Within his own ranks there were also, he complained, dastardly intriguers: two of them, Abdullah Shahari and Mohammed Habarwah, who had defected to the Italians, should have their throats slit for their tale-telling. Meanwhile, he openly admitted, he had wreaked terrible revenge on their families and celebrated this with a poem of self-constituted praise. He also warned Cordeaux against intriguers such as the hated Risaldar-Major Musa Farah, ISO, 'son of Egarreh', a born trouble-maker. As always his letter ended on a high note:

> let us be friendly and give back to each his property . . . I am prepared to accept all that you decide justly . . . see both sides . . . You, Cordeaux, be the peacemaker.

This apparent reasonableness was followed by downright arrogance, a letter demanding that the British remove themselves post-haste from the Ain Valley, and making no secret that he was urging his Warsangli allies to force the Dolbahanta to come in on his side. These insolent letters were openly sent through the country of the Dolbahanta so that the latter might be impressed by the Mullah's contemptuous treatment of the British. Cordeaux, faced with this Dervish resurgence, and with the Colonial Office failing to take up Italy's original offer of a joint blockade of the Warsangli coast, instituted one of his own in November 1908. At the same time operations of the King's African Rifles were directed into the Ain Valley and forces were brought over from Aden to garrison Las Khorai. This show of British strength brought some wavering of Warsangli support for the Mullah, and halted Dolbahanta defections to his cause.

More disturbing for the Mullah at the end of 1908 was the action of two apostates, Abdullah Shahari and Deria Arraleh, who returned from Mecca with a letter from Sheikh Salih, head of the Salihiya Tariqa there, denouncing the Mullah in the strongest terms: he had sinned against Allah and the Prophet; he was a veritable kaffir, an unbeliever and a madman. This denunciation, coming from a high religious figure, hurt the Mullah more than a military defeat. He claimed that it was a conspiracy between Abdullah Shahari and Salih's secretary, whereby the latter turned what was a mild rebuke from Sheikh Salih into a virulent condemnation. The letter could not so easily be dismissed. It gained considerable circulation in the Protectorate, and the British missed an opportunity in failing to get the Grand Mufti of Turkey to add his omniscient voice to this denunciation, and in failing to protect disenchanted followers of the Mullah who, when their coup against him failed, suffered a terrible fate.

By the beginning of 1909 the Mullah had recovered from this temporary setback and the Dervishes were again on the move. The Nogal and Ain valleys fell to them, loyal British-protected tribes fled to Haisam and Hudin. More men of the King's African Rifles were now brought in from Nyasaland and East Africa and a full infantry battalion held in readiness at Aden. Cordeaux and the Inspector-General of the KAR were all for extending operations into the Ain Valley and bringing in a camel corps from India. They argued that the entrenched-coast mentality could not be maintained and that the military framework so ridiculed by Churchill was now crumbling. The Treasury, however, would have no more costly expeditions against the Mullah, and, scarcely a year after its consideration of Churchill's report, the Cabinet met again to ponder the Somali problem.

At this stage a number of hare-brained proposals from Colonial Office officials and outside advisers as to how to end the Mullah menace were put forth. Why not a man-to-man approach to him? Appeal to his good sense, tell him the British were aware of his problems and the need of his people for adequate grazing ground and scope for their traditional raiding. Show good-will towards him. Make him an attractive offer: in return for peace he would be pardoned and given an annual subsidy of £2,000, a form of Danegeld. Sir A. Pearse, who claimed to have met the Mullah in Berbera (there is no evidence for this claim) 'in olden days' and felt he thoroughly knew him, offered to go in person, accompanied by a devout Somali and a 'good military man', to palaver with the Mullah, drawing out his innermost aspirations, and thereby securing 'complete restoration of peace . . . and with the Mullah persuaded to leave us alone'. It was an idea out of the empyrean and was treated with disbelief at the Colonial Office and by men on the spot in Somaliland. As for giving an annual subsidy to the Mullah, he would only use it to re-arm. Truly the month of March 1909 was a month of madness.

The inanity of Pearse's suggestion was highlighted when, in the same month, Cordeaux received a letter of the most irreconcilable kind from the Mullah. The latter, while openly admitting the looting of stock from the Ishaak who had resisted his bird-calls, claimed that this looted stock was his due, to be shared out among loyal Dervishes. He then proceeded to point out British derelictions: they made too much of that terrible man, Risaldar-Major Musa Farah, they owed the Mullah blood money for the Dervishes they had killed in the Nogal country and they should return the stock and arms they had captured. Finally, they should get out of Somaliland. Cordeaux rebutted the Mullah's allegations and studiously avoided reference to his demands that the British should get out. Instead, Cordeaux stated that if the Mullah really desired peace he should cease interfering with 'British tribes' – those under British protection. The Mullah made no reply to this, and matters seemed at an impasse, with battle lines drawn.

The militia scheme had failed, and so also the Illig Agreement, the administration was demoralised and on the verge of collapse, and transport was in short supply. The Dervish threat was mounting. Where could a lasting solution to the Mullah problem be found, apart from outright war or washing of hands of the whole thing? Could not wisdom and experience in dealing with similar problems elsewhere in the Empire be drawn on? The luminous figure of Wingate in the Sudan might provide the answer.

If Sir Reginald Wingate (1861–1953), Governor-General and Sirdar of the Sudan, a territory not unlike Somaliland, could lend his weighty authority to what the Colonial Office itself seems to have already decided on as the right policy, it would win their case. The Colonial Office view was that Wingate, if faced with this policy as a *fait accompli*, would accept it, even though it went against his personal convictions.

There was much to be said for bringing in Wingate. His military authority and august presence as Sirdar would impress the Mullah. The Treasury viewed his appointment with benign eye, for his work in the Sudan had brought it from a state of anarchy to one of stability and economic advance, and his use of native authorities there had given a good underpinning to local government. Wingate appointed an interesting partner for his Somali mission. He was General Sir Rudolf (Baron) von Slatin, Inspector-General of the Sudan, a most impressive figure, a mystic whose religious oscillations had taken him in and out of Islam and were a cause of much puzzlement to his friends and admirers. Deeply immersed in the ways of Islam and knowing his Arab proverbs (including the lovely couplet 'Grief before three things ever flies apace/ 'Fore water, foliage and a lovely face'), unworldly yet withal a capable administrator, he would be a valuable adjunct to Wingate's more practical acumen. On home ground in Somaliland a third figure, Cordeaux, with his unique knowledge of Somali affairs, would make up what was meant to be a powerful trio. Cordeaux's inclusion in the mission would also show that the designation of Wingate, an outsider, to lead it, was no reflection on Cordeaux's conduct of affairs in the Protectorate.

Wingate's instructions, dated 15 April 1909, directed him to evaluate the Somali situation and to recommend a policy for the future administration of the territory. The Secretary of State indicated that an organised campaign against the Mullah was out of the question and so also military occupation of points in the interior. He let it be known that the Government favoured complete withdrawal, or at least partial withdrawal, to the coast, and was prepared to give the Mullah an annual subsidy, subject to his good behaviour. It would be a form of indirect rule. Wingate was left in no doubt as to the narrow limits within which he was to make suggestions.

On arrival at Berbera at the end of April 1909, he immediately got down to business. In a letter of 30 April to the Mullah, written in Arabic (in which language Wingate was fluent), he addressed him as 'Fakir Sayyid Abdullah bin Mohammed Hassan' (the prefix, 'Fakir', being used here, not in the usual pejorative sense of a mendicant, but in the true Muslim and highly austere religious sense), and with the salutation, 'May God keep you.' This flowery opening dispensed with, Wingate bluntly proceeded to blame Sayyid and his people for the aggression and wrongdoing between 'your Arabs and our Arabs'. Although Cordeaux was all for further military action against the Dervishes, he, Wingate, would restrain him. He reminded the Mullah – and was God not his witness? – that the British were magnanimous and could easily have taxed the interior of their Protectorate but had refrained through benevolence and their being imbued with what was 'right and just'. Wingate reminded the Mullah that he had only 25 days at Berbera (he stayed nearly two months) and, though in a hurry, was prepared to meet such wise and faithful men as the Mullah might send to discuss 'all questions'. The envoys would be assured of *aman* (safe conduct), guaranteed by Allah, the Prophet, Wingate and HMG. With poised touch Wingate rounded out his letter:

> Your envoys should know the Arabic language, as that is the language we speak ourselves, and we wish to talk with them without the necessity of using interpreters.

Wingate's letter was delivered by two messengers whose subsequent fate (the same as befell all bearers of bad news) can only be guessed at. Sayyid, ignoring Wingate's warning that he had only 25 days at Berbera, waited nearly two months before replying, and then in the form of four letters delivered to Wingate by an aged Dervish, a fanatical

Wadad, Hirsi Koshin. This messenger professed great unworldliness, and claimed that he was only a servant of God, although Wingate found him 'clearly unacquainted with the true tenets of Islam'. The Mullah's letters which he had brought were empty of content, more invocations to Allah and the Prophet to witness his desire for peace, despite British provocation. In the face of this, Wingate left for England at the end of June 1909, by which time he had submitted to the Colonial Office two tentative reports, dated 12 and 17 June 1909.

Wingate's final report was completed in August 1909, after his arrival in England but, along with the two earlier reports, remained in a shroud of secrecy almost up to the Second World War. They were held in such perdu that Jardine, writing in the early 1920s, was denied access to them. This secrecy arose partially from Wingate's and Slatin's severe strictures on Protectorate officials. (Cordeaux had been patently uneasy with the two eminent figures of Wingate and Slatin hovering over him during their visit.) Slatin had lent a willing ear to the complaints of Somali elders that Cordeaux ignored their traditional role in Somali tribal affairs. Wingate, proud of his command of Arabic, poked fun at Cordeaux and fellow officials for their lack of knowledge of the Somali language – how could they purport to understand the Somali without knowing his language? A more cogent reason, however, for the secrecy surrounding the Wingate mission's conclusions was that they were clearly opposed to the Colonial Office view. The mission made a clear recommendation for entrenchment, as against withdrawal to the coast, which the Colonial Office had already decided on and had believed the mission would support.

Wingate's denunciation of the Pestalozza agreements was more to the liking of the Colonial Office. Wingate and Slatin claimed that these agreements, to which the Mullah had been a party, had given him murderous scope, for he had used Italian protection under these agreements to raid British-protected tribes, and the Italians, with Machiavellian cleverness, had sought to embroil him with the British, declaring that, as a rebel, he was no longer their responsibility. They also led the Mullah to believe that the British had incited them, the Italians, to seize a dhow carrying the Mullah's goods. The Colonial Office was of the view that ending the Pestalozza agreements might force the Italians into a more active defence of their territory.

Wingate's reports throw much light on the nature of British administration in the Somaliland Protectorate, as seen by high and experienced personages from another African territory similar in many respects to Somaliland. Their aspersions on Cordeaux and colleagues for their lack

81

of knowledge of Arabic and Somali languages reveal their unawareness as to what small currency Arabic had in Somaliland, that Somali was an unwritten language, and that even in its oral form there was little instruction available at the time. There had been no Christian missionary activity in Somaliland to speak of, nor had there been any translation of languages and compiling of dictionaries, etc., such as usually accompanied missionary activity in a new country. Wingate and Slatin, largely unaware of this, were led to criticise British officials in the Protectorate for over-reliance on native personages, who in turn were heartily disliked by their fellow Somalis. A prime example of this was Risaldar-Major Musa Farah, who held a high post at Burao. He was looked on as a British stooge.

Wingate and Slatin affected an intuitive understanding of Islam and the Arab world to which Somaliland purportedly belonged, and they saw much there that was familiar to them. Like the Sudan it was a poor land, largely desert, with no agriculture or commerce worth the name, and its people, largely Islamic in religion, were nomadic pastoralists. Slatin, half-oriental in mode of thought, less pragmatic and imperial-minded than Wingate, spoke vehemently against vandalising native culture. The Somalis should be left embalmed, like a fly in amber, in their timeless way of life. He saw much to admire in it, and did not want too close supervision of nomadic society, for this tended to produce a degeneration. Tribes previously alert to defending themselves would become de-energised under too close British protection. Slatin reckoned that on the whole it would be no great loss to either Somali or the British if the latter departed, for they had made their regime unpopular. The term 'home rule', much in the air *à propos* Ireland at the time, might be extended to the Somalis in a mild form of indirect rule. If the British were to stay, theirs should be a skeletal administration confined to Commissioner, Superintendent of Police, Director of Customs, Financial Secretary and a few District Commissioners at the coastal towns.

A prime example, in Slatin's eyes, of British insensibility in the matter of Somali religious feelings was allowing a Roman Catholic mission openly to proselytise in Berbera. The sight of convert children running around Berbera with a medal or scapula round their necks was an affront to Allah and the Prophet and anathema in Islamic eyes. Slatin denounced this tactless exhibition of Christianity in a solidly Islamic society, but he overlooked the fact that these convert children were mostly waterfront waifs rescued from Berbera harbour, and who had been given food and shelter by the Christian mission. There were no

Right: Sayyid Abdi Krim (one of the Mullah's sons: photo taken 1945)

Below: De Havilland 9 (two-seater) day bomber converted to ambulance

Left: Camel with field artillery

Below: Mounted *illalos* (tribal police)

Above: Dervish look-
out towers (also used
as granaries)

Right: Taleh fort
from the air

Above left: Richard Corfield

Above right: Memorial to Richard Corfield at Marlborough College

Below: The Mullah's memorial in Mogadishu

parents available to be consulted in the matter of their conversion to Christianity.

The Wingate mission conceded that the British administration in the Protectorate laboured under severe handicaps. They pointed out, as had Churchill, the sore need for direct telegraphic communication with the outside world. Nothing had been done to right this anomaly since Churchill had drawn attention to it. There was an active arms trade which went on almost unchecked apart from a British patrol at sea from Muscat to Zanzibar. The International Arms Conference, which was to meet on 4 December 1909, should be apprised as to the need for joint action by all the Powers to stop the arms trade in the Horn. The mission, however, saw little hope of French and Ethiopian co-operation in the matter. Above all, the long war of attrition with the Mullah had deflected precious resources and time from the development of the economy and education and communications.

The Mullah was both the hub and the crux of the Somali problem. The ideal for Wingate and Slatin would be if he took up a peaceful life in the Ain Valley and desisted from raiding British-protected tribes. This would allow British troops to be withdrawn from the Ain Valley, leaving only a few military dispositions elsewhere, as at Sheikh, which could be used as a relief centre for the British regiment at Aden – a welcome change from the heat of that place. Their presence at Sheikh would have a salutary effect and would enable the local troops based there to patrol elsewhere. Burao could be abandoned. Such arrangements would lift an enormous burden from the shoulders of the British administration.

In return for this boon, which would make the Pestalozza agreements irrelevant, for which much thanks, the British would grant the Mullah trading facilities and access to their ports. It would be a happy arrangement all round. The only flaw in it was that the Mullah's intentions were unknown.

His movements were unpredictable except that kinship and family still exercised their pull: when severely pressed he would always fall back on his mother's people, the Dolbahanta in the north, or his father's folk, the Bagheri in the south. If to the latter he might move farther south-easterly, towards Ethiopia, acquiring fresh influence among the tribes of the upper Shibeli and Juba, although the lower, tsetse-ridden Juba area might deter his advance in that direction. For the meantime, however, the Mullah was quiescent. Could it be that he was in awe of the powerful Sirdar from the Sudan? Or was he only biding his time, watchful of Wingate's actions? In September 1909, when the Sirdar had left the country and the Mullah's aged emissary to Wingate had returned empty-handed, Sayyid signalled his anger by putting to death a messenger carrying a letter from Cordeaux in which he urged the Mullah to pursue the path of peace. In late September Burao was attacked and a number of *illalos* (scouts) slaughtered.

By October 1909 the Cabinet had considered Wingate's reports and made its own decision as to policy for British Somaliland. The essence of Wingate's recommendations were that only if the Mullah were vanquished should there be withdrawal to the coast, and in no circumstances should there be complete evacuation of Somaliland. This would be disastrous for British prestige, would undermine her position at Aden and sever its provision line with Somaliland, and give the Mullah fresh life. A subsidy to the Mullah was also out of the question: it would only lead to ever-increasing demands from him. To vanquish the Mullah would mean a forward policy, joint British/Ethiopian/Italian action, arming of tribes and letting them loose on the Mullah, and the time was not ripe for this: the Italians were unready and the Ethiopians unsure. Wingate thought a chance had been missed at Jidbali by not pushing home the victory there. Only if the Mullah were disposed of could the British contemplate withdrawal, although they could use the threat of withdrawal to stimulate the Italians into playing a part in keeping order in the Horn, and until this was achieved the present military dispositions, with some minor alterations, must be maintained. Once rid of the Mullah and the Dervishes, a complete reorganisation of the military and revamping of the administration could take place, giving more responsibility to the natives and developing the economy.

Wingate's second report, dated 17 June 1909 (a postscript to his main report of 12 June of the same year) had attached to it four of the Mullah's letters and British replies to them. The Mullah's letters repeated the well-worn theme: the British were responsible for the mutual hostility between themselves and the Mullah. The latter's watchword had always been 'peace'; there were the same old tergiversations and delaying tactics, meant to prolong a situation which the Mullah knew to be costly for the British. The British, in reply, stated that the Mullah's letters offered nothing concrete, and that the Mullah must desist from interfering with British-protected tribes. In the face of the Mullah's continued recalcitrance, Wingate's and Slatin's postulations and recommendations were mere marginalia.

By October 1909 the decision to withdraw to the coast had been taken. This meant the end of the Illig Agreement, and when Italy was informed of the decision to withdraw, she protested vigorously. Had she not always fully accepted responsibility for Sayyid as an Italian subject, and had she not co-operated with the British, and were not their interests intimately allied in Somaliland? Her protests were in vain, and Italy was officially informed that HMG considered that the Illig Agreement 'is *de facto* at an end and it seems that as a matter of self-respect we are bound to say so.'

6

WITHDRAWAL TO THE COAST, 1910–13

CHURCHILL'S advocacy of withdrawal to the coast, so vehemently decried at the time, was put into effect by the Government in January 1910. It would have been expected that Cordeaux, with his long experience in Somaliland, would have presided over the process of withdrawal. Joining the Indian Army in 1894 as a young man, he had been appointed Assistant Resident at Berbera in 1898, and then, successively, Deputy Commissioner (1904) and Commissioner, and Commander-in-Chief in 1906, holding the latter post until 1910. He probably knew more about Somaliland than any other European officer at the time. However, it was thought that Cordeaux was long overdue for a change from the trying climate and trials of Somaliland. His subsequent high postings were in lush territories, far removed from the rigour of Somaliland: Uganda (1910–12), St Helena (1912–20), Bahamas (1920–to retirement).

General Sir William Manning, successor to Cordeaux and who was to effect the withdrawal, arrived at Berbera in early January 1910. Following a short reconnaissance of the interior, he reported on 9 February 1910 that the situation was optimistic. The Mullah's star was on the decline. The Dervishes were divided among themselves, apart from the main body of staunch supporters in the *haroun* (main base) in Italian Somaliland. Many of the Darod had not only deserted the Mullah's ranks but were ready to try their hand against him, and Manning claimed that they should receive British support, much more than the capricious Warsangli in the north who dithered as to whether their loyalty lay with the Mullah or the British. As for the Bagheri in the south, who usually came down on the side of the Mullah, they should be contained by the Ishaak with British support, although Manning was not averse to some rough usage of the Ishaak by the Dervishes – it would evoke their dormant virility and throw up a necessary leader.

As for the Ogaden, on the Ethiopian border, their precise relations with the Mullah were unknown.

Summing up, the three main fronts of the Dervish threat were the Warsangli, Bagheri and the force concentrated with the Mullah. Throughout February 1910, Manning issued arms to pro-British tribes to meet this threat. Manning feigned to see what the aftermath of withdrawal would be: a situation much like that existing in Italian Somaliland, with little control over events in the interior, and forcing pro-British tribes to defend themselves, thus fostering their self-reliance and cohesion.

The withdrawal, which began on 6 March 1910, and was to be completed in three weeks, presented a melancholy scene. As the 6th Battalion, King's African Rifles, moved coastwards, across the parched desert, hastening to beat the rainy season, a violent thunderstorm broke, causing much panic among the mounts and stampeding the camels. Previously dry water courses were now torrents, water perils to be surmounted. The British officers had seen nothing like this, even in India. Borne along on a last mad gallop, banners streaming behind them, and with the plodding ox-carts far in the rear, they finally reached the outskirts of Berbera, to the infinite relief of the Indian soldiers, glad to depart the hell-hole of the interior.

Berbera hummed with activity during the withdrawal: returning Somali forces, disbanded police, *illalos* and *akils* (tribal headmen), Indian forces from the recently disbanded 6th Battalion, awaiting posting to guard duties at the coastal towns. Concurrent with the withdrawal and as a removal of an irritant to Muslim sensibilities, the French Catholic mission at Berbera and its recently established branch in the interior were closed down in April 1910. The mission was permitted to take its few converts to a new site in Aden and was duly compensated for the interdict on its activities in British Somaliland.

Withdrawal signified the contraction of Imperial responsibilities in Somaliland at a time when Imperial expansion was much in the air elsewhere. It was not to the liking of either public or Parliament at home. It seemed a retreat similar to that which had taken place earlier in the Sudan with sorry consequences, and it meant the letting down of loyal tribes whom Britain was sworn to protect: 'It was one of the most deplorable acts ever committed by a British Government,' proclaimed *The Times* (8 April 1910). Italians and Ethiopians were alarmed that the withdrawal would result in a rampage of uncontrolled tribal war in the British sphere which might spill over into their territories. Their fears were realised.

87

A two-year period of lawlessness followed. There was Dervish resurgence and tribal in-fighting, razzias as of old, raiding of stock, and paying off of old debts. Apart from a brief period when the Warsangli were roughly handled by the Italian and British Mijjertein and the Bagheri were repulsed by pro-British tribes, Manning's optimistic forecast for the future was not fulfilled. Manning at one stage fell for a report that the Mullah had died and that there was confusion in Dervish ranks. Alas it was untrue! Manning's roseate picture of the future possibly arose from his desire to show that the situation in Somaliland was so improved as to no longer need his presence there. In the upshot he did leave, in June 1910, for Nyasaland.

On the eve of his departure the dragon reared its head. Gadwein supporters of the Mullah attacked coastal customs posts at Hais, Mait and Karam, and gave gross insult when, in defiance of Manning's threat to bombard Hais, they exhumed and burnt the body of a British soldier buried there.

Manning's successor, Horace (later Sir Horace) Byatt, a man of peace and reserved common sense, was faced with Habr Awal attacks on caravans, tribal war between the Habr Toljaala and Aidegalla and camel raiding in the Ogaden by the Habr Yunis. A statement in the House of Commons that the Mullah was 'completely broken', was soon belied when, in July 1910, the Mullah moved from Illig into the eastern Nogal Valley, causing much panic. Tribes ousted by this advance turned on their neighbours. Meanwhile the arms trade flourished. The British, constrained by their policy of withdrawal, lost prestige, and their erstwhile loyal Somali employees, worried about their families and property in the interior, now defected. The cosmopolitan trading community – Indians, Arabs and Jews, at Berbera – found their wares rotting and unsaleable. British inactivity appeared to cause ever-growing anarchy.

Despite Byatt's action in sending a British warship to Hais in August 1910 to punish the culprits guilty of the aforementioned desecration and levying a fine on Hais, unrest grew. In September–October 1910 the Dervishes won major battles against the Mijjertein and Warsangli, worsted the Dolbahanta and established a post near Bohotle, 'one of the most valuable and important watering places in the Ain Valley'. A joint British–Italian approach to Ethiopia thwarted the Mullah's attempt to win over local chiefs on Ethiopia's eastern border. Their attempt, however, to get rid of a Warsangli chief, a supporter of the Mullah, by deporting him to Mombasa failed when the culprit escaped and reappeared later as a hero among his own people.

In an attempt to rehabilitate himself following the rebuff and denunciation he had received from Sayyid Mohammed Salih of Mecca, the Mullah sought to rally wide support for a jihad against the infidel. His messengers were sent as far afield as the Marehan near British Jubaland, and European officials in that area suspected the Mullah's hand behind anti-colonial movements there. Intercepted letters revealed that the Mullah was in touch with a leading sheikh in the Yemen who sent him stonemasons to construct the Mullah's prize fort at Taleh. And he urged Muslims far and near to join in a jihad against Europeans, of whom the Italians were the ultra-infidels. Such now was the Mullah's renown that a small Muslim community (including some from German East Africa) pursuing university studies in Berlin sent him a letter avowing support for his sacred war. This letter also fell into British hands. Untoward rudeness of Somali employees at Berbera towards the British was associated with a report that the Mullah was about to strike at Berbera and drive out the British. It caused much panic and scuttling among the trading community.

Amid increasing signs that the encampment system was a failure, and with transport and trade disrupted by inter-tribal feuding, British prestige was at a low ebb in 1911. Byatt's attempt to win support against the Dervishes by visiting the coastal towns and issuing arms and subsidies to coastal tribes brought little result. Dervish resurgence and tribal disintegration continued. There were murders and preying on caravans, stories of mutilations and atrocities, and of refugees so destitute that they were reduced to cannibalism. The high point of terror came in February 1912 when the Dervishes penetrated Berbera, leaving a mysterious cabbalistic sign, the letter H, on trees and buildings, and causing great panic in the town. When the Dervishes ousted the Dolbahanta from Bohotle they turned it into a Dervish base in British territory, from which they could control the rich pasture in the Ain and Nogal valleys and communication with the Bagheri country, whence came arms and followers. The picture was stark in the extreme. Indian troops from Aden were insufficient to garrison all points.

By March 1912 the Colonial Office was bemoaning the lack of an Englishman who could rally the tribes of the interior against the Mullah. It now heeded Byatt's cry about the folly of withdrawal and abandonment, and the need for a flexible striking force to meet the hit-and-run tactics of the Dervishes. Byatt wanted a camel corps, similar to the Bikanir Corps, which would operate within a 50-mile radius of Berbera. Byatt had to argue his case well, for the failure of the militia system was still in mind. But when Byatt skilfully stressed the cheapness of the camel corps he won over both Colonial Office and an ever-watchful

Treasury. Approval of a 150-man Camel Corps came in June 1912, and this along with 320 Aden troops and 200 Indians from the disbanded 6th Battalion, King's African Rifles, made up the Protectorate's total forces.

The Mullah saw this military reorganisation as a preliminary to a major expedition against himself. Having failed to bring over the Ogaden and concerned as to the vulnerability of his forces at Bohotle, he withdrew to the east, and concentrated his *haroun* near Gerrowei, on the Italian frontier. From here he penned letters to Byatt with the usual ornate openings of 'Praise be to God' and 'Prayers and Salutations to our Prophet Mohammed', and stressing his desire for peace: 'when can there be the necessary meeting on this subject?' These epistles ended with the usual reminder that they came 'from the slave of God and the poor man'. Byatt's reply was terse. The Mullah could prove his desire for peace by abstaining from war and raiding and by stopping his call to British-protected tribes to join him in a jihad. Otherwise the 'powerful help of the British Government' would be against him, and 'May God give you wisdom to listen to these words.'

The formation of the Camel Corps was a prolonged affair. Riding camels and saddlery had to be obtained from India. There was drill and musketry training at Berbera. The Camel Corps was made up of two companies, each of four sections of 18 men. In addition there was a Maxim gun team. Richard Corfield, the young political officer who commanded the Camel Corps in its role as a constabulary force, had served in Baden Powell's Scouts in South Africa and had previous experience as a political officer in Somaliland and Nigeria. It was with much enthusiasm that he returned to Somaliland to take up his new appointment.

Lawlessness abounded throughout the Protectorate while Corfield was recruiting and training his force. Dervish attacks had driven inland tribes into the northern half of the Protectorate where, competing for limited pasturage, they were warring with each other. G. F. Archer, Acting Commissioner, witnessed this state of affairs when he visited the northern ports of Las Khorai and Hais in August 1912.

In early December 1912 the Camel Corps, basing itself at Mandera, 42 miles south-west of Berbera, took the field. Its first task was to protect the important Berbera–Hargeisa caravan route, much preyed on by raiders. Byatt's instructions to Corfield were in the form of a pep talk. He reminded him that the creation of the Camel Corps did not reverse the policy of coastal concentration. It was to act within a 50-mile radius of Berbera. It was not to close with the Dervishes at any time, and, if threatened by attack from the latter, was to retire to the coast.

This placed the Camel Corps in an almost impossible situation. It soon found itself pursuing raiders and when success was in sight having to call off the action. In the Ain Valley to the east, where the Dervishes were giving the Dolbahanta a difficult time, and the latter were threatening to go over to the Mullah if they did not receive British help, the Camel Corps could do nothing. The area was well outside their designated range of action. Corfield was soon asking what was the actual role of the Camel Corps? Time and again the Camel Corps had to stand aside during Dervish raids on pro-British tribes. Both Byatt and Corfield chafed exceedingly in these circumstances, and began to doubt whether the Camel Corps had any role to play.

In the face of Byatt's constant urging that the Camel Corps be allowed to operate outside the 50-mile limit, Harcourt, the Colonial Secretary, grudgingly gave permission on 24 January 1913 for the Camel Corps, in the event of emergency, to operate as far as Burao in the Nogal Valley direction, Ber (about 100 miles from Berbera) being the extreme limit, but not to enter the Ain Valley. The fiction that the Camel Corps was a coastal constabulary had been abandoned.

Meanwhile letters continued to come from the Mullah, written in his usual flowery style, and containing protestations of peace and much scolding of Byatt for not listening to the Mullah's words. Had not the latter shown much altruism in returning looted stock to pro-British tribes and punishing Dervishes who raided without his orders, although it was difficult to restrain Dervishes 'who have gone beyond my control'? In reply, Byatt commended the Mullah for his action, but more was needed if his words of peace were to be taken seriously: if the Dervishes did not attack pro-British tribes then the Camel Corps would assuredly not attack the Dervishes. In this spate of letter-writing by the Mullah, one of his letters, meant only for Muslim eyes and which fell into British hands, shows his style. It opens with prayers and salutations to the Prophet and thanks to God from this poor man of God who is writing to the wise men of the Gadwein. He reminds them of the punishment of Hell and bliss of Paradise which hovers over all their actions. He, the Mullah, has direct contact with God, and his prayers can secure condign punishment for enemies of the Gadwein. Some of these enemies had already died or became infidels or were wasting away as a result of his prayers. He invokes God's name thrice over to bear witness that he is a pilgrim, a fighter and man of sincerity. However, he can not restrain his bitterness towards the Dolbahanta, those wicked Dolbahanta whose consciences are not clear nor their hearts directed towards God.

Just as the entry of the Camel Corps into the field was a new departure for the British so also was that of fort-building which the Mullah started in 1912. The idea of using a Camel Corps against the Dervishes was a new and supposedly effective answer to Dervish tactics. Instead of sending infantry against them as in the 1901–4 Expeditions, the British would now fight them on their own terms and ground, and beat them at their own tactics. The Dervishes, seemingly aware of the new British approach, paralleled it with their own, namely, fort-building. For the British, familiar with military strongholds, attacking forts was much preferable to pursuing the Dervishes into the farthest corners of the Protectorate. It meant a change from the old fear of ambush on the march, and the time-honoured practice of forming a square to meet the headlong rush of the enemy amid dust and confusion, waiting for the attack. Now the initiative would be in their own hands.

The Mullah's cohorts raised stone forts at Laba Bari (in Bagheri country) and at Bohotle and Damer. Taleh in the eastern Nogal Valley, however, was his masterpiece. In January 1913 he moved his *haroun* to Taleh from Gerrowei, and henceforward it remained his headquarters. To construct this remarkable edifice he had the loan of stonemasons from his friend the Sheikh of the Yemen who had so enthusiastically supported him in the 1910–11 war against the infidel. Building stone structures was not beyond the ability of the Somali or their predecessors, as many stone structures throughout Somaliland testify. But at Taleh, the long experience of the Yemeni in constructing immensely strong forts was drawn on without the realisation that Somaliland was much different terrain from the Yemen, where such strongholds served an admirable purpose.

Why did the Mullah take to fort-building? It meant a complete change of warfare from his previous hit-and-run tactics against the enemy. The Sultan of the Yemen had extolled to him the value of strong fortresses as impregnable defence against an enemy, and was prepared to loan him his personal masons for the task of building such. The Mullah was an easy convert, for in his early travels he had seen many such fortified defence structures, and the formidable nature of strong forts greatly appealed to him. They would be a trenchant response to the Camel Corps with which the British hoped to gain advantage over his own nomadic type of warfare. A powerful fort would stand up against any major expedition launched against him. Great forts would give witness that the enemy had no monopoly of such defences and they would signal Sayyid's high prestige.

British withdrawal to the coast left the Mullah with his own spheres of influence to administer and protect, and for this and possible future confrontation with the British, permanent centres were necessary. The Mullah's increasing infirmity and obesity (a result of elephantiasis), which made it a painful exercise for him to move about or mount a horse, meant that he could no longer pursue strenuous nomadic warfare. If his campaign was coming to an end his last stand would be made in dramatic fashion. Whatever the many explanations for his fortress-building, Taleh was an impressive structure by any standard.

Seen from the air (as it would be later, in 1920) it had a lunar crater-like appearance. Approaching it on the ground it showed up as a strange complex of square bastions with cone-like projections on their tops. Close up, the massively blunt proportions of the whole gave an impression of Norman and Eastern architecture combined. There was an imbalance in its whole assemblage, as though lop-sided, tilted from south to north, especially when approaching it from the south-east. Its stronger side, from the west, south and round to the south-east, from where attack was anticipated, was a most elaborate defence, making up the main fortress complex. It was ringed by a stone wall of enormous strength and thickness and this was surmounted by 13 forts of great size and strength, 40 feet high, 12–14 feet thick at the base, and about 6 feet wide at the top. Nine of them had cone-like projections (similar to the wind-funnels seen in Persia and other Middle Eastern countries, or the tower-dwellings of the Yemen), the rest were roofless and had a truncated pyramid-like appearance. The forts were linked together by blocks of thick-walled corridors and series of vaulted chambers, built into the thickness of the ramparts, and with embrasures widening inward into the parapet and through which a gun could be fired.

Within the encirclement of the main structure was a hexagon-shaped area made up of a complex arrangement of double bastions, traverses and an elaborate system of guard-chambers and wells – the latter full of pungent water, well-spiced from the droppings of goats and camels. On the eastern side of this complex was an irregular oval in which rude huts and shelters were sited; nearer still to the western side was ample space for hundreds of head of stock. There were also numerous grana-ries filled with millet from the Mullah's gardens at Gaolo, 12 miles distant from Taleh; and also a garden, irrigated from the wells within. Everything indicated that the fort had been constructed with a long siege in mind. The north and north-eastern side of the whole fortress complex consisted of a simple wall with square bastions and enclosures and chambers, on a diminished scale in comparison to the western and southern side.

Perhaps the outstanding feature of Taleh, approaching it from its weaker side, the desert on the north-east, were three massive outlying forts – some 200 yards distant from the main complex – as though to correct the imbalance of the whole and to compensate for the weakness of the main fort on the side nearest to them. They were monumental in size, 50 to 60 feet high and of great square bulk – walls 12 to 14 feet thick at the base, and 6 feet wide at the top – and were topped by cupolas. Isolated from these three outriding forts, and some 100 yards to the north-east, was a small acorn-shaped structure, perhaps an advance surveillance post or an overflow granary. These outlying structures on the north-east were powerful obstacles to any attack on the main fort on that side which would be heralded from afar by the approaching dust clouds of an advancing enemy. They had one great disadvantage, an inexplicable oversight: they were not connected with the main fort by tunnels.

What heroic work went into the building of Taleh, a great fortress, ultimately to be left to the winds of the deserts and the ghosts of silent places! Was it a great tactical blunder on the part of the Mullah to tie his fortune to the construction of such military defences? Archer noted that whereas, before the building of Taleh, 'searching for the Mullah was like searching for a needle in the proverbial haystack,' now his whereabouts were easily determined.

The confidence he gained from the construction of forts such as Taleh may explain the paranoid tone of the Mullah's letters to Byatt in April 1913. In one of these he requested a personal interview with Archer, a face-to-face meeting. What a wonder of wonders it would have been if it had come about! After the usual opening and blunt salutation 'To the British Consul', he proceeded to warn against mischief-makers on both sides who made settlement between them difficult. There were spies, renegade Somalis whom the British should be on guard against. There were deserters from the Mullah, self-seekers who spread 'idle stories' to suit their own purpose. Did not Byatt know, as he, the Mullah, knew, that the Somali's view is a malicious one, 'and as black as his own skin'? He slated a number of culprits – Abdullah Shahari, Deria Arraleh (murdered by the Mullah in 1907), Adan Egal (a renegade from the 6th Battalion, KAR), and his cousin, Mohammed Nur (a Mijjertein gun-runner) – all sent at one time or another as peacemakers: they had all failed him. With a touch of the quixotic, the

Mullah proposed that they should 'converse mouth to mouth', and he, the Mullah, would come with ten men or fewer to any place Byatt might name. The Mullah was desirous of a settlement and peace.

The Commissioner pondered over the Mullah's proposal. Was it inspired by the success of the Camel Corps and apprehension as to a pending major expedition against him? Was it treachery – the arrival of a large force under the guise of peace? Yet it was worth the risk. Byatt took up the Mullah's proposal, and in a reply which reached the Mullah in late April 1913, he agreed about the damage caused by mischief-makers, and that it was best to have a face-to-face meeting. Such a meeting should be as soon as possible, and Archer suggested it take place at Sheikh in the month of Jomada (April or May), for, soon after this, Byatt was off to see the 'Big Government' in England. The Mullah should come with ten unarmed men or even one man. If he came with many followers this would mean not peace, but war. With the letter sent off, Byatt prepared an agenda for the proposed meeting. Its main points, agreed to by the Colonial Office, were: discussion as to the future location of the Mullah (was it to be within or outside the Protec-torate?); trading facilities for the Mullah at the coast; checking the arms trade; status of the Mullah in British eyes; and a subsidy or pension for him, subject to his good behaviour.

The proposed meeting never took place. The Mullah's overtures were a ruse to avoid a Camel Corps attack, for his horses were unfit to take the field owing to horse-sickness. When the bearers of the Commissioner's letter arrived in the Mullah's *haroun* on 24 April 1913, he perused it and then destroyed it and put the envoys in chains. Luckily for them they managed to escape and lived to tell their story at Berbera. The Mullah was later to claim that he had not followed up the proposed meeting because Byatt's promise of protection and *aman* was a mere ruse.

Rains were abundant in the Nogal and Ain valleys in the spring and summer of 1913. Dervish ponies waxed well on good pasture and so also did the stock of friendly tribes, despite constant fear of Dervish attack. Corfield, camping at Burao, eager to protect the Bohotle–Burao road and operating in an enlarged field of action, forced a settlement on feuding tribes and the return of looted stock. So successful was he that by March 1913 the contingent of Indian soldiers returned to Aden. Byatt, impressed by all this, tended to give Corfield a freer hand, despite a nervous Colonial Office. Byatt went on leave in June 1913, and Archer, who took over as Acting-Commissioner, arrived in the same month. Archer was fearful lest Corfield's impetuous nature led to rash action, and was much alarmed when in June 1913 Corfield moved into the field in full strength, eager to protect the Bohotle–Burao road and restore confidence in the fleeing tribesmen. Archer gave stern warning that the Camel Corps' operations must be confined to the immediate vicinity of Burao in the Nogal direction, with Ber as the extreme limit. To go beyond this was 'entirely foreign' to instructions. In case of 'grave and imminent danger' Corfield must always be ready to fall back on Burao immediately. Privately, Archer warned Corfield that the consequence of any rash action on his part would rest on his own head.

By early August 1913 Corfield chafed exceedingly under the constraint imposed on him. Archer, alarmed over the advanced position of the Camel Corps at Burao at a time of high Dervish activity, went there with Captain G. H. Summers (26th King George's Own Light Cavalry) in command of the Somaliland Indian Contingent. They arrived on 8 August 1913 when a large Dervish force, raiding south-east of Burao and towards Idoweina, was causing great alarm among pro-British tribes. Corfield and tribal elders entreated Archer to act against the Dervishes. Archer, suspicious that reports of Dervish activity were concocted by *akils* to bring in British action, would only agree, and with much reluctance, to a reconnaissance by Corfield, and he detailed Summers to accompany him as a restraining influence.

The Camel Corps made an impressive sight when it moved out of Burao on the afternoon of 8 August 1913, with Corfield and assistant officers in the lead, and followed by a contingent of 110 mounted camelry and pony men, all armed with single-loading M. H. carbines and a full number of rounds in each man's belt and a goodly reserve in their saddle bags. They carried also a precious Maxim with 4,000 rounds of ammunition packed in cork-lined tin boxes. In addition the 150 followers could muster between them a dozen or so rifles and 10,000 rounds of ammunition. This compact force was joined *en route* by 600 spearmen and 2,000 riflemen from pro-British tribes. The overall impression was one of vigour and purpose.

As the force moved south-eastwards in the direction of Ber, it learned from retreating tribes that a large Dervish force under Yusuf bin Abdulla Hassan (the Mullah's brother) was driving a vast herd of looted stock towards Idoweina. Corfield sent out a posse of 15 mounted men to confirm this. Meanwhile he scanned the horizon with his field glasses for sight of the enemy. At about 7 pm, when darkness was falling, and at about 10 miles from Idoweina, he put away his glasses. Just then a scouting patrol returned with the report that a large Dervish force of over 2,000 rifle-armed footmen and hundreds of mounted men were moving on Idoweina with vast numbers of looted stock. Darkness had now fallen, and wearied by their rapid march from Burao, the Camel Corps halted for the night, about 4 miles from Idoweina and with the glow of the Dervish camp fires some few miles away clearly visible.

A *zariba* was made, the Camel Corps formed up in columns of sections, with the camels in the centre and the Maxim at the ready. Full military precautions were taken against a night attack and there was hushed expectancy as to what the morrow might bring. The night silence was broken only by an occasional shot from the enemy camp and restless stirrings of the herded camels and ponies. It was a radiant African night with a bright moon and myriad stars looking down upon the scene. None could envisage what the night might bring nor where Death would stake her claims.

A sudden whispered warning from the sentries set the whole camp alert. Muttered assurance soon came, however. It was only a force of some 300 Dolbahanta wishing to join them, intent on recovering their looted stock. Ammunition from the precious reserves was distributed to these new recruits. Corfield was restless and consulted with Summers as to whether he should make a night attack on the Dervish camp or wait until dawn and place his force across the Dervish line of withdrawal. Summers reminded him that the Dervishes were aware of the presence of the Camel Corps, and that the latter were not trained for night attack, and he advised reconnaissance only and a readiness to withdraw. Corfield brushed this aside; he was determined on action, and announced that the attack would be at dawn. That same night he sent off a message to Archer at Burao to this effect.

When dawn broke on 9 August 1913, the Camel Corps, already standing at arms for over an hour, marched out of camp in a long column with the cherished Maxim in front. As it proceeded in a southerly direction there could be discerned in the increasing light, dust clouds raised by vast droves of looted stock herded along by the Dervishes. They were in a line parallel to and to the left of the Camel Corps. What Summers perceived through his field glasses to be a party of Dervishes proved a false alarm. It turned out to be a band of ostriches, which, even at this distance, could be discerned as exhibiting that leaden colour of their naked parts peculiarly distinctive to the Somaliland ostrich.

A genuine sighting came at 6.30 am, when the advance guard reported a party of Dervish horsemen half a mile away, causing the Camel Corps to veer more southerly and alter formation, ready to form square in case of ambush. Half an hour later, at Magalayer, near Dul

Madoba (black hill), having come up in front of the advancing path of the Dervishes, the Camel Corps dismounted and formed line of action. Corfield and Summers consulted and decided that position should be taken up about 200 yards forward, just where thick bush gave way to open ground across which the Dervishes were advancing. With the Maxim to the fore and mounted for action and camels in the rear, and the 300 Dolbahanta on the extreme left flank, an advance was ordered. The pace of the fast-approaching Dervishes, however, was miscalculated and the Camel Corps were caught in a most difficult position, in dense bush and unable to form square. The result was disastrous: a floundering skirmish line with unprotected rear and flank. At the first shot the mercurial Dolbahanta fled incontinently, carrying with them the precious supplies of ammunition. No surprise ambush could have been more disastrous. It was still early morning 7.00 am and light was obscure in the thick bush and amid raised clouds of dust.

The Dervishes came on in waves, spurred on by their unnerving battle cry of 'Mohammed Salih'. As each wave threw itself on the Camel Corps and fell under the latter's fierce fire, another rose in its place, ever pressing forward. A few excitable spirits among the Camel Corps, unable to stand the strain, darted forward in the interval between the waves of attack, and had to be rescued and brought back. Suddenly, caught unawares by a sharp change of Dervish tactics and weakened by the flight of the Dolbahanta, the Camel Corps were enveloped on their right flank. The result was disarray and panic. Some 25 of the Camel Corps fled, later to be dismissed with ignominy from the service. More serious, the Maxim gun, on which so much depended, was scarcely manhandled into position before it was silenced by Dervish fire. Corfield struggled manfully to unsnarl the feed block, and while doing so was shot through the head and killed instantly. The time was about 7.15 am. Summers, aghast at the loss of his commander, strove to effect an orderly withdrawal and at the same time put right the Maxim, but its Susee spring box was hopelessly damaged. Their ace card, the Maxim, had gone. A last desperate stand was made by forming a small *zariba* with the heaped-up bodies of the dead ponies and camels. The Camel Corps would go down in a glorious defeat.

All was a wild confused mêlée: desperate hand-to-hand fighting in smoke and dust, stabbing and firing at close range. Summers, bitterly cursing the trap into which they had fallen and should have avoided, slumped in a pool of blood, for he had been thrice wounded. Surrounded by dead bodies, dropped rifles and expended ammunition, he continued to rally his men from his bended knee. The mantle of leadership now fell on a civilian, Dunn. The beleaguered little band, faced with endless rushes from the frenzied Dervishes, were now prepared to meet their Maker, when they were given miraculous reprieve. The frenzied Dervishes suddenly withdrew and galloped off, their eerie war cry fading in the distance. What had caused them so abruptly to break off their attack? Was it the sight of Dunn's white shirt with its sleeves torn and waving like canonicals in the air, along with Dunn's strange gesticulations giving the impression of some Old Testament figure, a Messiah-like apparition, to strike terror in the hearts of the superstitious Dervishes? Or was Dervish ammunition, so wildly fired during their excesses and headlong rushes, near exhaustion? Even the Dervish spearmen, good Dervishes though they were, who welcomed death in battle and were stirred on by the promise of an ensuing Paradise, inexplicably called off the attack. They retired at a critical moment when they might have penetrated the *zariba* and captured the disabled but still coveted Maxim. How often were similar scenes and unexplained actions enacted in the history of the Empire!

Amid the unreal calm that followed so suddenly on this scene from Hades, the remnant of defenders looked at each other in dazed wonderment and surmise. In the *zariba* the dead were more in number than the living. Among the survivors were Mr Dunn, looking almost comically surprised that he had come through it all, Captain Summers, in sore need of medical care, and some 40 fighting men, scarcely any of whom went unscathed, and were slightly or seriously wounded. Of seven personal servants – 'followers' – only one was living: Corfield's two attendants (including the loyal Dualeh who had followed his master from Somaliland to Nigeria and back) lay dead at his side. Out of 110 Constabulary who had so blithely left Burao the evening before, 10 had fallen out on the road, 35 had been killed in action, 17 were seriously wounded and 24 had deserted.

On the wider field of battle the smell of death pervaded. The Dervishes had seeded the ground with their fallen. Out of the grand host of 2,000 Dervishes who in high élan had set out to annihilate the infidel, 600 were no more; 200 were wounded beyond repair, and for those left lying on the field in the pitiless heat, merciful death could not come too quickly.

For the pitiful remnant of the Camel Corps there remained the melancholy task of burying their dead, including Corfield, on the scene of battle. They scarce had strength for this, shallow though the graves were. Such was the superstitious awe of the Dervishes, who marvelled at the heroism of the small band of defenders, that they did not disturb or mutilate the bodies of the dead, as was their custom. A small British party which returned to the spot ten days later to re-inter Corfield's remains in a deeper grave in a spot known only to the British, found the site undisturbed. Left with the ghosts of the dead, the legend grew that around the grave of Corfield Sahib stood guard his faithful 'boys'.

Having destroyed the badly injured camels and ponies, and having confirmed that the Dervishes had moved southwards with a vast herd of stock including 25,000 camels, the remnant of the Camel Corps, exhausted and half-crazed for water, set out on the endurance trek of 6 miles to Idoweina, which was reached at 4 pm the same day. Bitter welcome did they find. The few pools of water in the sandy river bed were fouled and browned by the droppings of Dervish camels and goats. However, they drank greedily of the putrid slime. For those who had so lately brushed with death it was as the elixir of life.

Meanwhile, at Burao at 9.30 am on the 9th, Archer received Corfield's message informing him of the intended engagement with the enemy, and then a further message later on the same day, announcing the severe reverse and the death of Corfield, and reporting that the remaining force, one British officer and 30 men, were in a parlous state. This was grave intelligence for Archer, already much on edge and worrying as to what rash action Corfield might have taken. Assuming that the Dervishes, though severely shaken, were still in the field, he set off at once with an escort of 20 Indian sepoys and a posse of riff-raff from Burao trailing behind, to act as carriers. It was a gladsome meeting when at 2 am on 10 August 1913 they met the returning survivors from Dul Madoba. Together they returned to Burao and thence to Sheikh.

Dul Madoba made headlines in England. Somaliland was brought to the attention of a public often only made aware of happenings in far corners of the Empire by news of major disaster or victory. The heroism of a small British force against Dervish fanaticism caught the imagination, and so also did the reckless daring of their commander, forgetting that it was this which had led to the disaster. Alan Ostler, gadfly reporter for the *Daily Express*, roved throughout the Horn in the summer of 1913, sending home such lurid reports of the dire effects of Dul Madoba on British prestige and the fillip it gave to the Dervishes that he was finally deported in December of that year. Ostler's instancing of Somalis in Aden spitting in comtempt at British officers produced a reaction that the mailed fist was the answer to such contumely. The *Pall Mall Press Gazette*, however, argued against any further British embroilment in 'this waste corner of the earth'.

Post-mortem on Dul Madoba was an easy exercise in hindsight. It was easy to point out Corfield's lack of experience in confronting Islamic zeal, and his grave mistake in entering into headlong collision with these desert fanatics. He should have exploited the mobility of the Camel Corps and harried the Dervishes, using their own hit-and-run tactics against them, to recover vast looted stock. What was overlooked was the almost impossible request that British officers would stand passively by when tribes whom they were pledged to protect were savaged by the cruel enemy.

Dul Madoba highlighted Dervish strength: in addition to the 2,000 riflemen, 150 horsemen and 150 spearmen at Dul Madoba there was an equal number of Dervish fighting men at Taleh and another 2,000 in the Ogaden. The Mullah could rally 6,000 horse and foot, riflemen and spearmen to his banner. Arms were readily accessible to him by way of Ethiopia and Jibuti. They also came from Arabian ports such as Mukalla, whence they were shipped to the Somali coast. The Dervish force that left Taleh on the eve of Dul Madoba was estimated to have 40,000 rounds. The Dervishes, rash and prodigal marksmen though they were (much more deadly with their native spear), expended great quantities of ammunition in times of excitement. As for Dervish mobility, the Camel Corps could scarcely match them. A Dervish force of 2,000 covered the 200 miles from Taleh to Dul Madoba within a few days, and without the Camel Corps at Burao being aware of their presence until they were within 40 miles of that place. These Dervish horsemen would have done credit to Pegasus himself. And they had crowned this rapid advance with their victory at Dul Madoba.

The Mullah gloated over Corfield's death. When it was rumoured that Corfield's sister was to lead an expedition against him to avenge her brother's death, he penned a coarse poem, containing self-praise for himself and pouring scorn on her, whom he likened to a lowly Midgan outcast: 'Let her continue to mourn.'

The Mullah's writ now ran to the farthest corners of the Protectorate. The 'friendlies' were cowering and there was no Camel Corps to bolster them up. Archer's report of 26 August 1913 presents a dismal picture: remnants of the Camel Corps trailing back to Sheikh and the inhabitants of Burao tagging after them, and a host of 'friendlies' flocking towards Berbera where a relief camp containing 2,000 people was already devouring precious rice stocks much needed by the Indian soldiery. Dervish strength was 5,000–6,000; the loyalty of pro-British tribes was in doubt – they had deserted Corfield on the field of battle. Even that admirable answer to a coastal policy, the Camel Corps, was a broken reed. Was there not now the probability that the Mullah would attempt to fulfil his long-threatened boast to roll back the British into the sea. It was a hard choice for the British: abandon all, or reverse the coastal policy to one of effective military occupation. A hard lesson had been learned. In the meantime Archer brought over Indian troops from Aden, a warship was assigned to the north Somali coast and the Camel Corps was increased to 300 under a new commanding officer and four additional officers. While these strengthening measures were undertaken, news of Dervish aggression continued.

They had razed Burao, so recently evacuated by the Camel Corps, their farthest penetration towards Berbera since 1900, and with thousands of head of looted stock had rejoined the Mullah at Shimber Berris, at the head of the Ain Valley and dominating its rich pastures, and with the pro-British tribes there at its mercy. 'Friendlies' were loth to leave the luxuriant grazing and arrived at a *modus vivendi* with the Dervishes whereby, in return for tribute and presents of their women in marriage, they were allowed to stay.

Meanwhile the Mullah continued his rash of fort-building, at Shimber Berris (garrisoned by his élite), Jidali, Urgai, Damer, Bohetle and Laba Bari (in Bagheri country), further strengthening of the Taleh complex, and some lesser forts elsewhere. In all, by the end of 1913 he had constructed nearly two-score forts. Dervish aggression emanated from these forts.

The proud Dolbahanta, formerly first line of defence in the Ain, but now a shadow of their former strength, were easy prey for Dervishes raiding from Shimber Berris; the Habr Awal and Habr Toljaala being raided in quick succession in October. The only recourse for these tribes, debarred from their traditional grazing in the Ain Valley, was to quit the Protectorate or flock to Berbera. British protection had failed them and they were much disheartened.

There was much soul-searching and pondering at the Colonial Office at the end of 1913 as to the right policy for their Somaliland Protectorate. There were arguments between coastal-concentration men and reoccupation-of-the-interior men, consultation with Byatt, present in London at the time, and dire prophesies from the Cassandra-like H. F. Prevost-Battersby (author of *Richard Corfield of Somaliland*) as to the consequences which would result from British weakness, penny-pinching and letting down the 'friendlies', and all this against a background of news of continuing Dervish raids near Ber and Burao. Sir Percy Anderson on 20 December 1913 was stirred into suggesting the use of aircraft against the enemy, working with the Camel Corps and reporting on Dervish movements. It was a novel idea at the time, but was taken up and warmly received by the Colonial Secretary, Harcourt (later Viscount), in mid-January 1914. A final decision, however, rested with the Admiralty, which would not endorse the use of aircraft without deeper study of technical and financial implications. War clouds were soon gathering over Europe, and the outbreak of the First World War placed such heavy demands on the Royal Flying Corps as to preclude any diversion of aircraft to Somaliland. Events in Europe would soon overshadow all.

In the midst of this cogitation in high places, Byatt returned to Somaliland in January 1914, to receive a letter from the Mullah, delivered by a messenger so impertinent that Byatt had him locked up. The letter announced in high-flown manner that the Mullah, with the full support of Allah, had partitioned the Protectorate between the Dervishes and the British, the hill of Shimber Berris being the boundary between them. And, 'like wood and fire', the two sides should stay apart. Byatt dismissed this impertinent claim with 'it is well known which country belongs to your fathers and that which belongs to the Government.' It was Byatt's view that the Mullah, fearing a British advance from Sheikh, and because of drought and poor pasturage, was playing for time and hoping to attract 'friendlies' to his flag.

Nevertheless the Mullah's extravagant claim to have partitioned the Protectorate spurred on Cabinet deliberations regarding Somaliland, and on 24 February 1914 Harcourt announced a new policy in the House of Commons.

7

REVERSAL OF POLICY,
1914–1918

ALTHOUGH the new policy meant a reversal from that of coastal concentration, the Camel Corps, which still caught the imagination owing to fine work elsewhere in the Empire, was retained and increased to 500 men. The Indian Contingent of the disbanded 6th Battalion, King's African Rifles, was reinforced with 200 Indian recruits. Burao and Shimber Berris were to be reoccupied. Harcourt's vivid account of conditions in Somaliland during the parliamentary debates following the announcement of the new policy was an education for those only vaguely acquainted with the subject. Harcourt highlighted the vainglorious stance of the Mullah in professing to have carved up the British Protectorate, and the need to quash his pretensions. He stressed the plight of British-protected tribes for whom grazing in the Ain Valley was vital, and who were now denied access to it by the Dervishes. The memory of the British defeat at Dul Madoba, if it had faded from the recollection of many MPs, was revived by Harcourt. He stressed the shattering blow it had been to British prestige and how it had unnerved the friendly tribes, leaving them without moral or material support. There was the danger that these tribes, disheartened as they were, would be forced into the Mullah's camp by some *modus vivendi* with the Dervishes. If this were to happen it would mean the end of British claims to her Protectorate. To prevent this eventuality the military strengthening, as outlined above, must take place and Burao and Sheikh and Shimber Berris must be reoccupied to enable the Camel Corps to protect the 'friendlies' and grazing in the Ain Valley. And this time there would be no limit as to the field of the Camel Corps' operations.

Before the new policy could be put into effect and, as it were, to pre-empt it, there took place, on the night of 12–13 March 1914, an event which caused 'great consternation and confusion in Berbera'. It showed the Dervishes at their boldest. Forty Dervishes, on their fleet Somali ponies, made a startling and daring ride of 150 miles from Shimber Berris by way of the Meriya Pass and Las Dureh, and entered Berbera in early morning darkness. They shot up the native quarter of the town, bypassing the Shaab (residential quarter) and garrison of the Indian infantry. Although the Dervishes vanished as quickly as they had come, they caused great panic in Berbera; many inhabitants sought refuge in the European quarter or dashed into the sea – hoping for safety on dhows riding offshore.* Although the raid was unnerving for the people of Berbera, the real damage, death and destruction was along the line of the Dervishes' route to and from Shimber Berris. British scouts and 'friendlies' were scattered and helpless in the face of this lightning raid.

The dread visitation set coffee shops in Berbera agog. A rumour that the raid was engineered by the local administration to ensure the reversal of the coastal policy did not allay a deep fear of its recurrence. The pace of reconstruction and strengthening of the military was now quickened, and the raid highlighted the need for British control over the interior. Four years of decline had to be halted and the British will to govern demonstrated. Archer, who succeeded Byatt as Commissioner and Commander-in-Chief in May 1914, was given this task. On his arrival the inhabitants of Berbera were still quaking from the recent raid, and he had first to allay their fears. Outposts of Indian infantry were established at Biyo Gora and Dubar, south and east of the town; 200 troops from Aden were brought in to man its redoubts; wire entanglements, costing £2,000, ringed the town; a company of the Camel Corps at Sheikh was brought in to serve as a striking force. Archer then turned to the organisation of the military and the reshaping of the Camel Corps.

The role of the Camel Corps, as defined by Lord Emmott, Under Secretary for the Colonies, in the House of Lords on 13 April 1914, was to keep order in the west of the Protectorate and prevent the advance of the Mullah on the east, ensuring that friendly tribes could

---

* On the evening of 12 March 1914, a *kharia-wallah* (Somali villager), a spreader of incredible tales, told the British authorities in Berbera of the impending Dervish raid. He was locked up for his pains. The following morning, to his surprise, not only was he given his liberty but a handsome present as well. A few years later he again warned of a Dervish raid and was rewarded for his intelligence. This time it proved false. Unmasked, he fled into the bush.

graze and water their flocks unmolested. The Camel Corps would be modified on military lines, and renamed the 'Somaliland Camel Corps'. Attempts to obtain recruits for it in Ethiopia, Arabia, Nyasaland and the Sudan proved singularly unsuccessful, owing to repugnance for service in Somaliland with its impossible climate and low salaries. The Sudanese, for example, much preferred service in the Anglo-Egyptian Army. The idea of a foreign element in the new Camel Corps was soon dropped. Instead, 450 Somalis were enlisted, with a reserve of 150 men of the Somaliland Indian Contingent: a combined force of 600 men – two companies of camelry and one of cavalry, the whole being under 18 British officers seconded from the Indian and Regular Army. The Somaliland Indian Contingent, 400 strong (less 150 attached to the Somaliland Camel Corps) and a temporary garrison of 400 Indian infantrymen, completed the total force of the Protectorate. Indian soldiers were pleased to serve in Somaliland, if they were stationed at the coast where food and amenities were satisfactory.

The formation of the Somaliland Camel Corps evoked much interest among Indian and Regular Army officers. The 18 officers who headed the new Camel Corps were, in the words of one of their number, Captain A. Carton de Wiart (later Lt-Gen. Sir Adrian Carton de Wiart, VC, KBE, CB, CMG, DSO, 4th Dragoon Guards), 'a mixed crowd, and I suppose our only common denominator was that we were all short of cash, a fact quite unnoticeable in Somaliland which was about the one and only place on earth where one could not use it.' The commanding officer of the Protectorate force, who arrived in August 1914, was Lieutenant-Colonel (later Major-General) T. Ashley Cubitt, DSO, Royal Field Artillery, an officer of high calibre and a fine leader of men. He exhibited those qualities which de Wiart held to be essential to the art of leadership, 'so often argued and probed since time immemorial . . . to me it rests simply in the quality of the man. He either has it or he hasn't: Tom Cubitt had it and the troops felt it and responded immediately.' He displayed a genial bonhomie and all the human frailties that made one love a man instead of just admiring him. Another officer deserving of special mention was Captain Ismay (later Lord Ismay), Cubitt's staff officer and second-in-command. Ismay had joined the Somaliland Camel Corps while in India and had assisted in recruiting Indian soldiers for service in Somaliland. Ismay was known as a thorough and dependable officer, of sound judgment, and made himself so indispensable that, despite his longing for action in Europe, he was retained in Somaliland until 1920. Fine old British regiments were represented among the officers of the Somaliland Camel Corps:

Lt. M. L. Hornby, 12th Lancers; Cologuon, a good hard man; and Captain A. S. Lawrence, City of London Yeomanry, an officer noted for the tame cheetah which accompanied him; G. R. Breading, later to be Lawrence's second-in-command; Captain H. W. Symons, King's Own Yorkshire Light Infantry; and C. A. L. 'Paddy' (later Lt-Colonel) Howard, 32nd Lancers, Indian Army, who was to command the Somaliland Camel Corps, 1920–21, and later a brigade in India. It was Howard who had interested Ismay in Somaliland, where he was to become his second-in-command. De Wiart considered Howard to be 'the toughest officer' he had ever met.

They were a superbly fit group of young officers, eager for the adventure Somaliland offered, and to serve their country in a challenging field. They arrived at Berbera in the 90-ton ship, *Falcon*, in late July 1914, seemingly unaware of the Armageddon that was about to descend on Europe. Soon finding themselves caught up in the wrong drama, far from the field of main conflict in Europe, Somaliland quickly lost its allure. Europe was the great stage and Somaliland irrelevant to it. Until they got back to Europe they would have no heart's ease.

These young professional officers arriving at Berbera were quickly impelled forward in their work of construction of the Camel Corps – by Dervish aggression. In mid-May the Camel Corps, 350 strong, advanced south-east from Sheikh towards Burao. Meanwhile the Dervishes, using Shimber Berris and Jidali as their bases, dominated the Makhir coast and immediate hinterland. By the end of September 1914 they had encircled the Warsangli and Gadwein on the west and south, leaving them hemmed in on the north and south by the sea and Italians. The Gadwein were forced to come to terms with the Mullah to gain access to their ports, but the Warsangli, under their sultan, Ina Ali Shirreh, would not deign to do so, and in consequence suffered a severe bruising at Dervish hands.

It was to end this state of affairs that the reorganisation of the Camel Corps proceeded apace, albeit against an ominous background of the First World War looming up. Archer, newly arrived, found his requests for a warship to bombard Dervish positions on the Makhir coast, and for reinforcements and arms, tersely dismissed with the reminder that he was lucky to have the forces he now had, let alone ask for more. With Colonial Office support the go-ahead was given in October 1914 for the reoccupation of Burao and Las Dureh, as a first step in ridding the Ain Valley of its tormentors, and to capture Shimber Berris. The headquarters of the Somaliland Camel Corps, now deemed a full military force, was to be at Burao.

Burao and Las Dureh were occupied with scarcely any resistance on 7 November 1914. The Camel Corps then got down to some hard training at Burao, in preparation for the capture of Shimber Berris. Strenuous training, relieved by game shooting, polo and hockey, was completed by 14 November, when permission came for Cubitt to attack. Following last-minute intense preparations, Cubitt, on the morning of the 17th, and heading a mounted column of 114 officers and 520 rank and file, marched out towards Shimber Berris. In the early morning of the 19th they reached their goal, and advanced on the three forts at the top of the escarpment.

Nature had contrived the ideal spot for the formidable fortress awaiting them. It was sited on a great brooding bluff, at the western apogee of the Bur Dub range, and 1,000 feet above a surrounding plateau intersected by deep clefts, and crossed by ridges covered by large boulders and thick scrubby bush. Shimber Berris dominated the landscape to the south and east, and was supremely designed by nature to guard the approaches over a 290-degree swathe and give coverage to a ravine below, the sides of which were honeycombed with caves which could shelter men and animals if driven from the forts above. The ravine also contained priceless wells of water. Little wonder that the Mullah deemed Shimber Berris a fortress rivalling Taleh. Throughout the winter of 1913–14, master masons spared from Taleh had supervised Somali labour in constructing three large blockhouses, storeyed in the Yemeni fashion, and each with its supporting smaller blockhouse. Placed as they were at the top of the escarpment, their formidable strength was not evident until close up. Each blockhouse was constructed of stone, strongly cemented with mud and with the solidity of a minor fortress, and with immensely stout walls, 20–25 feet high, 20–30 feet wide, and 10–12 feet thick at the base, tapering to 4–6 feet at the top. The whole presented a most daunting challenge to any besieger. Each blockhouse had a small door, the threshold of which was about three feet above ground, and with a great stone slab as a lintel bearing the superincumbent weight of the wall above. The parapets of the blockhouses, as well as the walls above the door lintels were pierced by down-sloping loopholes, guarding all approaches. An investment of Shimber Berris would be a costly enterprise.

This was the prospect which greeted Cubitt's column as it ascended the western approach. The Camel Corps was within three miles of its objective before the Dervishes were aware of its approach. Although now was the moment when the enemy's rushing tactics could have been used to good advantage, they made no attempt to molest the advancing column, and it was not until the head of it was within half a mile of the central fort that the Dervishes opened fire. At a point about 500 yards from the fortress the column dismounted amid a storm of abuse and much pot-shooting from the Dervishes. Cubitt and his officers consulted as to the tactics of assault. The Indian Contingent was more experienced in such matters, but Cubitt gave way to de Wiart, who held that the Somali Company, restless and difficult to hold in check, should also be unleashed on the fortress.

The leading company at once deployed for attack, and the ensuing scene was like a military tattoo. The noise of Dervish cries and rifle fire from the battlements was terrific. Amid this the British forces charged right up to the walls and fired through the loop-holes at point-blank range. Unable to force an entrance they withdrew, only to charge again and again. After a series of these recoils de Wiart proposed that he, Ismay and three other officers should rush the door after the machine guns had played their fire to clear the gallery above. With great dash, while avoiding falling masonry, the door was reached. It proved impervious to entrance. Attention was then turned to the two other forts and at about 11 am they were jointly rushed. The fort stormed by the Indian Contingent under Howard was quickly cleared. The other, however, despite three charges by the Somali Company under de Wiart right up to its walls, withstood the assaults, during which Captain Symons had the back of his head blown off by a soft-nosed bullet of the type used by the Dervishes. De Wiart, when he was within a yard of the fort's door, and gallantly attempting to scale the wall of the door, was seriously wounded. He was sewn up on the spot by an accompanying medical officer. Attempts to batter the door down, amid a hail of fire and richocheting bullets at point-blank range, failed to achieve success. Ismay and Hornby managed to retrieve Symons' body. More fierce charges were made, right up to the walls, and then falling back to get second wind, charging again and then recoiling before the fanatical resistance of the Dervishes. All at a pace so hot that scant thought could be given to the consequence of over-daring. Riflemen in the galleries above continued to be the main menace, and there was a lull in the fighting while they were cleared by the machine guns. Again there were more unavailing charges, amid brighter volleys of rifle fire and acts of personal bravery, and a sensation of thrill, primitive and devouring, on both sides.

The fighting continued until 3 pm on the 19th, when, having failed to force an entrance and the Dervishes meeting demands to surrender with derisive contempt, Cubitt called off the action and retired to about a mile away. Then, since light was failing, they withdrew to camp about 8 miles south to take stock of the position and to attend to their wounded. Unknown to the British, the Dervishes, shortly after this withdrawal which they thought was a British ruse, evacuated the first fort they had held so ferociously. On the 20th the Camel Corps withdrew to Bohotle, from where Cubitt sent to Burao for the only large field gun available, an ancient muzzle-loading quick-firing 7-pounder which had last seen service in 1879. This antediluvian cannon arrived three days later, on the 23rd, and the attack on Shimber Berris was renewed. The gun was brought into action against fort number three by Captain Dobbs, at a range of about 200 yards, and three or four direct hits were scored. They did little damage, but the defenders were apparently so unnerved by the concussion in the confined space that they fled.

Cubitt and his officers, surveying the now deserted Shimber Berris, could see the terrible toll they had exacted from the Dervishes. How now the Mullah's wisdom in building forts? Looking at the massive, vacant structure, Cubitt's first thought was to blow it up. Lack of precious explosives precluded this; neither did he have sufficient troops to leave a post at Shimber Berris. With one last look at it, the British forces withdrew to Burao on 24 November 1914. Two weeks later came the surprising news that Dervishes had reoccupied the forts. How tenacious were these Dervishes! And how attached were they to their forts!

The task of clearing the Dervishes out of Shimber Berris had all to be done again, and this time it would be more difficult. For a cruel fate at the Mullah's hands awaited the survivors of the garrison who had failed to hold the forts against the British. It was reported later that they were castrated. The Dervishes who replaced them at Shimber Berris were thus steeled to hold on at whatever cost.

What had come out of this first attack on the forts? Was it a realisation that the Camel Corps had not fulfilled expectations? It had not anticipated encountering forts. The presence of animals during the attack had hampered the assault while performing no useful role. It was a job for the infantry, liberally supplied with explosives and a mountain gun, and backed up by a transport column and ample water to enable the attacking force to remain in situ for four or five days in case repeated assaults were necessary.

Archer left for England at the end of November 1914 to argue this view at the Colonial Office. He argued well and, although getting no infantry, was assigned explosives, field guns and machine guns from

Aden and the valuable assistance from there of an officer and platoon of the 23rd Sikh Pioneers, trained in the use of explosives. Archer's request, considered very novel at the time, for a long-wheel-base Rolls Royce for desert travel (he thought this would have a surprise effect on the Dervishes) was refused as too frivolous. Nevertheless the mobile force that sallied forth from Burao, and concentrated some 5 miles south of Shimber Berris on 2 February 1915, was admirable for the task in hand. From the professional point of view the setting would not have been out of place on the north-west frontier of India.

The assembled force consisted of 570 rank and file, Indians and Somalis, under 15 British officers. The six machine-guns were carried by mules, and the two 7-pounders on wheeled carriages hauled by mules signified formidable firing power. Mule transport in this respect was much superior to camel transport.

Advancing in two columns on 3 February, and from the south as in the previous attack in November, the British force discerned that the Dervishes had already partially constructed new forts on the hilltop of Bur Dab: these and the most southerly of the Shimber Berris forts were unoccupied and quickly blown up. Darkness now falling, a short withdrawal was made. On the morrow, 4 February, it having been decided that to cross the hilltop to the two forts on its northern side was not to be risked, the Dervishes being now well alerted, a quick, shift of tactics was made. Re-forming in one column, and rapidly detouring through a pass 5 miles west of Shimber Berris, by late morning the British force, to the surprise of the Dervishes, suddenly appeared and soon concentrated on the rising northern slope. The two remaining forts at the top of the hill, held by the enemy, overlooked the ravine, at the farthest end of which was another fort commanding the precious well, also held by the Dervishes who infested the caves of the hillsides.

No time was lost in attacking. Each of the flanking forts guarding the ravine at the top was invested by a company and after a short bombardment was rushed and taken, but not before its occupants escaped. Observing the Dervishes reappearing in the ravine below, it was discovered that they were doing so by way of an almost hidden passage through a *nullah* (dry watercourse) which fanned out on the northern slope of Shimber Berris. When the British passed their own forces and guns through this *nullah* the enemy directed heavy fire on them from the fort and caves as soon as they appeared in the ravine. The heavy guns of the British were now brought into play and along with the machine-guns they rocked the ravine with their fire. It was all

111

at close range and the trajectory flat: the noise was deafening, and the damage incalculable. Soon the defenders of the fort at the end of the ravine could be discerned hastily retreating up the ravine to the caves.

Uncertainty as to whether any Dervishes remained in the fort was soon dispelled when the Pioneers, approaching to detonate a charge of 150lb of gun cotton against its walls, came under intense fire, just before its defenders were blown sky high, amid flying debris. As one observer remarked: 'The whole building seemed to rise skywards and collapse in a tangle of enormous boulders.' Fire from the caves now being reduced to desultory potshots, hand grenades were tossed into them. The concussion for the occupants must have been terrific, wreaking instant death. All Dervish fire now being silenced there only remained the task of blowing up the two flanking forts overlooking the ravine. The time now being late afternoon, and with a sense of finality of a job well done, the British column withdrew in smart manner to its camp some 5 miles away. There had been five hours of continuous fighting. Rest was now in order for the weary men and animals.

On the following morning, 5 February 1915, Cubitt returned to examine Shimber Berris in daylight. The hilltop was strewn with the rubble of the forts. Down in the ravine the empty caves were still smelling of gunpowder. Dervish dead, whole and dismembered, some 72 in all, were left to the elements. They had fought well. British casualties were light: no dead British officers, only five wounded; four rank-and-file killed, and 18 wounded. Detailing a tribal post at Shimber Berris, Cubitt led his column back to Burao, where he arrived on 8 February 1915. The victory had been a laurel crown for the Camel Corps; and for the Somali soldier it had been a restoration of his reputation so besmirched at Dul Madoba. Vain, volatile, a freebooter at heart he might be, but as a brave fighter with remarkable powers of physical endurance he had no peer. His morale was much uplifted by Shimber Berris.

As for the Dervishes, their old fighting zeal had diminished, their marksmanship – never spectacular – deteriorated even more. Their ammunition was short, their forts destroyed; routed from the Ain Valley, their activity now shifted eastwards, to Taleh, Jidali (temporarily vacated from June to August 1915) and to the grazing ground between the Makhir coast and Galadi. In the face of this, Archer, in a tour of the northern coast in May 1915, wooed the Warsangli and Mijjertein. The Mullah, in turn, warned them that the Koran declared that those who joined the kaffirs themselves became kaffirs. Despite this dire warning, defection continued from his ranks, much hastened on by his cruelty and a severe drought that destroyed their flocks. The hinterland thus temporarily enjoyed unwonted peace, and the Camel Corps patrolled deep into the Ain Valley. Archer, feeling events moving in his favour, floated a rumour to the effect that he was in a strong enough position to assist in opposing the Turkish advance into the Aden Protectorate. Archer would keep up the pressure on the Dervishes. This was, however, impossible because of the war in Europe. Large forces were not available. Officers were rejoining their regiments back home, and those in Somaliland pined to be with them. Summers, who succeeded Cubitt as commanding officer, was perforce committed to an interim defence policy, a holding arrangement.

Archer now took the singular and imaginative step of informally dividing the Protectorate into two zones, one for the Dervishes and one for the 'friendlies', demarcated by a line running from Ankhor, on the Gulf of Aden, south-east to Badwein (at the western extremity of the Ain Valley) and continuing south-west to the intersection of the southern boundary of the Protectorate with the 46th meridian, an overall distance of 200 miles.

The Somaliland Camel Corps and mounted Indian Contingent, based at Burao and Ber, were to secure this partition, helped by some hundreds of scouts strung along the arc of the protected zone, and with infantry forces garrisoning Berbera, Burao, Hargeisa, Las Dureh and Las Khorai. Reliance was chiefly on the Camel Corps, fleet and mobile, inured to arduous marches – they could cover 120 miles in 40 hours without water. Their surprise attacks jolted the Dervishes.

While this weakening of the Dervishes continued, events in Ethiopia had an impact on Somaliland. They took an anomalous turn when Prince Lij Yasu, grandson of Menelik, succeeded to the throne in December 1913. Immature and silly he might be, nevertheless it came as a shock to the Coptic Ethiopian government when this unripened fledgling announced his conversion to Islam. Soon it was rumoured that Christian churches were to be turned into mosques. Coming in the face of the ancient enmity with Islam, and his treasonable act in forsaking the religion of his fathers, this was more than the theocratic Coptic government of Ethiopia could brook. Lij Yasu was denied the traditional coronation as Negus Negusta (King of Kings) and literally drummed out of the kingdom. He took the easiest escape route available, eastwards to the more congenial territory of Harrar whose governor, Sadik, was sympathetic to Islam and the Dervishes. Donning Arab habit and observing Muslim prayers, Lij Yasu gathered around him Muslim advisers, including Somalis.

Lij Yasu's apostasy to Islam boded well for Germany's flirtation with the Muslim world during the First World War. German consular agents (including the learned Professor Frobenius) at Addis in 1915 (purportedly arranging plans for a German takeover of British East Africa and the Somali coast which would link up with the Turks in the Aden Protectorate) made the most of the disturbed situation. They fostered the idea of Lij Yasu's heading a great Muslim empire, embracing the Horn and Ethiopia and co-operating with, and parallel to, that of Arabia and the Turks. The Mullah would have a key role in all this. Relations between the Mullah and Lij Yasu warmed. The Mullah's wise men could point to a passage in the Koran fortelling a relationship between himself and Lij Yasu. Soon there was talk of marriage between the Mullah's daughter and Lij Yasu, and the Mullah was invited to extend his sway over the Ogaden region up to Ethiopia. What did Lij Yasu expect in return for all this? Hoping to return to Ethiopia, he overestimated the Mullah's importance, seeing in him a redoubtable opponent to any dismemberment of Ethiopia that might take place in a post-war conference on its future.

The Mullah was riding a crest as far as external developments were concerned, even if his Dervishes were suffering reverses at home. When, on 29 April 1916, news of the fall of the strategic British fortress of Kut, 180 miles up the Tigris, and the surrender of a large British-Indian force to the Turks reached the bazaars of Berbera by way of the date dhows from Basra, no subsequent success of the Allies in Europe, not even the recapture of Kut by the British in March 1917 could counterbalance what was deemed to be, at least in the selective hearing of the Somalis, a severe reversal for British arms and prestige. The Mullah was supposedly in contact with Ali Said Pasha, a high-ranking Turkish officer at Lahej in Aden, and was apparently willing to place himself under Turkish protection, and would even sign a formal treaty to this effect. In June 1916 there appeared in Ethiopia a German manifesto urging Muslims to destroy the enemies of their religion. There was reference to the Mullah, who, as the Sword of Islam, had a special role to play in casting the infidel out of the land. Muslims in the Horn vibrated at this message. The Mullah, fooled into vainglory by all this flattery, renewed his taunting letters to the British, offering to make peace between them and the Turks. He already possessed a Turkish flag to fly over his fort at Hais, in readiness for the arrival of the Turks in the Horn.

Archer had a general idea of the grand plans of the Germans and of Lij Yasu's machinations. Could Britain not extract advantages from the disturbed Ethiopian situation? The British and Ethiopians were both Christians, and much could be made of Ethiopia's holding out as a Christian bastion in a sea of Muslims! If the exigencies of war so dictated, Archer would have the British enter Ethiopia. In the meantime he would extend British Protectorate boundaries westwards and amalgamate Harrar with the western region of the Protectorate. Hargeisa would be the half-way administration centre between Harrar and Berbera. He already had a likely British vice-consul and administrator for Harrar in mind, in the person of Major A. S. Lawrence, now commanding officer of the Camel Corps, a prickly customer whom he would fain be rid of. Harrar would fully occupy Lawrence's talents! Archer, to counter pro-Turk and Islamic influence, directed Summers, Acting Commissioner, to meet Ogaden tribesmen at Hargeisa in June 1916, to present a more acceptable version of the First World War and assure them that the British would enter the Ogaden, if necessary, to protect British interests. Lij Yasu countered by holding his own meeting of Ogaden tribesmen at Jigjiga. Archer then moved the British headquarters from Berbera to Sheikh, a delightful spot much loved by heat-soaked officials from Berbera. Sheikh remained the British headquarters for the rest of the war.

Perhaps Archer's most imaginative move in this propaganda war was to send a party of Somali elders to Egypt in July 1916, to learn how Egypt and Mecca had rebuffed Turkish overtures, and to hear that a renowned Islamic leader, Shereef Hussein of Mecca, had sided with the British. They would also see for themselves the full might of the British Empire. They would see great British warships but no sign of German or Turkish vessels; they would see prisoner-of-war camps and many German and Turkish prisoners. British control and jurisdiction was supreme in the Red Sea and Suez Canal areas. The elders rounded out their visit with a wondrous journey by rail from Ismailia to Cairo, the magical city of western Islam, and it too was under British control. The contrast between their own harsh land and this dazzling world and British power made a great impression on the elders, and was not lost in their telling of it in the bazaars of Berbera on their return.

Archer, in August 1916, anticipating the break-up of Ethiopia and its repercussions in the Horn and on the illicit arms trade based on Jibuti, put forth contingent plans for the annexation of Harrar and Ogaden, and the purchase of Jibuti from the French, in exchange for terrritory, possibly in West Africa. He saw East Africa and the Horn as a whole. Events in Jubaland could not be separated from those in Somaliland: the death in February 1916 of Elliott, a British administrator, in Jubaland was connected with the Dervishes in Somaliland. An active war against the Mullah was part of the East African campaign. Amid all this cogitation on events concurrent with those in his own Protectorate, Archer was bargaining, unsuccessfully as it turned out, for the construction of a motor road from Berbera to Burao in return for his supplying 8,000 camels to the Allied forces in Egypt. The Treasury was not amenable to such barter arrangements: anyway the cost of such a road, £60,000, was out of the question. As for providing heavy transport for Somaliland, demands elsewhere made this impossible.

Archer was right in anticipating the break-up of Ethiopia. Lij Yasu had practically vacated his kingdom, had failed to Islamise his subjects, and had moved eastwards to Harrar and Jigjiga. About the same time a rumoured joint Ethiopian–Dervish invasion of Hargeisa sparked off a ruthless massacre of Muslims at Harrar by Ethiopian Christian soldiers. It was feared this was all a prelude to a jihad against infidel rulers in the Horn. Then came the overthrow of Lij Yasu on 27 September 1916. He escaped to Amhara, in the north, where a large army was raised to defend his cause. But when this was routed by a Shoan army, Lij Yasu's career was finished. His open declaration of apostasy from Islam at this juncture irreparably lowered his status in the eyes of both Muslim and Christian. To the Mullah and his followers Lij Yasu had never been a true believer and there was always much scepticism as to the genuineness of his adherence to Islam. He had now shown himself to be a mere tergiversator.

Archer was also right in anticipating Lij Yasu's overthrow. In this Ruritanian world there now appeared an Empress, Woizero Zaudito, Lij Yasu's aunt, with Ras Tafari as regent and heir. It was a government friendly to the British. In February 1917 Archer, fresh from a holiday and marriage in England, attended Ras Tafari's coronation with the veteran British minister at Addis, Wilfred Thesiger, at his side. In an atmosphere of hardly veiled international rivalry in the midst of barbaric splendour in this African Tibetan world, and where the Russian mission wielded great influence through its operation of a first-class hospital and free treatment for a much-infected and diseased population, Archer endeavoured to put his case. He raised the matter of the ineffective Ethiopian administration in the Ogaden, arguing that a British administration there would be to the advantage of the Ethiopians, for Ethiopian sovereignty would still be recognised. Ras Tafari was well disposed to the suggestion, but not his ministers. According to Archer it was difficult to do business in Ethiopia, where every question was shelved with little prospect of solution. Further break-up of Ethiopia was expected. In this event, claimed Archer, Britain should occupy areas contiguous to the British Protectorate, namely Harrar Province and the Ogaden. If she did not, Italy would do so. Colonial Office response to Archer's suggestion was that matters of such high diplomacy were best left to trained diplomats. They were not within the purview of a mere Commissioner of British Somaliland.

A poignant episode attendant on the extension of the European war into the Horn was the sad tale of a German tinker, Emil Kirsch, a repairer of the new-fangled invention, the typewriter, which had quickly found favour in the newly fledged administrations in African territories. After much travelling about in South and East Africa plying his trade (he was especially skilled in the alignment of type bars), the outbreak of the First World War found Kirsch in Jibuti, employed by French companies and the skeleton French administration. As an alien in enemy territory, he was faced with internment and quickly betook himself up-country – to Addis – travelling over the newly built stretch of the Jibuti-Addis Ababa railway. At Addis Ababa he found congenial employment in a milieu favourable to Germans, and among a sociable Austrian–German–Turkish group. For the next two years Kirsch was happily employed at Addis Ababa.

It was a sorry day for him when, in August 1916, a few weeks before his own downfall, Lij Yasu, as a demonstration of his friendship with the Mullah, loaned Kirsch on a five-month engagement at Taleh. Kirsch was to receive favoured treatment in return for applying his high skills in repairing the Mullah's weaponry, especially the Maxim guns captured from the British. Lij Yasu gave his own word as bond for the personal security and safe return of Kirsch at the end of his period of engagement with the Mullah. Little did poor Kirsch know what awaited him.

After travelling for many nights and days through the cool uplands of Ethiopia, down into the Ogaden and through the wastes of the Nogal Valley, Kirsch reached Taleh. Here he was given quarters in the main fort, but it was quickly apparent that he was held under duress. Scarcely rested from his long and arduous journey, he was immediately ordered to repair defective rifles. This was not beyond his capabilities, but he was then asked to perform the impossible: make good the Maxim guns captured from the British. They were of the 1898 vintage, with impressive brass cooling covers, and kept well-polished in true army tradition, but unable to fire more than five rounds without jamming. Although of long-standing use (they had a role in the Second World

War as weapons for home defence), Kirsch had no component parts for them, and to manufacture new ones was beyond even his Teutonic ingenuity. Despite all his efforts he could not conjure even the faintest stutter from the impotent weapons after they had jammed. When he also failed to produce bullets and ammunition out of thin air, his star quickly waned. His mentor and protector, Lij Yasu, was now deposed, and there was no one to whom Kirsch could turn to for help.

He was abandoned in a cruel and alien world. The Mullah, finding that his new-found mechanic could not perform what was demanded of him, refused to see him, or even tolerate his near presence, lest he, the Mullah, be contaminated by breathing in the same air as an infidel. Kirsch's pleas that he could do nothing without spare parts and raw materials fell on deaf ears. There then ensued daily floggings, much cursing and reviling. His five months' engagement to the Mullah had long since elapsed, and he pleaded in vain to be allowed to return to Ethiopia. Cruel mutilations inflicted by the Mullah on offenders among his own followers were vividly displayed for Kirsch's benefit and as a reminder of what awaited him if he continued to displease the Mullah. By now Kirsch was wellnigh demented at the thought of the fate which awaited him. His mind turned to possible release from this intolerable position: death, *sua manu*, or escape from Taleh. He resolved on the latter.

The easiest and most direct route to safety was northwards to Bunder Kassim on the Gulf of Aden. But this would take him through Dervish country. He thus decided to make for Bunder Alula, the most north-eastern point of the Horn where he could surrender to the Italians, Germany's late ally, and would at least be assured of humane treatment. To reach Bunder Alula, however, would mean crossing stark and difficult terrain. Having already hardened the soles of his feet by going barefoot or wearing sandals, Kirsch decided to flee unshod, thus leaving no spoor that could easily be followed by the Mullah's trained scouts.

On the night of 18 June 1917, Kirsch and his faithful servant Ahmed, a native of Nyasaland, aided by a tough rope and grappling iron, surmounted the massive wall of Taleh fortress. Provisioned with a small amount of water and grain, and some goat's cheese, and equipped with a small German compass which Kirsch had carefully secreted while at Taleh, they set out in the dead of night, in a north-easterly direction, heading for Alula, 300 miles distant.

There ensued days of struggling through an aggressively cruel desert. Food and water ran out, and there was no replenishment. The dust was blightingly hot and no sirocco could surpass the oppressive winds.

118

The scorching heat, blistering feet, absence of shelter or escape from the blazing hot sun and sand-blasting winds was an ordeal human flesh could not withstand. At last Kirsch could proceed no farther without long periods of rest. In a month's travel they had traversed only 250 miles. Finally, although he was not aware of it, when within attainable distance of his goal (some 50 miles from Alula), he sank exhausted to the ground. Aware that the end was near for himself, Kirsch exhorted Ahmed to persevere ahead and escape from this accursed land. Loth to abandon his master and still hoping to find precious water, Ahmed reeled on step by step. After about 3 miles' struggle, wonder of wonders! – he found a *nullah* and struck water. His own parched body could scarcely absorb enough of the precious liquid. Slaking his thirst as rapidly as possible, he scooped up enough water to fill his water bag, and struggled back to his master. He found him dead, propped up against a miserable thorn-bush under whose feeble shade he had crawled for shelter. Far from homeland and family, poor Kirsch had found a merciful death. The desert sands which Ahmed heaped over his master's body at last sheltered him from the cruel sun which had dogged his steps since his escape from Taleh. Kirsch's diary survived, and from this and Ahmed's tale as told to incredulous Italians at Alula, the story was pieced together. It was later confirmed as true, by deserters from the Mullah's cause who came over to the British.*

While this saga of poor Kirsch was unfolding, the British were much involved with Ina Ali Shirreh, Sultan of the Warsangli since 1905. Son of an Indian father by a Somali mother, he displayed much capacity for duplicity and double dealing. Although averring loyalty to both the British and the Mullah (who had married his sister) this did not deter him from raiding Dervish stock in early 1916. This brought terrible and quick retribution. On the night of 6 May 1916, a massed and screaming multitude of 2,000 Dervishes descended on Las Khorai, quickly capturing the wells on the outskirts, and then falling on the town itself, slaughtering over 300 women and children. The remainder of the town, including the sultan's palace, withstood the attack. That same night a few Warsangli escaped by sea and brought the news to Aden after a remarkably quick journey of two days. The result was that HMS *Northbrook*, under Commander Turton, arrived at Las Khorai on the morning of 10 May. Her appearance caused great consternation

---

*Kirsch's escape map and compass fell into the hands of Captain H. L. Ismay (later General Lord Hastings Ismay), Camel Corps, who refers to Kirsch as an extraordinarily brave man.

among the Dervishes, and they beat a hasty retreat to the pass in the foothills leading to Jidali, some 30 miles distant.

The Dervishes fleeing over the stretch of maritime plain presented a marksman's paradise. The *Northbrook*, running inshore and parallel to the coast, brought her big guns into play at a range of 6,000 yards. The trajectory was clear, the shells high explosive lyddite. The damage was catastrophic. The shells were dropped among the fleeing Dervishes as though hand-lobbed. The dense clusters of Dervishes were scattered like chickens in a storm. Attempts to re-group were immediately prevented by succeeding shells dropped in their midst. Never did a man-of-war wreak such havoc! The scuttling, fragmented mass of Dervishes finally reached the narrow pass, only to find a terrible nemesis awaiting them there, for the *Northbrook*'s gunners now had a clearly defined and stationary target. The range and trajectory were quickly found. The narrow pass was the only route of escape for the panicking Dervishes. Only a few shells were required. In moments hundreds of bodies were piled up, effectively blocking the entrance to the pass and cutting off access to it for those Dervishes struggling in the rear. The success of the *Northbrook* demonstrated that naval power could strike on land equally as effectively as the Camel Corps.

Following this defeat of the Dervishes at Las Khorai, that place, although in the territory assigned to the Dervishes, was occupied by a company of Indian troops in September 1916. This closed a valuable outlet to the Dervishes and brought the wary Warsangli under British surveillance. What an inhospitable station it was: windswept and with open roadstead, and with landings only possible at favourable times of the year, and then at a distance of 700 yards out at sea, and with a pick-a-back transfer through the heavy surf. The sultan's palace, the only edifice of worth in the place, was now converted into a garrison and fort, well-sandbagged and moated, and with outlying barbed wire entanglements. The forces quartered here were entirely dependent on imported supplies even of wood, mainly from India. The motley and now melancholy Warsangli, a shadow of their once ebullient selves, scrambled eagerly for the few crumbs that might fall from the provender of the troops. Despite their near starvation, the Warsangli, owing to religious scruples, disdained to eat fish, although these abounded in the nearby sea. Multifarious plagues beset the troops, the heat was intense, rising to 120°F, and there were sandstorms and flies. The great influenza epidemic then beginning to rage over the outside world also hit this remote region. There was no recreation or sports to relieve the tedium of the troops. Above all, the chilling isolation affected morale.

There was no communication, telegraphic or otherwise, with the outside world for weeks on end. How often and how anxiously did the British officers in this god-forsaken place scan the sea horizon for the welcome smoke of a steamer, the harbinger of mail and provisions for this forlorn outpost of the Empire. However, Las Khorai justified its existence in that it freed the Warsangli from Dervish torment.

The Dervishes did not tamely accept their reverse at Las Khorai. In late May 1916, a Dervish force of 1,000 riflemen severely mauled a party of Musa Aboker who foolishly ventured too close to Taleh. To offset their defeat at Las Khorai the Dervishes constructed another fort at Baran, 30 miles to the south. Still seeking an outlet to the sea they clashed with the Mijjertein in December 1916, only to be severely trounced. By early 1917 there was no refuge for the Dervishes in the north-eastern corner of the Horn. In March 1917 the Mullah penned a letter of wishful spite to the British. After boasting about the damage inflicted on the Mijjertein and Warsangli, and declaring that the British were the perverts and prostitutes of this world, and gloating over their imagined defeats at the hands of the Germans and Turks, the Mullah rounded off with a contemptuous gesture: he was sending 200 skins in payment of an old debt owed to an Arab in Berbera. What really irked the Mullah was the British closure of seaports to him.

Dervish setbacks continued throughout 1917 and into 1918. In the Ogaden the Mullah lost a strong supporter and fellow Muslim in the death, in June 1917, of Kedani, an underling of Lij Yasu, and an avowed follower of the Mullah. Their defeat at Las Khorai had caused the Dervishes to shift their activity south-westward to the Jidali–Baran, Burao–Bohotle triangle, but here an epidemic of dysentery and a prolonged drought wrought their toll. Seeking to rally his supporters and impress the British, and to replenish his depleted stock, the Mullah raided to within a few miles of Burao. There was then much pursuing by the Camel Corps, sharp fighting and capturing of stock; only too often such pursuit ended in a vision of fleeing clouds of dust disappearing over the horizon. Overall, the Dervishes suffered severe reverses near Burao and in the western Ain Valley in early 1917, and again at Bohotle and El Danano in early 1918; they achieved only minor success when they raided unguarded *kharias* of the Dolbahanta. The most significant encounter by the Camel Corps with the Dervishes was that at Endow Pass on 9 October 1917.

The Camel Corps presented an impressive spectacle as it moved out in strength from Burao in the early morning of 5 October 1917, in response to news that a large Dervish force of 500 men was raiding in

121

the Eil Dur Elan area. Ten British officers, young but, by now, tried men, 347 rifles and a strong six-machine-gun contingent under Major G. R. Breading reached Eil Dur Elan on 8 October, only to hear that the Dervishes were quickly moving north-eastward. Further pursuit, mostly at night, by Captain H. L. Ismay, (21st Cavalry, Indian Army), with 150 pony rifles and two machine-guns, brought contact with the enemy at daybreak on 9 October. They had driven their looted stock through two very narrow and difficult passes which they were now protecting as rear-guard action against any attempt by the Camel Corps to force the passes. Ismay, directing an irregular levy against the western pass to divert the Dervish attention, launched his real attack against the eastern Endow Pass, held by 300 Dervish riflemen entrenched on its crest and in nearby caves to cover the withdrawal of the looted camels.

Ismay commenced action at 9 am on 9 October. He was joined by Breading and the remainder of the Camel Corps at 10 am. There was quick and quiet consultation. Its termination was marked by the violent outburst of the six machine-guns. Their withering fire quickly removed the snipers from the crest and it was then turned on the caves which were effectively cleared out. The enemy, caught in the file, slowly retreated towards the summit of the pass, driving their stock before them while tenaciously opposing the advance of the Camel Corps. It was a repeat of the Las Khorai action of the previous year. Soon it was late afternoon and darkness was falling. The looted stock were already well into the pass, and once through it and on to the plateau on the other side, pursuit would be impossible through the Gud Anod hills. The Camel Corps were down to two days' rations, and far from their base and quite exhausted after 70 hours' gruelling pace and furious action. Pursuit was called off.

The Dervishes had been severely mauled. Their dead and wounded lay deep in the pass. Rifles galore had fallen into British hands. On the British side there were no dead, and only a few wounded. There was quiet elation at the victory so easily achieved. The Mullah, who had already lost many men at Shimber Berris, Las Khorai, Ok and Karumba, had now suffered another major defeat. Desertions from his ranks were increasing. Since Dul Madoba he had lost five-sixths of his men, recruits were no longer available and sources of arms and ammunition were closed to him. In the Ogaden he had lost a supporter in the death of Kedani. To offset his weakening position a new Dervish fort was completed at Wardair in Ethiopian territory in March 1918, and manned by 400 Dervishes under the Mullah's brother, Khalif. It is tempting to conjecture whether the Mullah at this stage was not already contemplating his final retreat. If Taleh and Jidali were lost he could still retire to the land of his father, to the south-west. Wardair betokened a shift of Dervish strength south-westward, thus menacing Ishaak and Habr Yunis, and indicating a break in the Gulf of Aden–Bohotle demarcation line. It meant a new arena of war for the Camel Corps, and raised the question whether it signified a new spate of fort-building by the Mullah. All this was not to be, however. The end of the First World War and events in the Taleh area prevented Wardair from having any real significance.

Based on Taleh in the eastern Nogal Valley, 60 miles from the Italian frontier, and with secondary forts at Jidali, Baran, Galadi and Wardair, the Mullah portrayed these forts as indicators of his strength, although it was rumoured that he was so weak that he planned to kidnap a high-ranking British officer for ransom and as guarantee for his own personal security. Although the Mullah affected to believe that the Turks were winning the war he did not claim, as did some Somalis, that the surrender of the Turks at Aden when Armistice came, was not in fact a surrender, but a prelude to a Turkish takeover of the government there.

8

THE 21-DAY CAMPAIGN

THE Armistice brought new optimism for the Protectorate administration. The years 1917–18 had seen a drastic weakening of the
Dervishes and at the same time a steady advance in the efficiency
and organisation of government departments, especially the medical
department. Local revenue had quadrupled and administration costs
had been held at £50,000. Both the Colonial Office and local administration hoped that, with the ending of the First World War, Britain
could give more attention to eradicating the Dervish menace. Heeding
Archer's request for a senior military man to advise on how this could
be achieved, the War Office sent out Major-General Sir A. R. Hoskins,
seasoned soldier, former Inspector-General of the King's African Rifles
in East Africa, and lately commanding troops in the Mesopotamian
campaign. Hoskins was a two-division man and believer in large troop
movements, not a Camel Corps man. At a dinner party for his mission
on their arrival at Berbera in December 1918, he was overheard to
remark that he envisaged a large expeditionary force for the task of
finishing off the Mullah. A quick reconnaissance with Archer of the
approaches to the Nogal Valley and plateau area overlooking Las Khorai
did not change his mind.

Hoskins' plan provided for three RAF squadrons* and six warships
for coastal action and three battalions of the King's African Rifles, two
Indian infantry battalions and an Indian cavalry unit, a company of
sappers and miners, five pack-wireless sets with 200-miles radius and
a general wireless set. There were to be 40 Ford vans for motor
transport and ambulance work, and a stationary hospital. There would
be two 3.7-inch guns and 16 Hotchkiss guns. Most notable was the
provision for an Aden-based flight of four-engined Handley Page bombers. Finally, there would be five companies (900 mounted troops) of
the Camel Corps.

The main striking column would advance on Taleh from the Ain
Valley, while subsidiary columns blocked avenue of escape. Two further

---

*The RAF was formed on 1 April 1918.

124

columns advancing from Las Dureh and Las Khorai would capture Jidali and Baran. The Italians, coming in with troops and provided with wireless communication with Illig, would block Badwein and Galkayu against Dervish escape, and would allow British troops to operate freely in the Italian zone. In the western part of the Protectorate pro-British tribes would attack the Bagheri and Galadi, while 5,000 Ethiopian soldiers at Jigjiga and Harrar would block escape in that direction. Royal Navy shelling of coastal positions and RAF bombing of Dervish forts would round out the grand strategy.

Hoskins' recommendations, along with Colonial Office comments, were in War Office hands by the end of December 1918, and were considered by the Cabinet on 24 January 1919. Immediate reaction was that they were overscaled and far too costly. The War Office was too engrossed at the time with demobilisation of armies in Palestine and Mesopotamia and deployment of transport there to give full attention to Hoskins' plans. Experience of previous Ethiopian and Italian co-operation raised doubts as to the wisdom of raising the matter at such an international level as to bring these two unreliable powers in. There was also uncertainty as to the future of British Somaliland in the anticipated reshuffling of territory in the peace settlement already underway. A transfer of the British Protectorate to Italy had been mooted, and Italian aspirations and unfavourable developments in the Ethiopian situation were such as to make co-operation from those quarters doubtful. The Colonial Office and the local administration view was that an expedition on the scale envisaged by Hoskins was unnecessary, and that there was no need for Ethiopian or Italian co-operation. As to Colonial Office and local administration reaction to the rumoured transfer of the Protectorate to Italy, surely in any post-war settlement it was out of the question that the Italians should be given the whole of Somaliland. When Hoskins returned home in February 1919, his recommendations had already been shelved.

Under Article XIII of the London Agreement, 26 April 1915, whereby Italy entered the war on the side of the Allies, it was declared that if France and Great Britain augmented their colonial possessions in Africa at the expense of Germany, there would be an adjustment in Italy's favour of the adjoining boundaries of French and British colonial territories with Italian possessions.

By the end of 1917 Italy was angling for these promised gains. Soon she produced her 'Maximum Programme', revealing her vaulting ambition. It embraced the Horn of Africa, including the sea approaches to Eritrea, and west as far as Kassala in the Sudan. There would be an enlarged Libya. Italy would be a formidable colonial power. That these Italian aspirations would not be met was indicated in a pre-Armistice statement of the Allies on 5 November 1918, wherein it was declared that annexation of territory was not their war aim. At the first plenary session of the Peace Conference at Paris on 18 January 1919, and at a meeting of the Supreme Council at Versailles on 7 May 1919, consideration was given to the application of Article XIII. Lord Milner, Colonial Secretary, was party to these negotiations and disposed to cede the interior of British Somaliland, but not the coast, to Italy. She, however, demanded all of British Somaliland and also Jibuti. The British Admiralty opposed cession of British Somaliland, owing to its strategic importance and possible future source of oil. France would not cede Jibuti, her only port on the Suez Canal route to the East and to Madagascar. With an Ethiopian delegation currently canvassing European capitals for support against anticipated Italian encroachment on Ethiopian territory, and with Ethiopia herself demanding outlets at Berbera, Zeyla and Bulhar, it was an anxious time for Italy. It was a bitterly disappointed Italian Minister of Colonies who complained to his Prime Minister on 30 May 1919 that the colonial question – of highest importance to Italy – had resolved itself into one of betrayal. Italy could only hope for rectification of borders in North Africa and cession of part of British Somaliland which it would be a grave mistake to accept: without its coast and without Jibuti as well, such a cession would bring burdens, not benefits to Italy.

At the Peace Conference, as a result of Italy's being too engrossed in acquiring Fiume, and her Prime Minister and Foreign Minister having to absent themselves at a vital moment to return to Rome to get parliamentary support for Italian claims, Italy lost out. None of the mandated territories was assigned to her. Orlando's cabinet fell on 19 June 1919.

On 28 June 1919 Germany signed the Treaty of Versailles whereby she renounced possession of all her overseas territories in favour of the principal Allied and Associated Powers, and these territories were placed under mandataries. The mandate system created by Article 22 of the Covenant of the League of Nations, which formed part of the Treaty of Versailles, came into force with the exchange of ratifications on 10 June 1920. Italy was left in the cold. She had not even managed to get Kassala, which she was certain would be hers. She did, however, obtain from France a welcome rectification of the Tripoli-Tunisian frontier and valuable railway and commercial privileges in Tunisia; and Britain assented in 1919 in principle to considerable adjustment of territorial claims in the Cyrenaican-Egyptian hinterland, and, by an agreement of December 1925, Egypt ceded to Italy the oasis of Jaghbub in the Cyrenaican hinterland.

In the upshot, Italy's 'Maximum Programme' was drastically reduced. In September 1919 Italy accepted the British offer of transfer to her, from Kenya Colony, of the western part of the Juba valley, a rich cotton-growing area, together with the port of Kismayu. Italian desire for a larger concession delayed a final settlement of this offer until 29 June 1925, when the Trans-Juba territory, comprising some 36,000 square miles and including the greater part of the Jubaland Province of Kenya Colony and also the port of Kismayu, was transferred to her by Britain.

While these matters of high international importance were being sorted out, the situation in Somaliland remained unsettled. Dervish raids continued in early 1919, and there was the complicated Warsangli-Mijjertein wrangle with its many counterclaims and disputes between these two tribes. The Warsangli, mercurial in nature, confronted by the Mijjertein on their east and the Dervishes on their south, confined to a narrow coastal strip and debarred from their nomadic life, were faced with an ineluctable choice. They could either subordinate themselves to the Dervishes and move into Dervish territory, or make peace with the Mijjertein and cross into territory administered by the Italians. Archer, in a bid to win over the Warsangli and their Sultan, Ina Ali Shirreh, a foxy intriguer, and to settle their disputes with the Mijjertein, visited Las Khorai, Bunder Kassim and Musha Aled in early February 1919. Reporting on his tour on 1 March 1919, following his return to Berbera, Archer expressed deep concern at the Warsangli plight: there was danger of their being forced into the Dervish camp. Failing the British delivering the *coup de grâce* against the Mullah, the Warsangli should be removed *en bloc* from their country. Even before the Colonial Office could digest Archer's report, events had moved decisively against the Dervishes.

OK Pass stands high in the list of British victories against the Dervishes, and on a par with that at Jidali in 1904. The message received by an Indian wireless operator at Burao in February 1919, reporting a powerful Dervish force near Rujimo, in the north-eastern Sorl Plain, caused Major Howard to move out of Burao on the same day, at the head of a mounted column, heading for the OK Pass in the Maritime Range, some 50 miles to the north-east. It was surmised that the Dervishes would concentrate there with looted stock before proceeding into the Sorl Plain to the south.

127

Having arrived at OK Pass on 27 February, Howard moved forward with two camel companies to reprovision at Eil Dur Elan, leaving Captain R. F. Simons, Loyal North Lancashire Regiment, with the pony company, to secure the Pass and to cover the stock of the 'friendlies' in the Guban. A party of 400 Dervishes, hovering near OK Pass and apparently unaware of this separate deployment of British forces, and misinformed by an artful old Midgan woman who told them that Simons' pony company's *zariba* was but a defenceless village, fell on it just before dawn on 1 March 1919. Simons was ready for them. His sentries were on the alert. Every sleeping man practically had his finger on the trigger. The native troops stood their ground and meted out heavy punishment. Their response to the Dervish attack was immediate and effective. There followed an hour of fast and furious fighting in which the Dervishes were driven off, leaving a mass of dead at the edge of the *zariba*. Simons immediately sent off a fast rider to Howard, while the pony company pursued the fleeing Dervishes and steered them towards Karumba Pass on the Rujimo–Las Adey track. At noon on 2 March 1919, the pony company called off the pursuit, being in need of rest and water.

The Dervishes, much elated at this withdrawal of the British force, and unaware that the main column under Howard awaited them, blundered into the trap. They were met by a deadly enfilading and raking fire from the advancing camel companies. Despite exhortations from their leaders to stand their ground, the Dervishes fled precipitately, abandoning captured stock, rifles and ammunition, and leaving 200 of their dead on the field. The British loss was two rank-and-file killed and one wounded.

The battle of OK Pass was surely the greatest defeat of the Dervishes since Jidbali in 1904. It demonstrated that the British had mastered hard and painfully acquired desert skills, so necessary in dealing with the Dervishes. Simons' cool and resourceful bravery won him the Military Cross, but he did not live to receive it or enjoy his much-earned leave. He died on his way home.

For the British the situation remained propitious. The successes of the Camel Corps at Shimber Berris, Endow Pass and OK Pass had boosted their morale, and their frequent arduous patrols had given them an ascendancy in areas long under Dervish control. The Mijjertein and Warsangli (the latter under a new and amenable sultan) were asserting themselves against the Dervishes, although not too much should be read into this, for they could not present concerted opposition due to their own internal quarrels.

In September 1919 the Dervishes – perhaps unaware of, or indifferent to, the possibility of air attack – inexplicably moved their headquarters from Taleh, their stronghold since 1913, to Medishe and Jidali, 125 miles north-west of Taleh (and not be confused with Jidbali), leaving only a small rump of Dervishes at Taleh. This move favoured the British, for it left the Mullah with less easy access to Italian Somaliland or the Bagheri country, and more vulnerable to attack from seaplanes or troops based at Las Khorai. The move to Jidali and Medishe was probably forced on the Dervishes also by Mijjertein and Warsangli raids into Dervish grazing areas to the south. Shortage of ammunition and the need to be near the coastal ports to obtain fresh supplies no doubt also played their part in the Dervish move.

The Dervishes, although much weakened after the battle at OK Pass, were soon collecting their strength. The Warsangli and Mijjertein, now squabbling and racked by divisions within themselves, could present no concerted opposition to the Dervishes. The new Warsangli sultan, Ina Ali Shirreh, failed to unify and protect his people, and was making overtures to the Mullah despite promises to Archer earlier in the year to refrain from such. He was summoned to Las Khorai where it was proposed to arrest him. Alerted in advance, Ina Ali Shirreh retired to his fort at Musha Aled, 30 miles inland. On 17 August 1919 the Las Khorai garrison swooped down on him. He was arrested and taken to Berbera, and then exiled to the Seychelles, a place where the British regularly sent difficult personages, such as Prempeh of Asanta, Kabarega and Mwanga of Uganda and, later in time, Archbishop Markarios of Cyprus. The British appointed as Ina Ali Shirreh's successor the aged Gerard Ali Shirreh, a mere figurehead.

Any hope the Mullah had of profiting from the failure of the Mijjertein and Warsangli to unite against him was short-lived. By November 1919 the Mullah's dispositions and their number (1,000 riflemen) in the Jidali area were known, his main force was in his *haroun* at Medishe (12 miles north-west of Jidali) and he held the forts of Surud and Baran.

Archer now began preparing the ground for what he termed the *coup de grâce*. He had not forgotten Hoskins' plan to use aircraft against the Dervishes, nor that their use had been contemplated in 1914 but had been ruled out then because of the war. Now, in March 1919, he brought up the idea again. He found a willing ally in the infant RAF, eager to demonstrate the unique and effective role of air power. Had not aircraft, working from both carriers and shore bases, co-operated with naval forces in the Dardanelles during the war? Air co-operation

129

had also been provided by the Navy in East Africa in July 1915, when seaplanes had been used in spotting the German light cruiser, *Königsberg*, and they had been used in the Red Sea in 1916 and in the Caspian Sea in 1919. Throughout 1919 air squadrons were in use in India's North-west Province, and they co-operated with garrison army units in the conflict with Afghanistan. In Mesopotamia, flying operations involved the use of DH9 and Bristol F2 aircraft, and these were currently in use against rebel Arab chiefs of Kurdistan in the northern territory, making good use of surplus explosives from the First World War. Archer, attending the Colonial Office conference in London on 23 July 1919, welcomed the view expressed, that success would depend on surprise and on the moral and material effect of bombing from the air. The new Air Ministry was approached on 26 July 1919, and had provided and costed a plan by 13 August 1919, when a decisive meeting was held at the Colonial Office. The Air Ministry stated that six aircraft with six reserves and 200 men could be provided for £10,000 a month, whereas a single airship, already discussed by the Admiralty, would cost £29,000. Airships had not been tested in tropical climates, and were not only vulnerable to the extremely high ground-temperatures there, but also presented a slow and large target which would be easy prey for tribal rifle marksmen. Air Marshal Sir Hugh Trenchard, Chief of Air Staff, and Lord Milner, Colonial Secretary, agreed on an air plan to put to an inner Cabinet group, including the Prime Minister and the Secretary of State for War.

War Office objections had to be overcome before Downing Street approval was given on 8 October 1919 for a full-scale expedition. The sanction of Admiralty and Air Ministry had to be obtained for warships and aircraft. Airfields had to be selected and prepared in Somaliland, and additional forces from the King's African Rifles had to be released. The aircraft carrier, *Ark Royal*, was directed to transport Z Unit (as it was known in the RAF) to Berbera soon after 1 December 1919. Thus October 1919 was a month of vital decisions. It saw the elevation of Archer from Commissioner to Governor, as though in anticipation of the fall of the Mullah and the additional territory that would have to be administered, consequent on this.

Unlike other expeditions against the Mullah, the War Office was not given control of this Expedition. Group Captain Gordon, 37-year-old veteran of 1914–19 seaplane operations, was chosen to command the air operations in Somaliland, and was directly under the Air Ministry. Z Unit of the RAF, which he commanded, was a flight of 12 aircraft, with six spare machines. They were DH9s (De Havilland 9s), two-seater day bombers, an improved version of the DH4 of the First World War. Carrying a 460 lb bomb-load and mounting two Lewis guns, they had a flight duration of 4½ hours at a top speed of 111 mph. A weak point in the DH9 aircraft was its BHP engine, and recognition of this weakness was evident in the spares sent out to Somaliland. (However, the gods seemed to have favoured the DH9 ambulance, for its engine gave no trouble throughout the '21 Days'). Back-up for Z Unit Flight was extensive: 21 motor vehicles, a medical team of 30 persons and the aforementioned flying ambulance, and 162 ground staff, aircraft hands, armourers, gunners and radio operators. The RAF in Egypt, with much experience in such matters derived from similar actions in the Middle East in the First World War, would provide 1,235 bombs and 15,000 gallons of petrol.

Ground forces for the larger area of battle would consist of the Somali Camel Corps, a composite battalion of 700 rifles from the King's African Rifles and a half-battalion of 400 rifles from the Indian Army. There would be temporary garrisons of Indian Army units. Less disciplined but invaluable was the irregular Somali Levy of 1,500 rifles, and 300 scouts (*illalos*), the latter grouped in small parties of 10 to 25, to collect intelligence about Dervish movements and relay this to the nearest garrison by wireless. These *illalos*, tireless, inured to hardship and imbued with the desire to loot and outwit the enemy, were a flexible and valuable arm for the British. Against these formidable British forces the Mullah could pit a hard core of 1,000 riflemen, ranked in formation and named after ten of his wives, and possibly 3,000–5,000 spearmen.

On 6 November 1919, two days after Archer returned from home leave, the bombs arrived from Egypt. On 20 November Gordon and an advance party of the RAF unit arrived at Berbera. Little secrecy attended these arrivals. Local officials had already disseminated reports that oil-boring operations were to take place at the sites of supposed oil deposits reported earlier in the year, a few miles south of Berbera and at Eil Dur Elan about 95 miles south-east of Berbera. The D'Arcy Exploration Company (later the Anglo-Persian Petroleum Company) after further testing in 1921 and 1924 decided they were not worth exploiting. But for the time being they acted as an effective ruse to mislead the Somalis. The preparing of airfields at these sites would supposedly be construed by Somalis as oil-drilling operations. Whether the 200 workers toiling under the sharp tongue of their foreman were taken in by this ruse is difficult to say. Some Somalis had already seen aeroplanes at Aden, although they were not likely aware of the demoralising effect of an air attack.

131

Final plans for the long-awaited Expedition were agreed at Government House, Berbera, on 12 December 1919. Archer, now Governor, was also Commander-in-Chief of overall strategy. This was as follows: In the first week of January 1920, Force A, under Colonel Summers, and comprising 550 men of the Camel Corps and 200 Indian infantry, would move to the Eil Dur Elan airfield preparatory to the airstrike to be made from there on Jidali and Medishe on 21 January 1920. Two days before this raid the Camel Corps would move eastward to Durdu Dulbeit, about 40 miles south of Jidali. Simultaneously, Force B, comprising 750 King's African Rifles and 200 Indian troops, and operating on the Las Khorai-Musha Aled line, would occupy Baran and prevent Dervishes escaping into Italian territory. When Gordon judged that the bombing of Dervish positions had achieved its aim, he would direct aircraft to co-operate with ground forces in rounding up and finishing off the now demoralised Dervishes. The Camel Corps would also join in the hunt.

The Royal Navy too would play its part. A naval landing party from the *Odin* and *Clio*, closely patrolling the seaboard and with an armed dhow off Mait to prevent the Mullah's escape by sea, would bombard and take Galiabur, a Dervish fort within a few miles of the sea. Meanwhile the Tribal Levy of 1,500 rifles would hold posts on the Mullah's line of retreat southwards to Bagheri, and would intercept Dervish fugitives and stock.

What a scene of activity was Berbera by mid-December 1919! Large droves of stock could be seen arriving from the interior. Five thousand transport camels had to be mustered locally (often on a hire basis: ripe invitation for fraudulent claims of compensation for neglect and loss of camels). Collecting such a number of camels was a difficult task, for the effects of sending 10,000 camels to the Egyptian Expeditionary Force in 1917–18 were still being felt. Men and provisions were landed at Berbera under a watchful eye against pilfering. Remounts, saddlery, Stokes guns and ammunition, water tanks – vast amounts of war stocks from India, Egypt and Aden had to be unloaded. Forces of the King's African Rifles were assigned to their posts at Las Khorai and other points. The arrival at Berbera on 30 December 1919 of the *Ark Royal* with the main force from Alexandria – 36 RAF officers, 189 other ranks, aeroplanes, mechanical transport and stores – signalled the end of secrecy of what was in store for the Dervishes.

Three aircraft were landed the same night as the *Ark Royal* arrived. Bad packing, missing bolts and nuts, torn wires and unsuitable radiators for the tropics were all now revealed. What now the experience of

Mesopotamia and Egypt! Only three bombers were ready by 7 January, the date set for the first air-strike. This was now postponed until 10 January 1920, and then postponed again. What a busy man was Archer! In the midst of all this preparation he had also, by early January 1920, brought over the Mijjertein sultan, Osman Mahmoud, to the British side with the promise of large rewards if he would capture the Mullah and his sons.

Still maintaining the pretence of secrecy, there were trial flights with the newly landed aircraft along the coast out of sight of land. That they were kept at bay and out at sea, so claimed some watching Somalis who witnessed these flights, was the result of the Mullah's soul force: if he had so wished, they claimed, he could also have brought them to earth by the same sheer force of his soul power.

On 19 January 1920, seven aircraft arrived at Eil Dur Elan from Berbera. When, in the early morning of 21 January 1920, six of these aircraft launched an aerial attack on Jidali and Medishe, it marked the start of a 21-day campaign which ended a 21-year war against the Mullah. In this first and crucial stage of the use of aircraft against the Mullah, engine trouble, which was their weak point, quickly beset the DH9s. Scarcely had the last aircraft taken off than the first was returning because of engine trouble. An additional problem for the pilots was that they were flying over unmapped country. The need for secrecy had prevented preliminary reconnaissance, and the out-dated War Office map of 1907, marked with much irrelevant and erroneous detail, was more of a hindrance than a help. The natural elements also seemed to have combined against them, for, unusual at this time of year, heavy cloud banks prevented all but one aircraft from finding the main target, Medishe, where the Mullah had concentrated his *haroun*, and was unaware of an impending air attack. However, those aircraft assigned to bomb Jidali found their target.

As regards the air attack on Medishe, the reaction of the Mullah and Dervishes when alerted to the drone of the approaching aircraft can only be surmised. Various stories were subsequently put about as to the fanciful ideas which supposedly went through their minds. One of these was that the Mullah was credulous enough to believe that the aircraft was a chariot sent by Allah to bear him to Paradise. Another, perhaps fostered by a Turk in the Mullah's camp, was that the approaching aircraft was a Turkish invention of war come to rescue their staunch ally. At Medishe, the close approach of the one aircraft was purportedly construed by the Mullah as a desire of its occupant to hold intimate converse with him. Thus donning his finest robes, he sallied forth on the arm of his uncle and close adviser, Amir, and took up a position under a white canopy, and awaited the august messenger. Such notions as to the friendly nature of this visitation from the skies, if they ever existed, were quickly dispelled.

When the lone aircraft, H5561, despite its faulty altimeter and a drifting bank of cloud which largely obscured Medishe, managed to break through sufficiently to drop eight 20 lb Cooper bombs and to machine-gun and photograph the supposed target, the first bomb (as revealed later by a survivor of the event), achieved results that were dramatic. The Mullah's party – his sister and uncle and an escort of ten riflemen – were practically blown sky-high: only the Mullah survived, although his fine white jubbah and green turban were much the worse from the explosion. This was war as the Mullah had never known it. Badly shaken and scarcely waiting to see the effects of the remaining bombs on his *haroun* (20 were killed and 20 wounded) he headed north, taking with him a small party of the faithful, and also the two precious machine-guns captured at Erigo and Gumburu years before, along with arms, ammunition and personal treasury. Taking refuge in a cave in the mountains 15 miles north-east of Medishe, he lay low, recovering his equilibrium and awaiting news of further developments in the field.

Bombing of Medishe continued on 22 and 23 January, although engine trouble continued to plague the aircraft; only three out of a flight of six being in action on the 23rd. The attack was heavy, with much strafing by machine-gun fire from as low as 300 feet, and dropping of 50 lb incendiaries. The result was drastic and quickly achieved: the virtual abandonment of Medishe by the Dervishes. Some of them made for the nearest caves; others could be discerned fleeing with their driven stock in the direction of Jidali, to which the aircraft now turned their attention. Before doing so they dropped propaganda leaflets on the heads of the supposedly demoralised Dervishes, and also on the nearby wells of Medishe. The leaflets contained a letter from Archer, and its dramatic delivery from the air was deemed an effective way of impressing the Dervishes. The letter was written in Arabic and was epistolaric in style. It likened the aircraft which delivered the letter to birds which could fly fast and far. It warned the Dervishes of destruction to come if they did not surrender unconditionally. Even if they did surrender there could be no *aman* (safe conduct) for some Dervishes, 36 in all; and prices of from 1,000 to 5,000 rupees were placed on the heads of the Mullah and his sons, dead or alive. These leaflets fluttering down on the heads of the wild Dervishes, although novel in manner, brought no effective response.

Bombing and strafing of Jidali from the air, which had commenced on 23 January, continued the next day, and there was an extensive reconnaissance that afternoon which showed Medishe and the nearby countryside as far as Jidali apparently deserted. It was now that independent air operations ceased. As of 25 January 1920, Gordon instructed his aircraft to engage in combined operations with land forces.

With Medishe taken by the British there remained only Jidali and Baran as Dervish strongholds in the north-eastern part of the Protectorate. It was against Baran that a King's African Rifles contingent of 700 men and 60 scouts, led by 23 British officers, moved out from Musha Aled on 20 January 1920. By early morning of the 23rd they faced the massive walls of Baran, and here they came under heavy Dervish fire which was quickly quenched by the machine-guns. It was now that there was brought into play a weapon new to Somaliland, the Stokes 3-inch mortar. Its inventor, Sir Wilfrid Stokes, could hardly have imagined when he devised this admirable piece of ordinance in 1914–15 (improved and used effectively in the First World War) that it would wreak severe damage on a Dervish fort in far-away Somaliland a few years later. The lightness of the 3-inch muzzle-loading Stokes mortar, the barrel of which, a light seamless steel tube, was designed to lob high-angle, high-explosive bombs, made it the ideal 'accompanying' piece. At 300 yards direct hits were scored on the towers of Baran by the two mortars, but the massive walls, however shaken, remained upright, making it impossible to assess the damage within. With night approaching the attack was called off, Colonel Wilkinson, commanding officer, withdrawing his force to a waterhole some 4 miles south, to await the morrow. The next day, 24 January, the attack was renewed, the Stokes being pushed forward and making direct hits within the parapets of the 40ft corner towers. The impact in the confined space must have been tremendous, yet the defenders continued to hurl maledictions and defiance at their attackers. That night, as the moon was about to set, and under machine-gun cover, 100 lb of gun cotton was tamped against a corner tower. Scarcely had the two officers who placed it there scurried away than a loud explosion followed. The results were not observed until dawn when a reconnoitering platoon rushed the main gate and occupied the three remaining corner towers.

Through the other, breached corner tower a number of Dervishes could be seen hurriedly escaping. They had waited until dawn, fearful of any trap laid outside for them. A few hand-to-hand struggles ensued before the fort was entirely cleared of Dervishes. Now could be seen the terrible toll wrought by the Stokes and the final explosion. Inside, sprawled in different attitudes of death, were over three-score dead, surrounded by their rifles. Three women taken prisoner related the terrible last hours of the Dervishes. Only ten had escaped and, of these, one picked up later died from his wounds. On the British side only four men and a mule had been wounded. Baran had fallen and the Mullah's line of retreat into Italian territory had been cut off.

Co-ordination of tactics between the RAF and ground forces was now the order of the day. On 26 January two DH9s landed with news of the Camel Corps advance from Eil Dur Elan to Eil Afweina preparatory to a move on Jidali. Ismay, having reached Eil Afweina on the 21st, prepared it as an advance base, with landing ground, hospital and supplies, including 3,500 transport camels. On the afternoon of the 23rd Ismay moved out, leaving Eil Afweina garrisoned by 130 Grenadiers with 1,700 reserve camels. It was an impressive force which moved forward against Jidali: 1,000 transport camels, Stokes guns, grenades and explosives, under an escort of a company of the Grenadiers. Four days' march brought them in sight of Jidali. As prearranged, four aircraft arrived the same day, 27 January, to soften up the fort. They straddled it with bombs, scoring hits on the north-east corner, and, flying at 300 feet, drove the fleeing Dervishes into low bush. They had been over the target for nearly two hours when Ismay arrived.

As Ismay advanced the Dervishes were kept down by machine-gun fire, and the Stokes mortars were brought into action. They breached the masonry and it was only the small chambers on the ground floor and the thickness of the walls which saved the garrison from annihilation. They still held out, singing and firing. That same night, while Ismay planned a renewed attack for the morrow when fresh explosives would have arrived, the Dervishes slipped away, leaving their dead and rifles. From a small boy, taken prisoner, Observer Officer W. L. Roberts, who had landed on 28 January, ascertained the events at Medishe and the story of the singeing of the Mullah's robes in the air attack.

The week's operations had finished off Medishe, Baran and Jidali. It was a swift and successful campaign. The demoralising effect of the Stokes was impressive, but it was more likely that Dervish withdrawal from Jidali had been part of the Mullah's plan for general evacuation of the area, rather than Dervish defeat. No Dervish prisoners had been taken and few deserters had come in.

News of the fall of Baran, and that that of Jidali was imminent, reached the Mullah and his followers hiding out in the Dalau Hills, 20 miles north-west of Jidali, on 27 January 1920. The next day the

Mullah, issuing two bandoliers to each Dervish, packed his treasure and the two precious machine-guns and headed south, his favourite wife riding behind him. Meanwhile the British, engrossed with the aerial bombardment, lost touch with the enemy, until news of the Mullah's *hegira* reached the British camp through a Dervish deserter on 30 January. It was assumed that the Mullah would make for Taleh; and, that same day, Z Unit was directed to scout there. The Mullah, using his old desert craft to good stead, watered at allegedly dry wells, at Danaan (20 miles north-east of Eil Afweina), on 29 January. The Camel Corps took up the pursuit (known as 'Maud') on 30 January, by which time the Mullah had a 40-hour headstart.

The Camel Corps reached Eil Dur Elan on the morning of 31 January after a 40-mile night march. Here the main line of Dervish retreat, well marked with discarded property, was crossed, and there were clashes with small parties of Dervishes driving vast herds of stock. The 'friendlies' fell with great relish on this prize which, in addition to hundreds of camels, included supplies of rifles and ammunition. Scouts reported the Mullah moving fast ahead of the retreating Dervishes. The pace quickened. The Camel Corps, pressing on, passed through Gud Anod and reached Eil Afweina by midnight, 31 January.

Here Z Unit reported on its recent air reconnaissance since combined operations had been sanctioned on 25 January. One aircraft had crashed, and the RAF had spent two fruitless days looking for Galiabur fort near the sea before it was finally bombed, presumably on 27–28 January. East and south-east of Eil Afweina in the general direction of what was thought to be the Mullah's line of retreat towards Taleh, there had been much strafing and bombing from the air by two aircraft. At one point, as later revealed, the Mullah had watched the bombing and destruction meted out from the air on a large Dervish convoy which included the Mullah's wives and sons and a vast herd of stock.

Since it was now assumed that the Mullah was making for Ethiopian territory, probably the upper Webi Shibeli region, and would halt for rest at Taleh on the way, on 1 February 1920 two aircraft directed their attention to Taleh, carrying out an air reconnaissance and taking photographs, scoring four direct hits on watching Dervishes, causing them to flee into the fort. Aerial photographs confirmed that Taleh was such a formidable fortification that massive explosives would be needed against this, the most impregnable of the Mullah's forts.* Z Unit's flying ambulance was now brought into diversified use. The flying hearse, as it was known, carried few wounded. It was more useful for carrying

*See p. 93 for the fort's dimensions.

heavy bombs. After ferrying wounded Captain Goodman of the Camel Corps to Eil Dur Elan for an operation, on 1 February 1920 it was directed to Berbera to fetch a 230 lb bomb for use against Taleh. There was much cursing at Eil Afweina when the bomb arrived without its firing pistol.

On 2 February one of the aircraft destined for Taleh was blown off course into the hills 160 miles from Eil Afweina. Despite these mishaps three aircraft carrying 13 bombs between them appeared over Taleh on 4 February. Three large 112-pounders were landed astride the fort's large main gate. Despite one aircraft engine twice cutting out, more hits were made with 20 lb bombs, and outside huts were set afire with a 50 lb incendiary. There was also machine-gunning of stock and Dervishes from the air, outside the fort. On 6 February the air attack was renewed with more machine-gunning and use of incendiaries. Gordon lamented that if he had more aircraft there could be night patrols, but engines had to be overhauled at night owing to the intense heat: 'We daren't look inside a plane cowling in the hot sun.' During this intense period of activity there was little scope for religious or political speculation: the struggle with the Mullah was primarily a military one, and preoccupation was with the job in hand. Shade temperatures were in the region of 110°F. There was an inadequate supply of heavy bombs – they had not reckoned on so formidable a target as Taleh. This caused Gordon to direct aircraft back to Berbera, and his provisional plan for a three-day bombing of Taleh, softening it up before the arrival of ground forces, had to be called off. Events continued to overtake planning, but in the end, despite much going awry, Taleh fell.

By 1 February 1920 the Jidali–Medishe area had been cleared out by the King's African Rifles and Grenadiers, hundreds of rifles had been captured and, as a healthy reminder of the Mullah's cruelty, they had come upon the remains of a Dervish roasted over a slow fire. The Camel Corps, reaching Eil Afweina on 31 January 1920, had then pushed on to Hudin by 2 February, covering 150 miles in 72 hours. Some 60 miles away that same night, the Mullah and 60 followers entered Taleh, the day after it had been bombed.

In the relentless forcing out of the Dervishes from the northern part of the Protectorate both the Navy and Tribal Levy played a role. When Z Unit had bombed the Dervish fort at Galiabur on 27–28 January 1920, in anticipation of a ground attack on it, HMS *Odin* and *Clio*, patrolling the coast, and in wireless communication with the force on land, were directed to Galiabur, where their presence would be a salutary warning to the Dervishes that no escape lay in that direction.

On 3 February 1920, Captain Gilbert Hewett landed with a force of 99 sailors and 140 Somalis at Sanak, some 10 miles from Galiabur. The next day, armed with 31 Lewis guns, two Maxims and a 12-pounder 4cwt field gun (instead of mortars), high explosive shells and Mills bombs, they made a short march through low hills leading from the beach to within sight of Galiabur fort. At a distance of 500 yards, when the occupants of the fort sighted them, the naval brigade spread out and surrounded the fort, the field gun was brought into play and its high explosive shells soon breached the fortress wall. Meanwhile Mills bombs and machine-gun fire kept down the return fire of the Dervishes. Although devastation within the fort must have been nearly total, there was no surrender; the few Dervishes who fled from the fort into nearby low bush did so under the withering fire of the Maxims. At midday on 6 February, the breach was stormed but the fort not taken until its defenders were killed or captured. They fought valiantly, well on to 200 Dervishes being killed and 24 captured alive. Hewett's losses were negligible. His forces re-embarked the next day. The action at Galiabur certainly deterred the Dervishes from heading for the coast.

The role of the Tribal Levy was likewise purposeful. Under the command of Captain Gibbs and Risaldar-Major Haji Musa Farah, this 1,500-man force was stationed at posts along the 100-mile Yaguri Gerrowei line, with Duhung, the half-way point, as the headquarters. In late January, Gibbs, endeavouring to block the Mullah's escape southward to the Bagheri, and suspecting that he might head for Taleh, directed 500 riflemen to Gaolo, 10 miles south-west of Taleh, to keep watch on that place. On 4 February tribal horsemen brought news that the Mullah had entered Taleh on the night of the 2nd, and that remnants of Dervish forces were converging on it. The tribal militia had killed many of them, including Haji Sudi (ex-naval interpreter) and Ibrahim Boghol (commander of the Mullah's forces in the northern area), and had captured much booty, including the Mullah's personal belongings, correspondence, jewellery, his prayer rug, great numbers of stock and many camel-loads of supplies, arms and ammunition.

Gibbs left immediately for Gaolo, joining up with the Camel Corps there on 8 February 1920. That same night the Mullah's son, Abdul Rahman, and his uncle, Haji Osman, deserted the Mullah's *haroun* and were brought captive into the British camp at Gaolo. From them it was learned that the Mullah, despite the 200-man Tribal Levy guarding Taleh, meant to bolt from there that same night, and make for the Ogaden. This betrayal of the Mullah's plans by his uncle and son took high courage, and they risked eternal damnation for handing over such

139

a holy man as the Mullah to the infidel. It required hard thinking on their part.

The Mullah's plan of escape, so they informed the British, was to sally out and drive back the Tribal Levy, and before the latter could recover they would make good their escape. And thus it turned out. When Gibbs and his 800 tribal footmen, with Camel Corps and supplies trailing an hour behind them, arrived at Taleh from Gaolo on the late afternoon of 9 February, they found the 200-man Tribal Levy driven back some 2 miles. They soon espied a party of some 80 mounted men, the Mullah and personal followers, swiftly passing out of Taleh's north gate and disappearing in a northerly direction. Somali scholars were later to describe this desertion of Taleh by the Mullah as an heroic escape amid a fanfare of trumpets. There was to be no going down to a glorious defeat for the Mullah. He readily abandoned the 90 Dervishes left to guard Taleh. However it was an escape by the narrowest of margins. If the Camel Corps had arrived at the same time as Gibbs, the Mullah would likely have been captured, and it would have meant the immediate and ignominious collapse of the Dervish movement.

It being useless to pursue the fleeing Mullah with men on foot, and it being now late afternoon. Gibbs, without waiting for Ismay to come up, unleashed his firepower on Taleh fort, already shaken by previous air attacks and inadequately defended by the rump of Dervishes holding it. The effect was immediate, a precipitous and headlong rush into the open by the occupants who were quickly dispatched. It was all over within the hour, except for a few snipers who were later cleared out or who escaped.

Ismay by now had come up, and in the deepening dusk he and Gibbs counted their prize. There were 45 Dervish dead, and as many captured, including Mohammed Ali, the Mullah's Turkish adviser, and four Arab stonemasons; there were hundreds of captured rifles, hundreds of camels and many ponies. The toll on the British side was light: nine wounded. However, for the British, the main prize, the Mullah, was still at large. That same night Ismay sent out a patrol to pick up his track. By midnight it had returned. Hard surface ground and darkness made tracking impossible. Meanwhile the Mullah had put 47 miles between himself and Taleh. Initially heading north, he then veered southerly, presumably making for the Ethiopian Ogaden. At break of dawn on the 10th, the Camel Corps, abandoning their camels for ponies, set out in quick pursuit. Pell-mell after the Mullah, over river-beds, *nullahs*, boulders and sand-dunes, thick scrub and thorn bush, they went, through blinding clouds of dust, scarcely stopping to examine the cast-off debris of the fleeing Dervishes. It was a thrashing pace under a pitiless sun, and the ponies were soon exhausted.

The tracks of the fleeing Dervishes repeatedly broke up only to converge again. This crazy pattern finally settled down 3 miles south-west of Galnole on the Italian frontier. It was difficult to know whether the Mullah was with the main party. As it turned out he had separated from it, sending it back into British territory, while he, his brother and the Mullah's eldest son, Mahdi, and three chosen Dervishes kept well to the east, observing utmost secrecy. Never was the Mullah's superb skill in evasive tactics more cleverly displayed. He never resorted to water-holes in person, ponies were watered only at night, there was a constant shifting to new positions so that even his bodyguards did not know what was afoot, lest they betray him. All the wily tricks learned through long years of desert warfare against the infidel were now brought into play with great effect. How quickly too had the Mullah caught on to the safety provided by crossing international boundaries, even if these boundaries were only marked by a few stone cairns. For refugees in flight they provided a previously unknown haven.

Ismay and the Camel Corps, pursuing by the light of the moon, moving southwards and keeping parallel with the boundary, and on the British side of it, arrived at a point on the frontier 3 miles south-west of Galnole on 11 February. The sick and unfit men were now sent back to Gaolo, and the same day Ismay set out again with 150 rifles, three machine-guns and two Stokes. The same afternoon, in a surprise enveloping movement, they wiped out an enemy watering party directly on the frontier, a few miles north-east of Gerrowei. Thirty Dervish riflemen and 14 others, including the Mullah's sons and relatives, were killed. Five of his wives and nine of his children were captured and subsequently sent back to Berbera. His large extended family had been steadily shrinking, and this loss was great, for among those captured was his favourite wife, Ena Ow Yussuf.

With this prize in hand, Ismay pushed on to Gerrowei. The early morning of the 12th saw another engagement. Placing the Mullah's wives and children under guard, Ismay gave chase to a Dervish force of horsemen and footmen who finally made a stand in a *nullah* near Gerrowei. There followed a cavalry charge in true Ismay fashion. Dervish footmen, heroic though they were, could not stand up to it and they went down like ninepins. Dervish horses were next to feel the terrible brunt of a cavalry charge, and they were galloped down almost to a man. Ismay was disappointed that again the main prize, the Mullah, was not among the Dervish party. He had eluded capture once more.

141

Patrols were at once sent out to pick up his trail. At midday on the 12th came news of the sighting of a party of Dervishes moving into the southern Haud. There followed a further winnowing out of the unfit and unwell. Ismay and a select party of 20 ponymen and one camel troop now set out on what was hoped would be the final pursuit.

Again the goddess of fortune eluded Ismay. A party of presumed Dervishes overtaken on 12 February proved to be an Ethiopian party under Fitaurari Bayenna, a known supporter of the Mullah. They went down fighting, only two surrendering. Little did Ismay realise that the Mullah had witnessed this action from a nearby hill, and that it had spurred him into mad flight. Moving with much haste, he entered unpoliced Ethiopian territory, into Bagheri country extending from Walwal south-west to the Webi Shibeli, and across the southern Haud to Galadi.

Ismay was in no position to continue the pursuit into foreign territory, even if he had been so inclined. On the late afternoon of 12 February the chase was called off. On 15 February Archer flew to Gaolo, and on 17 February Churchill, in London, was informed that the 'friendlies' had done really useful work, although the Mullah was still at large. In 21 days the Dervish forces, after as many years of war and defiance, had been brought low. Only the Mullah, his eldest son, Mahdi, a brother and a few leading Dervishes had escaped. Six of the Mullah's sons, five of his wives, four daughters and two sisters had been captured. How sadly contracted now was his once powerful family! The Dervishes' main wealth – their stock – was largely in British hands or those of the 'friendlies'. Arms lost to the Dervishes in previous combat had been recaptured: the Mullah's personal possessions had been seized, including his prize trophies, the two machine guns from Erigo and Gumburu. His forts, those vaunted bastions which were meant to turn the tide against the infidel, were now in British hands. Only the stark walls of Taleh remained, and these too were demolished by the Camel Corps within two months of the Mullah's flight from there. Explosives belatedly arrived from Egypt, and originally meant for the air attack, were used, too, in this final demolition of Taleh by the British.

A small price had been paid by the British in the final phase of the 21-day campaign: 4 killed, 11 wounded, and 13 deaths through sickness. The Royal Navy and Royal Air Force (the latter's flying hearse had scarcely been needed) came through unscathed. Z Unit left Eil Dur Elan on 24 February and, after a few prestige flights, dipping their wings in flippant salute over Berbera, left for home on board an aircraft carrier, in April 1920.

142

One writer (Jardine, p. 316) claims that the British public had forgotten the Somali war long before this final phase which brought it to a successful conclusion; and so it seems, for news of the Mullah's downfall, although acclaimed in the press and some quarters, did not arouse undue interest in the public at large. There was some bemusement over the garbled news reports that came from Nairobi, one of which stated that tanks had played a key role in encompassing the Mullah's downfall, and another that, now that the Mullah was defeated, a railway would be built inland to Bohotle and thence to Harrar. There were not at the time plans for even the slightest filament of a railway in Somaliland. More absorbing for the British public at the time, rather than concern over events in Somaliland, was the coming Boat Race. The London of 1920 was still suffused with post-war euphoria and slowly turning to peacetime roles. It could scarcely generate enough enthusiasm to celebrate the downfall of the Mullah and the Dervishes. Officers returning home from service overseas found London an attractive place; a haunting nostalgia for it had been with them during long years abroad, and music hall tunes had kept running through their heads. Tired and emotionally exhausted by war and strain, they had little time or interest in Somaliland or anything connected with it. Mullah and Dervishes should be forgotten as quickly as possible.

What was pleasing, however, especially for the House of Commons, so recently agitated over this foray into adventurism, was the small cost of the campaign: a mere £83,000, and but for the recent revaluation of the rupee (from 1s. 4d. to 2s. 11d.) in which it was costed, it would have been much smaller. This expenditure, in terms of results achieved, so claimed the Under Secretary for the Colonies, was scarcely paralleled in Imperial history. And what thoughts must Churchill, Secretary for War and Air, have had, looking back over the years since October 1907, when, as the young Under Secretary of State for the Colonies, he had visited that benighted land and made recommendations for its future. Following similar successes in air-bombing of tribesmen in Afghanistan and the Sudan in 1919, and planning for a Cape-to-Cairo air route, the success of the RAF in the Somaliland campaign argued well for Churchill's holding of both War and Air portfolios.

The role of aircraft in the final campaign against the Mullah had caught the imagination of many persons in high places. Undue claims for its importance brought a warning from one writer as to the 'perilous' belief that 'savage peoples' could be managed from the air: troops and police were the vital agents in such matters, not an airforce. Closer examination of the campaign showed that it was the terrible nemesis of the Camel Corps and Tribal Levy, fleet and mobile as they were, and using the same tactics as the Dervishes, which had shaken the nerve of the latter. It was the appearance of the Camel Corps and Tribal Levy at Jidali and Taleh which put the Dervishes to flight. There were also the six years of reverses, the abominations of the Mullah's executioners, the gradual disillusionment with the Mullah's cause, apart from a hard core, which had worn down Dervish numbers from 6,000 in 1913 to scarcely 1,000 in 1919. Also the ending of the First World War had enabled hitherto unavailable forces to be deployed against the Dervishes and to back up the fixed determination to eradicate once and for all this menace. Despite all this, many continued to see the airforce as the prime factor in ending the threat of the Mullah and his Dervishes.

In May 1920 Churchill argued for a key role for the RAF in Mesopotamia. At the Cairo Conference of March 1921, when the whole question of mandated territories and Middle East policy was under review, Lord Trenchard proposed a force of eight squadrons to control Mesopotamia, and in 1922 the RAF was given control of operations there. Henceforth the use of aircraft in overseas operations became a recognised part of Imperial policy. In Somaliland, aircraft were again used in 1922, at Burao, to deter an uprising of tax revolters there. An RAF detachment of two aircraft were stationed at Burao for aerial work during the Anglo-Italian boundary survey of 1929–30. They were used again in the mapping and surveying of the Anglo-Ethiopian boundary in 1932–4.

9

DEATH OF THE MULLAH

THE satisfaction over the scene of the fleeing Dervishes, harried by the Camel Corps and Tribal Levy, was short-lived when news came that the Mullah was still alive and that the drama was still not played out. The Mullah's movements from 9 February until his arrival at Galadi in early March 1920, as monitored by military headquarters at Burao, were marked by points running down through the Haud/Ogaden region: Halin, Damot and thence to Galadi. Here the Mullah and his party were joined by the Mullah's brother, Abdi Sheikh, and another of his sons (the Mullah at times could not remember which of his wives was the mother of certain of his offspring). Dervish notables in the party included Majdi Mohammad, Abdul Aziz, Abbas Musa and Yusuf Sheikh, and there were 70 Dervish riflemen, picked men all of them.

From Galadi the party proceeded west to Wardair fort and thence to Gorahei on the Tug Fafan, arriving there about 21 March 1920. Cordially received by his clansmen, the Bagheri, some of whom purported to remember his father, the Mullah decided to settle among them and resume the struggle when it was opportune. He was soon recruiting new followers in this so-called 'accursed no man's land', the refuge of malcontents and trouble-makers and the home of the fanatical Ogaden tribesmen.

The masters of these potential trouble-makers among whom the Mullah settled were a select band of several hundred well-armed Dervishes, led by the Mullah's half-brother, Khalif. Since 1903 they had based themselves at fortified points – Walwal, Wardair and Gorahei – from which they had terrorised and dominated the Ogaden Somalis, and had provided the Mullah with arms and ammunition from Ethiopia. The Mullah always knew that there was safe retreat among these restless brigands who were, however, a thorn in the flesh of the Ethiopian administration which claimed control over the region. The Ethiopians had never taken to life in this territory which they claimed as their own. The feverish lowland climate and the lawless Muslim tribesmen (with supposedly a fighting strength of 45,000 men) presented an ineluctable challenge for the Ethiopians who, despite urgent British representations, declined to administer the territory firmly. This corner on the upper Shibeli remained a bolt-hole for criminal fugitives from as far away as British East Africa. In early 1920, at Moyale in the Northern Frontier District of what is now Kenya, a party of 25 *askaris* of the King's African Rifles, after murdering their officer, Lieutenant Dawson-Smith, escaped with their arms, including a machine-gun, and found refuge among the Abdulla section of the Ogaden on the north-west bank of the upper Webi Shibeli. The Mullah's move to this region shortly after caused much alarm in British East Africa.

In this locale, denuded of family, property and his main fighting force, the Mullah, such was his reputation and resourcefulness, still managed to rally around him a core of hard fighters, including his half-brother, Khalif. It seemed that he might again pose a formidable threat to the British. Archer, apprehensive of this, on 15 February 1920, and referring to himself as the British Wali, sent a letter to the Mullah via a deputation consisting of one of the Mullah's wives, an uncle (Haji Osman), a sister and the chief Dervish executioner. The Mullah was reminded in the letter that the British had been victorious in the recent war with the Germans and Turks. Ras Tafari and the Mijjertein sultans were friends of the British. He, the Mullah, however, was isolated and weak from heavy losses, a dispossessed leader, with no forts, property, stock or family, but the British were magnanimous and would offer him the olive branch. If he surrendered within 40 days of receipt of the letter, he would be given safe conduct to his own *tarika* (religious community) where he could follow his own *din* (religion).

The Mullah's reply, sent from Shinileh, 40 miles west of Gorahei, and which reached Archer on 25 March 1920, was cool and stubborn in tone. He, the Mullah, would not kneel to the British. He was the oppressed without cause, a Hashimi by descent, Saffei in doctrine, a Sunni and of the Ahmedieh *tarika*. As to Archer's version of their relative strength, he could not affirm this – it was in God's hands. If the British wanted peace they should offer some consolation as regards his family, who, the Mullah claimed, had been sent overseas (they were in fact in Berbera at the time and were later freed). The Mullah stated that his hands were clean of wrongdoing. Intimating his acceptance of Archer's terms, he insisted that he himself should choose his place of residence, among his own people, and if allowed to do so, he would give the British no further trouble. On the whole the Mullah's reply was auspicious.

146

Archer, however, surmising that the Mullah was playing for time while endeavouring to raise support in the Ogaden, pretended to take the Mullah at his word. He sent off a ten-man deputation to the Mullah, consisting of prominent sheikhs and akils under the venerable Sheikh Ismail Ishaak of the Salihieh *tarika*. Although such a mission was traditionally assured safe-conduct, the deputation was panic-stricken at the thought of what might await them in the Mullah's camp. In their minds it meant certain death at his hands, and so convinced were they of this, and so also were their relatives, that the latter lost no time in distributing the deputation members' possessions among themselves, as soon as the mission had departed on 9 April 1920. They were presumed already dead.

The letter that was carried to the Mullah from Archer, dated Burao, 7 April 1920, repeated the previous offer of a *tarika* for the Mullah, but in more detail. The *tarika* would be in the western part of the Protectorate and under British jurisdiction, leaving the Mullah free to make the Haj (pilgrimage to Mecca) and with much autonomy, subject to his satisfactory behaviour. His possessions and family would be returned to him. He would abstain from interfering with other tribes and must confine himself to administering the Sharia in his own *tarika*. Thus he could live in immunity for the rest of his days. Bitterness of war would give way to the consolation of comfort and peace. If the Mullah accepted these terms he should return with the British mission so that *aman* could be sealed with Archer in person.

It is tempting to speculate on the nature of such a meeting between Archer and the Mullah and what it might have achieved. It would have been the first meeting between the Mullah and a European since that with Pestalozza, back in March 1905. Could anything have come of it? Was it really to be imagined that the Mullah would abide by such a limitation on his freedom after so many years of unrestrained power, pillage and booty: years during which he construed Allah to be always on his side?

Sixteen days' travelling time brought the deputation to the Dervish fort at Gorahei, on 25 April 1920. To their relief they were hospitably received, and notice of their arrival was sent on to the Mullah at Shinileh. With much trepidation they reached the outskirts of Shinileh on 28 April. There began those strange antics which were to bedevil the mission's stay in the Mullah's camp over the next few days.

They were at first greeted in silence by an advance party from the Mullah, and beckoned forward, when suddenly they were frightened out of their wits at being enveloped by a gyrating band of armed horsemen who appeared from nowhere. The mission was then quickly disarmed. There then followed a most disconcerting hour of silence during which they were kept immobile, and then suddenly came a bewildering order that they should announce in a loud voice that they were the vanguard of a large British army, come to support the Mullah in an attack on Ogaden tribesmen. It later transpired that this was a ruse to impress an Ogaden deputation then in camp to discuss an alliance with the Mullah, and so hurry them into the process of agreeing to one.

It was only after these preliminaries were over that the party was led to the Mullah's camp a short distance away. Here, to further befuddle their wits, they were made to circle it in both directions a number of times at a fast pace. This enabled them, however, to assess the layout of the camp. It was a sprawling place, with huts sited well apart, that of the Mullah being more so and well canopied under a clump of trees, supposedly a shield against aircraft attack, for the Mullah had not forgotten the lesson of Medishe.

The circlings of the camp had now ceased and the mission found itself confronting the Mullah at a distance of some 75 yards, face-to-face with the terrible man at last. The party, possibly the only Somalis to converse with the Mullah in a formal manner in his latter years, was to provide the best and last description of him for the outside world. The Mullah was a big man physically, about 6 feet in height and still showing evidence of the powerful figure he had been in his earlier years. What most impressed the mission was his immense belly, so paunch-like that he had to sit on the ground in a most uncomfortable fashion, with his legs straight out in front of him. As to his countenance, despite his own frequent aspersions on the Midgans, there was something negroid in the Mullah's own face: it was much darker than the usual copper-coloured Somalis, and much darker than that of his half-brother, Khalif, sitting next to him, and who was also much shorter in stature. This distinction between them likely derived from their having different mothers.

The Mullah's dark face was marked by alert yet brooding eyes. Most striking, however, was the singular disfiguration on the forecrown of the Mullah's head, frequently alluded to yet rarely confirmed. The mission now gave witness to it. The two firebrand marks on his forehead and the high, bony, scar-like ridge above them, the result of that operation performed on him as a boy by a medicine man, lent a mark of terrible distinction to this awesome figure. Sitting in the midst of the tired old rump of Dervishes, the remainder of his once proud and select band, now so shabby, unwashed and exhausted, the Mullah stood out as an impressive figure in his gleaming white *tobe*.

Hypnotised by the sight of the Mullah, while they were still mounted and held in one spot by their Dervish escort, and in enforced silence, the mission seemed transfixed, scarcely noticing the minutes ticking away. This cat-and-mouse game continued throughout the long hot tedious day. It was a game in which the Mullah was much practised and he endured it better than his victims. Alternating periods of long silences interspersed by his scrutinising the ground, wagging his head to and fro, to the accompaniment of low groan-like 'tut-tuts'. What thoughts were going through his head? The members of the mission were in suspense. His first question, without warning, was extremely disconcerting. Was this a meeting of Christians or of Muslims only? It threw the mission into disarray.

They were not sure whether the Mullah was referring to infidels or apostates among their number. In either case they would not be allowed to converse directly with him and this would ruin the whole purpose of their visit. They thus gave no answer to this question. The Mullah then demanded that old Sheikh Ali Guhara give the names of the mission, and these the Mullah scratched down with a thorn on the bare arm of an old man sitting impassively beside him. The pantomime continued. There now arose on all sides from the thick bush the Mullah's weird battle hymn, 'Mohammad Salih'. It was a clumsy ruse, a party of singers moving around the camp and meant to give the impression of numerous supporters. And to add to the impression, some 150 horsemen, mainly Ogaden, solemnly circumambulated the camp, trailed by armed footmen at measured distance, and all to the accompaniment of shrill maledictions hurled down on the infidel. Then, at a blast of a Somali horn, a large conch shell, a veritable Triton's horn, the whole mass came to an abrupt stop.

The Mullah, then rising, raised expectations that he would give a display of his much vaunted horsemanship, a feat of his old bareback riding. Alas this was not to be. He thought better of the idea, and it was mercifully deferred. Instead the Mullah moved slowly round behind the visitors and sat with his back to theirs. Another blast on Triton's horn and they all swung round facing each other again. This was play-acting at its best, a farrago of nonsense. There now ensued a dramatic interchange between the Mullah and Sheikh Ali Guhara. The Mullah, ignoring the latter's honorific of 'Haji', again demanded that he read out the names of the mission. And as these were read out the Mullah feigned great shock. He railed at each in turn. Were not the marks of

149

their degeneracy evident in their faces. One had lost his good looks since becoming an unbeliever. And the face of another, said the Mullah, apparently forgetting the darkness of his own skin, had become as black as a *galla*'s (an unbeliever). Still another (whose father was the most distinguished sheikh in Somaliland) was ignored as a nonentity. The Mullah's special venom, however, was reserved for poor old Sheikh Ismail Ishaak, high religious leader, most venerable and of great piety. He was vilely slandered, taunted as being illegitimate and of servile birth; he was no true Dolbahanta and had no right to pass himself off as a sheikh; and, monstrous accusation, he had been guilty of gross acts of obscenity, affirmation of which most vile charge came from Ogadens prompted for the occasion. Having, as it were, destroyed the revered religious leader, the Mullah then proceeded to lambaste all mankind as infidel. He excommunicated them all. He only was the true Muslim and supreme exponent of the Koran. All others, even those at Mecca, including his old mentor, Mohammed Salih, whom he claimed to have raised up to high recognition, had become craven. Those who would follow the Prophet should follow him, the Mullah, Sayyid. They should give up all, family and property. All else was a sea of infidels. He chided those who sided with the British, for the latter would suck their blood without their being aware of it. Somali scholars in after years would describe the Mullah's harangue as a perfectly sane, albeit fiery speech. At the time it seemed part of the mumbo-jumbo, the rigmarole, which the mission was forced to witness.

Despite these weird goings-on, the visitors lived well. They dined on great bowls of rice, tender camel meat, milk, honey, and drank the finest Ethiopian coffee. The Mullah's uncle was directed to be the special taster of their food, lest some ill-wisher poison them.

The next day, 30 April 1920, the Mullah, after blaming the apostasy of the mission on Musa Farah, an explanation to which they only too readily acceded, he re-admitted these supposedly renegade Muslims into the bosom of Islam. There was a ritual of re-baptism, the Mullah affecting to read a passage from the Koran: 'There is no God but God and Mohammed is the Prophet of God.' And now that they were Mohammedans again, with good red blood in their veins, he would present them with wives, and wrote down the names of ten girls, and they, the visitors, in return should do likewise for him; and so, entering into this fiction, they affected to write down the names of such. It was here that the Mullah revealed his chagrin, for the mission had brought back only the Mullah's little daughter, and he had expected the return of his wives. 'You have brought back none of my wives – nothing but this little cat.'

On the fifth day after their arrival, 4 May 1920, the Mullah dictated his reply to Archer, sounding off to his amanuensis in a loud voice so as to impress the listening Ogaden and implying that he was dictating peace terms to the British. There was much reference to his supposed vast wealth, to his great arsenal, including machine-guns, to his veritable treasure trove of gold and precious stones, exotic feathers, and learned books: Croesus-like wealth, which the British must return to him. So also must they return his men who had been captured or who had deserted, and they must pay blood-money for the 40 of his children, 'infants and innocents', they had killed. They must also return his forts and his land. He referred to the British offer of enticing peace terms, that he would have his own *tarika*, and would be assured of ease and repose in his last years. He refused the bait. He preferred to go down fighting. He demanded complete and unconditional surrender by the British.

The Mullah's reply throws much light on his interpretation of recent events. He blamed the Italians for causing trouble between himself and other tribes by distributing arms to the latter, thereby forcing him to move into British territory to seek 'peace and quiet'. And when he was on the point of making peace with the British, the latter 'without any cause or fault of mine', attacked him with 12 'birds', four of which they had borrowed from the French: 'a great abuse to a man in my position'. The Mullah claimed to have destroyed six of these 'birds' and two British officers, one of whom was a very bad man named Lawrence (Major A. S. Lawrence, still very much alive at the time the Mullah was dictating his letter). The British had returned the four borrowed aircraft, thus only two remained. From the Mullah's letter and from what the mission had learned, it was evident that the air attack was still much on the Mullah's mind. He did not mind the birds' 'droppings', some of which had fallen on his white canopy, but did not touch him. What really hurt were the letters in Arabic which Archer had directed to be dropped from the air at Medishe, and in which the Mullah was described as 'Mohammed bin Abdullah, Ogaden, Bagheri, *rer* (clan) Hamar'. 'That was dreadful! Do I look like a Bagheri, *rer* Hamar? They are Midgan, outcasts. Do I look like a Midgan?' And here the Mullah, referring to what he termed his own beauty, indulged in some Rabelaisian remarks. In a flight of fancy he adverted to his blood relationship with Lij Yasu, 'Prince of Abyssinia', for was it not stated so in the Koran? Finally, ending his letter, he stated, despite his foregoing rejection of it, that he was 'quite willing' to undertake Archer's settlement, but made no mention of details.

The next day, 5 May, the Mullah decided to move camp to Burgayer, 12 miles to the west, but not before the mission was to witness the terrible spectacle of a picket who had deserted his post being mercilessly flogged and then burnt to death. It was meant to be a lesson for the visitors. On their departure they also witnessed a pathetic attempt by the Mullah to display his horsemanship. So gross was he in weight and so sapped in vigour that he had to be lifted bodily on to the back of an aged mount. He then flew off with much ado, followed by six women on ponies floundering after him. What a falling off from his great days!

After seven days at Burgayer, the mission was allowed to depart on 12 May 1920, carrying the Mullah's reply to Archer. Their send-off was better than their reception. The Mullah, in hearty mood, provided them with ample food and transport, and gave them a last reminder as to the promised girls.

On their return journey, two weeks on the road brought the mission to Burao, on 26 May 1920, where they were greeted as returned from the dead, and it was with much chagrin but albeit feigned happiness that their relatives received them, for they had already shared out their possessions. By 28 May they were at Sheikh, relating their experiences to the British. They depicted a paranoid Mullah, much declined in health, but still very dangerous. The aura of a jihad still lingered over his camp. The Ogaden and Khalif's Dervishes were rallying around him and a new resurgence of Dervish raids from across the Ethiopian border might be expected at any time.

Confirmation of this soon came, for hot on the heels of the departing mission, the Dervishes launched a raid into British territory from the Ogaden on 20 May 1920. In the next few weeks came news of more such raids. What was thought to be a spent force was still very much alive. It must be smashed. The man to do this was at hand in the person of old Haji Waraba, who had his own quarrel with the Mullah to settle, and who was imbued with the killer instinct. He was given a free hand to raise a tribal force of 3,000 riflemen from among the Habr Yunis, Habr Toljaala and Dolbahanta, and assisted by 100 Camel Corps men. They were fighters all of them.

Entering into what was almost a jihad in reverse, and picking up support on the way from those who had suffered at the hands of the Dervishes, and marching mostly at night, they reached the Mullah's camp at Gor'ah, west of Shinileh, in late July 1920. They were half-expected, but the Mullah and his forces, to the number of 800, did not envisage retaliation on the scale that now emerged. There was the sudden rush and storming of the camp in the half-light of dawn. There were no effective leaders for the Dervishes. Khalif and Mahdi (the Mullah's eldest son) had recently been cut down by smallpox, and the Mullah himself was nearly immobile from ill-health. Despite this the Dervishes stood their ground. Only a few fled. The remaining Dervishes were practically wiped out, and 700 rifles and 60,000 head of stock were captured. Old Haji Waraba, however, was robbed of his prize. Breaking into the Mullah's tent, he was seconds too late: there was only a hot cup of tea, unfinished. The Mullah was on his travels again.

His last movements are not too clear. It appears that he fled southwards to Shoga, and then to Imi on the upper Webi Shibeli, where he arrived in early August 1920. Here he settled down with 300–400 followers, on Guano Imi, a hill near Imi, and overlooking the Webi Shibeli, where they built a series of forts by October 1920. This activity brought a reaction from the nearest Ethiopian garrison, whose Fitaurari inquired as to the Mullah's presence. The latter then sent peace offerings, claiming that he was a refugee from the British and sought protection in Ethiopia and requested help and provisions. The Fitaurari's response to this was to place the Mullah's messengers in chains. Soon after this came the final tragedy for the Mullah.

The encampment at Imi was struck down by smallpox, influenza and then famine. Fatalities were widespread, and the Mullah met his rendezvous with death on 23 November 1920, after six days' illness. (Various dates later given, viz. 21 December 1920 and January 1921, possibly arose from the dates the news of his death reached the British.) The Mullah was buried in a small tomb with a dome over it, in a small hut in the central fort, the doors and windows of the hut being blocked up with bricks. Thus at Imi, far from his former scenes of battle, and remote from his father's and mother's people, this turbulent spirit was laid to rest. What the British had failed to do, nature had accomplished. It was a tame ending: 21 years of warring with the infidel, to end in so prosaic a fashion.

With the Mullah's death the heart went out of the Dervish movement. Disintegration soon followed. Many of his followers had also succumbed to the epidemic. Others returned to their tribal areas in Somaliland, or submitted to the Ethiopian authorities. Small, sad remnants continued to roam the country, reduced to mere mendicants. A few, however, the hard core, implacable last-ditchers, moved south into the region between the upper Juba and upper Webi Shibeli, far removed from

British or Ethiopian jurisdiction, here perchance to dream of making a bid again one day for their old ascendancy.

As for the Mullah and his purported madness, 'Who is to say what is madness?' asked *The Times* of 19 March 1921, reporting the Mullah's death and proffering the view that he was 'no more mad than the rest of the world'. The passing of time and the fading of memory would smooth out and dim the recollection of the harshness, the despotic cruelty and the irrational behaviour of the Mullah, leaving only the picture of an unyielding patriot and fighter, a national hero.

The murder, turmoil and strife which had characterised the Mullah's career did not end with his death. There was still much arms-holding, and there were 'lots of rifles' about. There always remained in the minds of many the possibility of another inspired Wadad rising up, to lead another jihad against the infidel. A nightmare thought, enough to make the nearest Englishman literally reach for his gun. Latent opposition to British rule among the Somalis made such a jihad not unlikely.

There was no great glee on the part of Somalis at news of the Mullah's passing in far-off Imi. Despite his cruelty, fearful tortures and the mad pace at which he had led them, they still saw him as the embodiment of their ideal of freedom and liberty. Such unbelievable tenacity as was his, and his refusal to acknowledge defeat or kneel to any man, made them admire him and explained his amazing ascendancy over them. Although the Mullah had claimed to owe allegiance to no man, Muslim or infidel, yet he himself commanded the allegiance of his followers. He fought under the banner of religion, yet his real strength lay in the spear, rifle and desert craft.

The news of the Mullah's death stirred surprisingly little interest in England. Scarcely a ripple! No public celebrations, no parades, no toasts of congratulation to King–Emperor marked the event. There had been no last dramatic cavalry charge, as had accompanied the defeat of the Dervishes in the Sudan. No great general like Kitchener had dominated the field. There had been no war correspondent of Churchill's stature to vivify events and to titillate the imagination of the reader by descriptions of the contest. Much had happened since the war with the Dervishes in the Sudan. There had been the Boer War and then, over-shadowing all, the First World War. These had come and gone after dominating all minds. These major conflicts had strained the resources of the nation. The affair of the Mullah had been, in comparison, a mere side-show, a gad-fly nuisance.

In the Somaliland Protectorate, with the Mullah out of the way, officials could now properly assess the potential of the territory, and see its development in relation to other territories in Africa under British control. They could see much that paralleled the situation in the Sudan at the time of the defeat of the Dervishes there, and where, following that defeat, the territory had been set on the path of progress. The parallel was too tempting. In the Sudan the strategy laid down to defeat the Dervishes had bequeathed to that territory hundreds of miles of telegraph and railway lines, and steamers on the Nile and its tributaries. Education had an easier path in the Sudan where there was familiarity with and much admiration for Arabic. Christian missionaries had been established south of Khartoum by the mid-nineteenth century, by which date Khartoum itself was a cosmopolitan centre. There was much to build on (in modern parlance, an infrastructure) in the Sudan: not so in the Somali Protectorate.

There are no great rivers tapping Somaliland's hinterland, nothing comparable to the Nile. The Protectorate had been drained by 20 years of warfare. Its economy was of negligible value. The material legacy from the Mullah's defeat was small, apart from some experience with wireless communication, telegraph connection with the outside world by way of Berbera and Aden, and a well-graded road from Berbera up through the Sheikh Pass to Burao, which had been constructed by the Indian Pioneer Corps during the operations against the Mullah. Post-war relics included a few military dumps and broken-down motor vehicles. The one novel feature that had been introduced as a result of the campaign against the Mullah was the aeroplane.

The country was pitifully poor. And it was not easy to awaken much enthusiasm in Britain for its reconstruction. There was no great fund of philanthropy such as had enabled Kitchener to raise money for the founding of Gordon College in Khartoum. Imperial grants-in-aid for the Somaliland Protectorate were already far too high, running at three times revenue (£45,000), and the imbalance was continuing. New sources of revenue must be found: customs and excise, port and harbour dues and court fines would no longer suffice. Where to find new sources of revenue? Various possibilities existed: to develop the reputed Daga Shabel oil fields and other mineral resources, and to divert trade from Jibuti to Zeyla by developing the latter's harbour (although the lack of water supply at Zeyla and its sterile hinterland made this highly unfeasible); to revive the plan for a railway from Berbera to Hargeisa. Some officials and politicians, such as Archer and Churchill, saw the solution to the Protectorate's economic and financial problems in its amalgamation with Aden. However, the Indian government, through which Aden was administered, had long memories of the tribulations associated with the administration of British Somaliland, and now, having got clear of it, would have nothing to do with a proposal for its amalgamation with Aden.

Officials in the Protectorate were also faced with latent opposition to British rule among Somali tribes. Even the Ishaak, so-called 'servants of the infidel', who had supported the British against the Mullah and had done well out of it, accumulating wealth and property and travelling abroad, enjoying education and possessing the most beautiful women in a land of beautiful women, were now, with the Mullah gone, standing on their own feet and showing their old insolence, independence and resentment against the British. They and other Somali tribes had a deep xenophobic fear of education administered by an alien government. Education officers were seen as Christian missionaries in disguise. The separation of education from religion seemed impossible for the devout Somali. There was no adequate base on which to build education, even at the most elementary level. There was no written Somali language; use of Arabic was rare, although it was highly esteemed. There had been a Christian mission at Berbera, but it had been closed in 1910, in deference to Islamic susceptibilities. A request as late as August 1930 for permission to reopen the mission was refused by the Colonial Office. Christian missionaries remained excluded from the territory.

There was opposition to the introduction of the Somali language in schools. This opposition and that against Christian missionaries was so extreme as to cause the Qaadiriyya and Salihiya sects to sink their differences and unite against the infidel, a sign of nascent Somali nationalism. The new trouble-makers for the British had potent weapons not available to the Mullah – new forms of communication, inspiration and contacts with Somalis overseas, superior rhetorical and metaphorical style, and, prior to its occupation by the Italians, sponsorship of much of this opposition to British rule from Ethiopia.

Of all the alien legislation introduced, such as provision for capital punishment (1924), and limiting the trade in the stimulant drug, *kat*, it was the attempt to introduce taxation which raised the greatest storm. Archer saw taxation as the way to introduce Somalis to the hard facts of life. Muslim leaders, however, declared payment of taxes to an infidel as contrary to Islam. There was also a rumour that taxation portended British withdrawal to the coast (as in 1910), leaving its collection in the hands of hated tax-collectors, the *akils*, Somali elders acting as government agents. Their origins in Somaliland went back to the time of the Egyptian administration at the end of the nineteenth century. There was now one *akil* for every 1,000 persons in the territory.

Taxation remained the bugbear. It brought such confrontation with the British at Burao in March 1922 that aircraft were directed there. The result was 'electrifying': the offenders, mainly Habr Yunis, quickly paid a hefty fine in camels. Archer, however, had little backing from the Colonial Office in the matter, for it was fearful of starting another Somali uprising. Thus thwarted, Archer was glad to be transferred to Uganda in September 1922, with the hornet's nest of taxation still buzzing round his ears. His successors were no more successful than he was in pressing taxation on an unwilling people. The affair highlighted the matter of security and the role of the Somali in the military forces of the territory, for was he not first a tribesman before being a soldier of the King? It brought a recasting of the Protectorate's armed forces. Indian forces were retained and the Camel Corps became the 7th Battalion (Somaliland Camel Corps) of the King's African Rifles. Two aircraft were retained in the Protectorate.

The perennial problem of trans-frontier grazing persisted after the fall of the Mullah, especially in the eastern part of the Protectorate. Although the Anglo-Italian Protocol of 1894* had defined the boundary between their respective spheres of influence (not demarcated by actual survey, concrete markers and stone cairns until 1929–30), it left much uncertainty as to the exact position of the 49th meridian which formed the eastern boundary of the British Protectorate. So much so that the War Office map of 1907 placed El Laghodie, assumed to be on the 49th meridian, 25 miles farther west of it, and within British territory. And the port of Banda Ziada on the Gulf of Aden, although immediately to the west of the 49th meridian, was for a time assigned to the Italians, before reverting to the British.

The Mijjertein had for centuries looked upon the Baran–Taleh area as theirs, and only retired from it when the Nogal was assigned to the Mullah when, for a brief time, he was an Italian protégé. When the Mullah died the Mijjertein resumed possession of this area and occu-

---

*The 1894 Protocol defined the boundary as a line running south-eastwards from Gildessa (about 30 miles north of Harrar) to the point where the 47th meridian intersects the 8° N latitude, and thence along that parallel to the 48th meridian and then to the intersection of 9° N latitude with the 49th meridian and then following that meridian directly north to the sea. The Anglo-Italian boundary line left the Taleh and Baran areas, traditional grazing ground of the Mijjertein, in British territory, and, following the Protocol, they continued to graze across that line from Italian territory, sometimes looting to the south and east as well. Likewise the Warsangli, and some sections of the Dolbahanta from British territory, grazed eastwards, upwards of 20 miles or so, into Italian territory.

pied the old Dervish fort at Baran in 1924, well inside British territory. In 1925 the situation was regularised when a British–Italian agreement allowed the Mijjertein to graze at Baran. The problem of trans-frontier grazing emerged again in 1926–7, when, to escape tighter Italian control, the Mijjertein fled into British territory, although finally returning to the Italian side in mid-1927. At the same time the Italians closed their borders to British-protected tribes grazing across into their territory. This final episode and the continued uncertainty as to the exact position of the boundary line resulted in the 1929–30 Anglo-Italian boundary commission which employed aircraft for aerial survey work. The result was an accurate definition of the 49th meridian and the placing of concrete markers and stone cairns along it and the southern boundary line as well, as far west as 47° E, 8° N. There was also the problem of trans-frontier grazing on the southern and south-western boundary of the Protectorate. The Anglo-Ethiopian treaty of 1897 had conceded the western corner of the Protectorate, the Haud (consigned to Britain by the Anglo-Italian Protocol of 1894), to Ethiopia. The boundary line skirted the north-east frontiers of the territories of the Girrhi, Bertiri and Rer Ali tribes. The customary grazing grounds of Somali tribes had thus been ceded to Ethiopia, although the 1897 treaty made provision for tribes on either side of the line to cross that line to resort to their traditional grazing areas. British officers at times crossed into Ethiopian territory to administer British-protected tribes resorting there for grazing. Conversely, the Ogaden tribesmen from the Ethiopian side raided and looted across the line into British territory as far as Burao. The British-Ethiopian boundary commission, 1932–4, was meant to end this state of affairs. Starting from 47° E, 8° N, and using aircraft for aerial survey work, it demarcated the boundary of British Somaliland westwards from that point, without specifying the trijunction point at either end of the Ethiopian portion. The Italian-Ethiopian boundary was still indeterminate in 1936, at which time the Italians were pushing deeply into the Ogaden and occupying water holes. This betokened a confrontation with the Ethiopians which would affect British Somali tribes resorting across the border to their traditional grazing grounds.

The collapse of the Ethiopian regime and the occupation of Ethiopia by the Italians in 1936 had far-reaching effects on British Somaliland. It brought the Italians well to the west and south of the British territory. The change of title from Commissioner back to Governor in 1935 had perhaps indicated the seriousness of the situation. However, the Italian occupation of the Ogaden brought advantages, not confrontation, for the Protectorate. A 'Transit Trade and Grazing Rights Agreement' between Italy and Britain in February 1937 gave British Somali tribes continued rights to their traditional grazing ground in the Ogaden (except for Walwal, which was outside the permitted grazing area). The Ethiopians had only conceded this as an act of grace on their part. The Italians would also share the cost of modernising Berbera port and would assist in road-building (at which they were excellent), which would attract increasing traffic to the Berbera-Hargeisa-Jigjiga and Zeyla-Aisha-Borama-Jigjiga routes from Italian-occupied territory, bringing more revenue to the British Protectorate. Improved roads and Italian administration in the occupied territories would result in trans-frontier tribes being disarmed and a decrease in lawlessness. The Camel Corps could thus be reduced, and the saving thereby directed to education and social services. The lapsing of the 'Transit Trade and Grazing Rights Agreement' in 1939, on the eve of the Second World War, was a pity. British-Italian co-operation in the Horn could have achieved much in the way of economic and social advancement.

The effect on the Horn of Italy's entry into the Second World War on the side of Germany was dramatic. British and French plans to oppose her from Jibuti collapsed when the French governor of that colony defected to the Vichy regime. Italy invaded British Somaliland in August 1940, and, in the face of this, Britain announced its abandonment. It was a poignant and historic moment for British officials in the Protectorate, and well described by Walsh, District Officer at Borama and namesake of that same Walsh who had introduced British administration so many years before.

With what bitter thoughts on that day in September 1940 did he watch from a hilltop overlooking his station, as alien troops poured into it. The Italians had achieved in a few weeks what the Mullah had failed to do in 21 years: the irony of it must have brought a rueful smile to the face of the Mullah's ghost.

This dramatic occupation of the Horn of Africa by Italy in 1940 was only exceeded by the drama of her capitulation within eight months when she lost not only British Somaliland but also her own Somaliland colony and Ethiopia. British military occupation replaced Italian rule in the Horn in 1941. Then, in 1950, by a quixotic turn of events, Italy was installed by the United Nations as the mandatory ruler of her former Somaliland colony, now designated a trust territory, on condition that it should become independent in ten years' time.

On 1 July 1960, what was formerly Italian Somaliland became independent. Five days previously the British had granted independence to their Somaliland territory to the north. In the same month, July 1960, the two Somalilands united into one territory – the Somali Republic. The fate of the Somalis now rested in their own hands. At last what the Mullah had striven to achieve over many years of arduous struggle had come to pass with comparative ease.

BIBLIOGRAPHY

Adam, F., *Handbook of Somaliland*, London, 1900.
Alberti, G., *In Somalia contro il Mullah pazzo*, Rome, 1935.
Andrzejewski, B. W., and Lewis, I. M., *Somali Poetry: An Introduction*, London, 1964.
Archer, Sir Geoffrey, *Personal & Historical Memoirs of an East African Administrator*, London, 1963.
Buchholzer, J., *The Horn of Africa*, London, 1959.
Burton, R. F., *First Footsteps in East Africa*, London, 1856.
Caroselli, Francesco Saverio, *Ferro e Fuoco in Somalia*, Rome, 1931.
Cato, C., *The Navy Everywhere*, London, 1919.
de Martino, G., *Relazione sulla Somalia Italiana*, Rome, 1912.
de Wiart, Lt-Gen. Sir Adrian Carton, *Memoirs*, London, 1950.
Drake-Broekman, R. E., *British Somaliland*, London, 1917.
Fitzgibbon, L., *The Betrayal of the Somalis*, London, 1982.
Gleichen, Count Edward, *With the Mission to Menelik, 1897*, London, 1898.
Golding, J. A., *The Golden Years*, Ashford, 1987.
Hamilton, A., *Somaliland*, London, 1911.
Hardinge, Sir Arthur, *A Diplomatist in the East*, London, 1928.
Herbert, A., *Two Dianas in Somaliland*, London, 1908.
Hunt, J. A., *A General Survey of the Somaliland Protectorate*, London, 1951.
James, F. L., *The Unknown Horn of Africa*, London, 1888.
Jardine, D. J., *The Mad Mullah of Somaliland*, London, 1923.
Jennings, J. W., and Addison, C., *With the Abyssinians in Somaliland*, London, 1905.
Lewis, I. M., *A Pastoral Democracy*, London, 1961.
McNeill, M., *In Pursuit of the Mad Mullah*, London, 1902.
Mainwaring, Brig.-Gen. H. G., *A Soldier's Shikar Trips*, London, 1920.
Miller, Captain G., *A Captain of the Gordons: Service Experiences 1900–1909*, London, 1909.
Morse, A. H. E., *My Somali Book*, London, 1913.
Moyse-Bartlett, H., *The King's African Rifles*, Aldershot, 1956.
Pease, A. E., *Travel & Sport in Africa*, London, 1902.
Prevost-Battersby, H. F., *Richard Corfield of Somaliland*, London, 1914.
Rayne, Major H., *Sun, Sand and Sandals*, London, 1921.

Rodd, J. R., *Social and Diplomatic Memories*, London, 1923.
Samatar, Said S., *Oral Poetry and Somali Nationalism: The Case of Sayyid Mahammad 'Abdille Hasan*, Cambridge, 1982.
Smith, A. Donaldson, *Through Unknown African Countries*, London, 1897.
Swayne, Major H. G. C., *Seventeen Trips Through Somaliland and a Visit to Abyssinia*, London, 1903.
Walsh, L. P., *Under the Flag and Somali Coast Stories*, London, 1932.
Wingate, Sir Ronald, *Lord Ismay, A Biography*, London, 1970.

Principal documentary and other sources consulted

Cruttenden, C. J., 'Memoir on the Western or Edor Tribes Inhabiting the Somali Coast of Northeast Africa', *Journal of the Royal Geographical Society*, XIX (1849).
Foreign Office Annual Series, 1893, No. 1208.
Foreign Office Annual Series, 1900, No. 2384.
Cabinet Papers, 37/63, Memorandum by Lord Cranborne on Somaliland, London, 1902.
Parliamentary Papers, No. 3, 1902, Correspondence respecting the Rising of the Mullah Mohammed Abdullah in Somaliland, and Consequent Military Operations, 1901–1902.
Notes on Somaliland, Nos 170, 171, FOCP 8040, Part LXXI, Oct.–Dec. 1902.
Parliamentary Papers, No. 1. 1903, Correspondence respecting the Rising of the Mullah Mohammed Abdullah in Somaliland.
Parliamentary Papers, Cd 1500, 1903, Despatches Relative to the Operations of the Somaliland Field Force.
Foreign Office Correspondence relating to the Rising of the Mullah Mohammed Abdullah in Somaliland and Consequent Military Operations, 1899–1902, London, 1903.
King's Regulations: Somaliland Protectorate, Berbera, 1904.
Parliamentary Papers, Cd 2254, 1904, Despatches etc., regarding Military Operations in Somaliland, Jan. 1902–May 1904.
Cabinet Papers, 37/70, Operations in Somaliland, 1904.
Africa No. 2, 1904, Trade & Commerce, Somaliland.
The Red Sea & Gulf of Aden Pilot, London, 1904.
'Somaliland Operations, June 1903–May 1904', *Journal of the United Services Institution*, V, XLIL, London, 1905.
War Office, *Official History of the Operations in Somaliland, 1901–1904*, 2 vols, London, 1907.
War Office, Military Report on Somaliland, London, 1907.
Cabinet Papers, 37/89, A Minute on Somaliland Protectorate, Churchill, W. S., November, 1908.
CO 535, Somaliland, Original Correspondence (including vol. on Wingate's Mission to Somaliland in 1909).

Bibliography

Cabinet Papers, 37/100, Sir R. Wingate's Reports, August 1909.

Somaliland Operations 1909, (Pamphlet 4295C) Royal Commonwealth Society Library, London.

Parliamentary Papers, Cd 7066, 1913, Correspondence relating to Affairs in Somaliland, 1913.

Ibid., Cd 7566, 1914, Further Correspondence relating to Affairs in Somaliland.

Somaliland 1897–1919, War Office, No. 106: Directorate of Military Operations & Intelligence.

Jardine, D. J., 'The Mad Mullah of Somaliland', *Blackwood's Magazine*, V, CCVIII, Edinburgh, 1920.

London Gazette, 1 November 1920.

Handbook on British Somaliland & Sokotra, Foreign Office, No. 97, London, 1920.

Italian Somaliland, British Foreign Office Handbook (No. 128), London, 1920.

Military Report on British Somaliland, London, 1925.

La Esplorazione dello Uabi-Uebi Scebeli, L'Italia Coloniale, Milan, 1932.

The Somaliland Peninsula (A New Light on Imperial Motives), Information Services, Somali Government, Mogadishu, 1962.

Gray, R., 'Bombing the Mad Mullah – 1920', *Journal of the Royal United Services Institute for Defence Studies*, London, Dec. 1980.

Ismay Papers, Liddell Hart Centre for Military Archives, University of London, King's College.

Thompson Capper Papers, Liddell Hart Centre for Military Archives, University of London, King's College.

FO 403 Series: Foreign Office Confidential Prints.

CO 879 Series: Colonial Office Confidential Prints.

Annual Report on Somaliland Protectorate issued by Colonial Office, London.

FO 844, Consul Archives, Somaliland series.

CO 607 Somaliland Miscellaneous.

CO 713 Somaliland Register of Correspondence.

The Wingate Papers, Sudan Archives, School of Oriental and African Studies, London.

The Slatin Papers, Sudan Archives, School of Oriental and African Studies, London.

The Geographical Journal, Vols. XIX (1849), LXXVIII (1931), LXXXIII (1934), LXXXVII (1936), London.

Daily Telegraph, London.

Pall Mall Gazette, London.

The Times, London.

GLOSSARY OF TERMS

Adi Sheep and goats.
Adone A negro tribe from the Webi Shibeli area.
Agal Nomad's collapsible tent.
Akil Headman of a tribal section.
Aman Peace; a guarantee of safe conduct.
Askari East African native soldier.
Buraad Roving band of robbers (highwaymen).
Chagul A canvas water bottle.
Dhow Sailing vessel.
Din Religion.
Diya Blood compensation.
Effendi Term of respect, i.e. 'Sir'.
Ergo A deputation; a mission, delegates.
Fitaurari Ethiopian military title.
Fitna Dissension and quarrelling, criminal intrigues.
Galla Pagan Africans conquered by the Arabs who invaded Somaliland in the 7th century. Looked upon as infidels, i.e. unbelievers.
Geel Camels.
Gerazmatch Ethiopian military title.
Ghee Clarified butter.
Gurgi Portable Somali hut of bent sticks and camel mats.
Haj Pilgrimage to Mecca.
Harem (Haram) The prohibited women's enclosure in a Muslim household.
Haroun The Mullah's headquarters and household encampment.
Heer Treaty or contract.
Herios Saddles (vs. Indian 'palans').
Illalo Somali scout.
Jihad Holy war of Muslims against infidels.
Jilib A tribal outpost.
Kasoosi Intimate associates and advisers.
Kharia Somali movable village.
Oll Somali tribal army.
Nullah A dry watercourse.
Rer A clan within a tribe.
Sab Minority groups such as Midgan, Tumals, and Yibirs.

164

Glossary of Terms

Sharia   The sacred law of Islam.

Tarika   Religious communities, settlements of Mullahs.

Tobe   Conventional dress of the Somali, usually of cotton cloth and resembling the Roman toga.

Tukel   Somali nomad's hut.

Wadad   Somali equivalent of Mullah.

Wadens   Well buckets.

Wagosha   Community descended from runaway slaves in Juba river region.

Wali   Governor.

Zariba   A temporary barricade or fence of thorn bush protecting a camp.

Zihr   Religious ceremonies.

INDEX

Index

Index

173